MATCHLESS & AJS

RESTORATION

MATCHLESS & AJS

ALL POST-WAR ROAD SINGLES & TWINS

RESTORATION

ROY BACON

OSPREY

Published in 1989 by Osprey Publishing Limited
59 Grosvenor Street, London W1X 9DA

British Library Cataloguing in Publication Data

Bacon, Roy H. (Roy Hunt)
    Matchless & AJS restoration
    1. Motorcycles. Restoration
    I. Title
    629.28'775
ISBN 0-85045-755-6

Filmset by Tameside Filmsetting Limited,
Ashton-under-Lyne, Lancashire
Printed by BAS Printers Limited,
Over Wallop, Hampshire

HALF TITLE ILLUSTRATION *The author at the helm of a 1960
31CSR at Silverstone with the owner hanging over the rear
wheel in borrowed leathers and helmet*

TITLE PAGE ILLUSTRATION *Two 1955 Matchless singles with
their Persian riders on tour and here in Adelaide*

Contents

*The start of the post-war singles line in the form of an
army G3L in Berlin by the Brandenburg Gate in 1948*

Acknowledgements

The fifth title in the restoration series produced its own set of problems in two distinct forms. First was the basic one of dealing with two marques which were almost, but not quite, the same in so many instances. Then, when I thought I was managing to live with this, along came the second in the form of the Norton engine and chassis parts to produce the hybrids.

Thanks to this latter there is a little overlap with the *Norton Twin Restoration* title in this series but not much and for that engine the other book is the recommended reading. Salient points have, I hope, been included.

Much of the material on which the text of this book was based came once again from my good friend Don Mitchell and his stock of second-hand motorcycle literature. I am equally indebted to Johnnie Walker of the owners club who kindly went through the manuscript to correct and comment as needed and also provided me with service information and machine data. His deep level of expertise helped me and should help all who dabble in the Plumstead products. Further help came from Bob Boaden who checked gearbox data for me even though this meant a visit to the depths of the garage on a dark night.

The pictures and line drawings came mainly from the EMAP archives which hold the old *Motor Cycle Weekly* files, for which my grateful thanks. Others came from the *Motor Cycle News* files, courtesy of editor Malcolm Gough, and a couple from my own files.

Some of the pictures would have carried the imprint of a professional and normally they would have been listed, as is the practice of both myself and the publishing house, but this is no longer possible due to the way in which the prints reach us. However, our thanks as always go to those who drove their cameras in the past when correct exposure owed more to the man behind the lens than the electronics in front of it.

Finally, my thanks to both editors—Tony Thacker who commissioned this one and Nick Collins who had to take it over, for their support during the book's production. Not forgetting Tim Parker who conceived the idea in the first place and the staff at Osprey who as usual did a superb, professional job in bringing the book to its conclusion.

Roy Bacon
Niton, Isle of Wight
October 1988

A line of 1959 model 14 AJS machines being sold to Portsmouth police, hence the single seat and provision for radio gear

Our policy

This book is written on the basis of a restoration back to original factory specification for the model and year. It is appreciated that not every reader will want to aim for this, but it is the only practical way to write the book.

Restorations can range from a mild check-over to a concours-standard rebuild, furthermore adding features and a finish never seen on a production machine. Alterations may be carried out, ranging from discreet rider improvements to major changes in updating the specification.

In all cases, and regardless of the final aim, it is hoped that this book will assist and guide the reader to produce the machine of his or her dreams. It is also hoped that the result will be sound in wind and limb, and every endeavour has been made to offer advice which is both helpful and safe. However, the onus is always on the reader to ensure that any machine he or she works on or rides is in a safe and legal condition. If you decide to carry out a modification, you must make certain that it will work properly.

Neither the author nor the publisher can accept any liability for anything contained in this book which may result in any loss, damage or injury, and the book is only available for purchase or loan on that basis.

It is worth remembering that each chapter of this book contains both general principles and specific information. The first can really apply to any make or model, while the second is very much applicable only to particular cases, such as a part made for a model that was only available for one year. This distinction is important—the reader will invariably find the principles in other material, but the particular appeal of this book is that it gives you the specific details that relate the general principles directly to your machine.

Machine year

Chapter 1 gives details of the way in which models are dated, which causes, for example, 1958 models to run from late 1957 to late 1958. It also covers the habit the industry had of using up 1957 stocks in early 1958 models to clear the bins at the factory. Because of these points, the text will use the model year without constant repetition that the feature or model was introduced late in the previous calendar year. Thus a late 1957 model is referred to as 1958 because that is the specification to which it was made.

The use of old parts is ignored by the AMC factory parts list and by this book. By definition they had to interchange by form and function, so any notes on parts have to bypass this area. Some further possible confusion was arranged by AMC who changed the form of the part number system once, so that identical items can be listed under two totally different numbers.

In all, this means that it is possible for an all-original machine with known history to have an incorrect item fitted, by its parts list. It is the owner's decision whether to keep it or to change to the correct listed part.

Engine and frame numbers take precedence over model year in determining when a change took place and have been noted where necessary. Parts lists, coupled with these numbers, are always the correct way back to the original specification.

Scope

This book sets out to deal with production road models from 1945 to 1969 specification, but not the AJS two-strokes or the road-racing 7R, G45 and G50 models. The G50CSR is not covered either, except in the sense that it used the CSR frame (which is) and the camshaft single engine (which is not).

The data quoted applies to standard UK-specification machines as these are the basis from which any factory variations were derived. Thus while the data will assist when dealing with a machine to USA or any other overseas specifications, it cannot be assumed to be exact. The same applies to all machines built for the police or civil defence as these had their own specification and could vary in detail from one order to the next.

AMC also complicated matters when they took over Norton by producing a whole series of models using the Norton twin engine in an AMC frame. This began with the Atlas scrambler, but in time led to the 33 and

G15 series and other hybrids. In general the AMC parts are covered, but not the Norton engine in any detail, for which the reader is referred to *Norton Twin Restoration* (Osprey Publishing). The content varied from model to model and this is a very tricky period to get involved in.

Neither prototype nor one-off specials are mentioned. If you are lucky enough to have such a machine, I am sure you appreciate its rarity and will look after it without my help.

Your skills

This book is not a workshop manual, nor is it a primer on being a motorcycle mechanic. It has to assume that you know how your machine works and have a good idea about how to maintain it. Also that you have a degree of mechanical aptitude and have worked on motorcycles to some extent.

In many cases a good restoration is a combination of skill, available tools and knowledge of techniques and tricks that get the job done. Together they equate to experience and no book can give you that. It can only advise that you do not attempt more than you can cope with, and adds the suggestion that with the right information, care and attention to detail this could be more than you think. Proceed slowly but with confidence.

Address list

Always a problem in a book as they tend to be out of date by publication.

If in difficulties, the 'agony' columns of the specialist magazines are there to help, so you can send them your query as long as you include some method of return postage.

Specifications

Many books of this type carry extensive tables of data to the fourth decimal place which have been compiled from endless hours of research. This, however, does not, as much of it is in *AJS & Matchless—the postwar models* (Osprey Publishing) and the rest in workshop manuals.

Before any restoration is attempted, it is recommended that data and information are collected to cover your model and its year. In many areas the four-figure dimensions are of little moment as parts are reamed to fit and made to size. Part of the art is knowing which ones matter and no book can teach you that, any more than it can show you how to paint a masterpiece or write an opera. Well, not one that is any good.

So there are no endless lists of bushes and bearings, gaps and settings, or tolerances and gauges. The figures and data that are provided are there to back up the manual you should already have and to help you sort out what you may have bought.

Note

To avoid constant detailing the machines will be referred to as singles, light singles or twins. The first are the traditional models built from 1945 onwards with separate gearbox and also known as the heavyweight singles. The second are the 248 cc and 348 cc models first seen in 1958, which appeared to be of unit construction although in fact the gearbox was clamped to the back of the engine. The last were all the twin models, whether fitted with AMC or Norton engines.

Furthermore, as the two marques were identical in nearly every respct, this can be assumed unless otherwise indicated, and they will be referred to as AMC rather than AJS and Matchless. Where appropriate, the models will be called by their suffix, such as C and CS, rather than the full type for both makes. If both are needed, the AJS will be given first—in any case, all Matchless codes start with the letter G and so can be easily recognized.

1 The start

AMC were very quick off the mark at the end of the war with a pair of AJS models announced in June 1945, and a similar pair with Matchless on the tank appeared a week later in July. There was a 348 cc and 497 cc model in both ranges, which leant heavily on pre-war design but included the wartime Teledraulic front forks.

This simple start was soon amplified to include competition models and then rear suspension. Late in 1948 the first parallel twins appeared, and early in 1958 the range was joined by the first light single. Both these types expanded to other models and these lines ran into the 1960s.

From 1965 AMC began to fit the big Norton twin engine to their cycle parts, and within a year or so this unit had taken over. These hybrids, and a sole example of their big single, were all that ran on to 1969. The AJS name stopped and then continued for a range of two-strokes, but the traditional models had gone.

History

At the end of June 1945, AJS announced the 348 cc 16M and 497 cc 18 models, while the G3L and G80 Matchless equivalents arrived in July. All were based on the pre-war ranges, which had crystallized during the war into the G3 and the G3L with Teledraulic front forks.

All models followed a very traditional English form and differed only in that the AJS had its magneto in front of the cylinder while the Matchless had it tucked in behind. Timing cover, tank badges and transfers just about completed the variations. Both engine sizes shared a 93 mm stroke which was to stay with them for a number of years.

Early in 1946, a small number of competition models in both marques and engine sizes were built, having a letter C suffix added to their type number. There were few changes from standard, but the tyres and mudguards were more suited to trials work and the silencer end was tilted up. In addition, the gearing was lowered and the lights removed.

There were only detail changes until the 1949 range appeared, but this included singles with rear suspension and twins. The first were the 348 cc 16MS and G3LS, and 497 cc 18S and G80S, while the twins were the 20 and G9 of 498 cc. The frame and many other cycle parts were common to these models, which shared several parts with the rigid singles.

Competition versions of the sprung singles appeared for 1951, further lengthening the model numbers which now ran to four forms, each of which came in two sizes and two marques to make 16 machines in total. The suffixes used continued as S for sprung frame, C for competition and CS for the two combined, and were added to the basic 16M, 18, G3L and G80.

There was a new gearbox for the whole range for 1952 and the Matchless single's magneto moved in front of the cylinder to be as for the AJS. Otherwise there were few alterations until 1956, when the rigid-frame models were dropped and a larger 593 cc twin was introduced as the 30 and G11. Prior to this, around 1954, the twin had also been produced in an enlarged 550 cc form, known as the G9B or G10, and sold for export only. Some home-market 20 and G9 models were later bored out to this capacity by their owners when it was found that suitable pistons could be obtained.

AMC caused some confusion with its model numbering at this point as the 16MC and G3LC both continued, but in a sprung frame, while the 16MCS and G3CLS changed to a shorter 85.5 mm stroke engine. The original engine was built for trials, while the second was for scrambles—its engine dimension was also adopted by the 18CS and G80CS scramblers. Only the road singles and one competition 350 kept to the old 93 mm stroke engine.

During 1956 the Burman gearbox of old was changed for the AMC one, also used by Norton, and for 1958 the road singles changed to alternator electrics. This also occurred on the standard twins but not on two further 593 cc models which came in for that year. These were the CS and CSR models, with the first being a sports scrambler and the second a fast sports road machine. During 1958 the 248 cc light single was launched as the 14 and G2, with just the badges to distinguish one from the other.

The first civilian models to come off the AMC line in July 1945 were these G3Ls

There were major changes to the twins for 1959 with the 593 cc models being replaced by 646 cc ones, listed as the 31 and G12. These came in four forms as standard, de luxe, CS and CSR, and were joined by four more with the 498 cc twin engine.

For the singles, the change was mainly one of type number as these were shortened slightly. One reason for this was that, as all had rear suspension, the suffix S was not needed. Thus the road models became the 16, G3, 18 and G80. The trials 350 became the 16C or G3C, while the shorter-stroke scrambles version altered to 16CS or G3CS. The 500 scrambler stayed as the 18CS or G80CS, and was joined by a 600 cc version listed as the G80TCS, which stayed in the lists up to 1962. In addition, this large single engine was used for a flat tracker, and there was also a 497 cc version of this specialized model. The light singles were joined by CS versions for scrambling, but these were both heavy and expensive.

The 348 cc scrambler did not run on for 1960, and nor did any 498 cc twin other than the standard build.

However, the four 646 cc versions did continue, along with all the other singles which had one addition. This was a 348 cc version of the light single which used many of their parts and was listed as the 8 and G5.

For 1961 a sports light single appeared as the 14S and G2S, while the 646 cc CS twins were discontinued. The rest of the range stayed, but at the end of the year the last of the 498 cc twins went, together with the 646 cc de luxe twins and the 93 mm stroke road single. This model continued as the 16 or G3, but with an even shorter 81 mm stroke engine, and was joined by a sports version as the 16S or G3S.

The long-stroke engine continued in the 16C and G3C trials model, but both the road and scrambles 497 cc singles kept to the 85.5 mm stroke. Of the twins, there was only the 646 cc model in standard and CSR forms, while there were now three 248 cc and one 348 cc light singles. During the year they were joined by a 248 cc CSR version, but the 348 cc one disappeared a month or two later.

That year all models had been given names, but this proved unpopular and did not last long. It was also the year that some 750 cc twins were built as the Matchless G15 or G15/45, and these used the AMC twin engine enlarged to suit. Not many were made, but there were two batches for export which used a combination of standard, CS and CSR parts.

Most of the range ran on for 1963, other than the S and CS light singles, but this range had changes for 1964. Out went the basic 14 and G2 models so only the CSR continued, as did the two 646 twins. Of the singles, the 348 cc one went back to the 85.5 mm stroke engine, and both it and the 497 cc model fitted Norton forks and hubs. The two competition machines were still there but the 348 cc trials model went at the end of the year.

The models powered by 745 cc Norton twin engines came in for 1965 as the 33 and G15 in standard and CSR forms. These also used Norton forks and wheels, so as the gearbox had been common to all marques for nearly a decade, there was not much AMC left. In fact, all but one had gone by the middle of 1966, the sole survivor being the Matchless G85C5 which replaced the CS models and whose frame was also used by the Norton P11.

For the last few years, this one single and various 745 cc twins were produced against a climate of financial problems and crises. The AJS 33 and 33CSR were only made up to 1967, but the Matchless ran for two more years. Early in 1967 the G15CS appeared and later that year the basic twin became the G15 Mk2. This model, together with the G15CS and the G15CSR, continued till 1969 when the whole line was dropped.

A 1947 AJS on display in the BOAC showroom window in Washington with English magazines of that time

Model choice

The range of AMC models offers the owner plenty of choice with a number of model types, engine sizes and years to select from. The choice is down to the individual and up to that person alone. The selection can be determined by a past memory, a desire for a particular model or to complete a collection, but for most it is settled by the money available and the machines on offer.

Spares for all may be a problem. The situation varies from model to model, part to part and day to day. Items that are impossible to find at the time of writing could be readily available when you read the words, or the reverse may be true. Owing to this variation, the text is written on the basis that spares are to be had, but that while the mechanics should be available, with occasional lapses, the cycle side could be much harder to find. However, they may be easier to re-create by one means or another.

Remember that some models were only made in small numbers, so their spares could be harder to locate. In addition, export specification models may pose problems even in the country they were destined for and worse outside it. A further pitfall arises if an attempt has been made to create a rare model from a more prosaic one or to convert from one specification to another. Very rarely will the change be complete, causing yet more headaches.

The AJS or Matchless can be obtained in many ways, but purchase from a dealer, following up small advertisements in a local paper or specialized magazine, by word of mouth, club grapevine or

Press test of a 1949 G3LC complete with its lighting equipment, alloy guards and tilted silencer

personal contact are the more usual methods. Alternatively, you may already have one you wish to restore or improve in some way.

You may not actually start with a complete machine but with a box, or boxes, of parts bought at an autojumble or from a local source. Often these are the hardest to complete as invariably parts are missing. The box is on sale because the last owner allowed

enthusiasm to run ahead of resources, stripped the machine and then gave up or was forced to stop. He is sure it is all there but has forgotten various parts already missing, lent, lost or strayed, and every one is a problem for the new owner.

The restorer must also decide what is wanted and what is possible, which may not be the same thing. A concours model may not be everyone's desire, but all should aim to get the machine in good running order, ensuring that it is reliable in use.

Aims can vary and may simply be to correct the

First AJS model 20 twin of 1949 with its saddle and pad rather than dualseat

faults of a machine in poor condition so that it is a pleasure to ride, even if its appearance is nondescript. They could be to repair damage to reach this standard, or might include changes to enhance performance, reliability or appearance. More usually, the aim is to restore the machine to its original condition or, in some cases, beyond that with more chrome, polish and sparkle than even a Plumstead show model.

The decision on the standard and style of the restoration belongs to the owner just as the machine does. Whether all-chrome, all-original or all-bituminous black, it is your choice and no one else's. This decision as to what to do depends on many factors, including time, money and facilities as well as the owner's wishes.

Assets

Motorcycle restoration or repair requires time, money and equipment, and it is necessary to have some amount of all three. Possession of a large amount of any one reduces the need for the other two, but will never remove them entirely. Thus, given plenty of time, the highest restoration standards can be reached using limited facilities and at minimal cost. A deep purse will allow the project to be farmed out and finished in a short time and without the need for much equipment. The ultimate along this road is just to hand the model and money over to a professional, which may sound easy but still calls for decision-making and organizational skills. Finally, anyone with really good facilities can complete a restoration cheaply and quickly by making or refurbishing the parts and tools needed.

It has to be noted, therefore, that all three assets do have to be present to some degree.

Abilities

The AMC restorer must try to make a realistic assessment of his or her abilities. Some of us are less well-blessed with manual skills than others, and it is very important to realize one's limitations early on and to plan ways around them. This can be equally satisfying as the object is to complete the project by the means that are available to you.

An example lies in the use of special tools. You must use these in certain instances and they can be bought, made or, alternatively, you can take your parts to someone who already has them. The method chosen depends on the money, facilities and time previously mentioned.

A person's level of skill varies from job to job and must also be taken into consideration. Your expertise in some areas may be to a very high standard whereas in others it may be lower, so accept that fact. You must judge the areas in which you have the required competence and those where help will be needed.

One answer to this problem is to lower the standard of the restoration. If you cannot do certain jobs and do not want outside help, the only answer is to settle for less than a concours finish. It is likely to be more satisfying to rebuild a basket case into a reliable machine than to attempt perfection and miss it due to personal rather than financial reasons.

A further factor to consider is the timescale of the job. The machine may be wanted by a particular date, in which case the planning must allow for some mishaps as these always occur. For your first restoration it is much better not to have any deadline, as even with the experience of several it can be hard to estimate when a project will be finished.

It is much better to allow for delays, particularly if you are aiming for a concours standard. If a straight rebuild is being done, it is easier to keep to a schedule as more of the work will be under your own control. Planning ahead can often reduce delays. A series of tasks that depend on one another and run in sequence should be started early to prevent a hold-up later on.

Wheels are a classic example as you have a whole series of jobs that can only be carried out in one set order, each task depending on the one preceding it.

Thus, the first stage of any restoration is to decide on a machine and determine the degree of restoration to be carried out. It always pays to think this through before committing oneself, and proper planning not only saves time and money but makes the work more enjoyable, turning a job into a hobby.

Receipts

It pays to keep the paperwork in order from the start. This is dealt with in more detail later, but it cannot be over-emphasized that you must be able to prove that you actually own the machine which sits in the garage, shed or front hall, depending on your workshop habits. It is therefore essential to obtain a receipt for the machine, or if it is built up from boxes of parts, get receipts for them and for all the major purchases you make. It will not do any harm to keep

the till slips of even minor items, logging all of these in your records.

This will help prove ownership, be a useful record should you wish to sell, show a prospective customer exactly what has gone into the machine, and perhaps frighten you at the size of the cost of a restoration.

The workshop

This has been the subject of many articles which seek to describe an ideal arrangement, but for most restorers it is either their garage or garden shed. Some lucky people have better premises and some much worse, but the work that comes from the shop may bear little relation to its size and facilities.

It is possible to produce a concours machine in a small draughty shed and many people have done just this. However, the job of restoring a machine is not an easy one and the exercise is supposed to be an enjoyable hobby, so it makes sense to be able to work in comfort at least.

There is seldom much you can do about the size of your workshop, but the smaller it is, the more you need to have it well organized. Whatever the size it must be clean, dry, warm and well lit. The first job is to stop the roof from leaking and the next is to check the floor and consider sealing its surface. Aside from the dust problem, which sealing greatly reduces, it also makes it much easier to find anything dropped on the floor. Normal concrete is gritty and finding small screws can be difficult.

With the roof and floor in order, the walls can be seen to. A coat of white emulsion greatly brightens the atmosphere and helps the efficiency of the lighting which must be good and fluorescent tubes are essential. They should be the daylight white type and may need to be supplemented by a bench light and a

The first springer single year was also 1949 when candlesticks were used to control the rear end of this model 18S

The great Fergus Anderson at Quarter Bridge while surveying the TT course using a borrowed 1950 G9

hand torch or wander light. It pays to wipe the tubes over occasionally as they tend to get dirty in a workshop, and any reduction in illumination is a handicap. If likely to be knocked at any time, they should be protected by a guard.

Some people share a workshop and this can be a great help, but only if you get on well and can work side by side. For some jobs a pair of spare hands can save a lot of time and trouble, while discussing a problem will often solve it.

Just as important as sharing with another person is sharing the restoration site with another machine. If the same shed has to garage a machine in daily use then sooner rather than later it will come in wet and dirty. This is not impossible to live with, but is a factor to remember when deciding what can and cannot be attempted at home.

Equipment

The workshop has to be fitted out, and the first requirement is a bench to work on which must be solidly built and firmly fixed in place. Next on the list is a machine bench with a means of running the motorcycle up on to it; finally, shelves of various sizes for the storage of parts, tools, equipment, spares and consumables, such as oil and grease are essential. Don't forget a place for a large, shallow box in which to store your gaskets.

The bench needs a vice and you may also wish to make up an engine stand. This can be constructed in wood or metal, its purpose being to stop the unit from falling over on the bench and possibly damaging itself. To be really useful the stand needs to be clamped to the bench, and the same effect can be achieved by holding the engine, or gearbox, in the vice. This leaves both hands free to do the work, but does emphasize the need to fix vice and bench

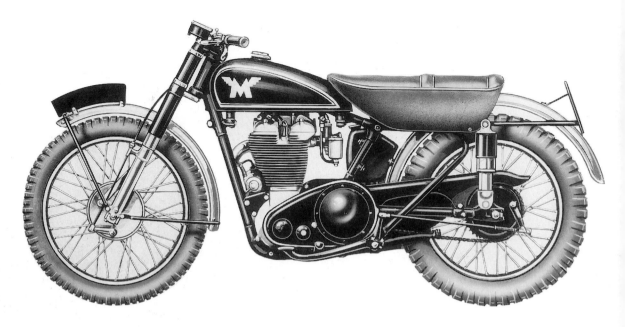

By 1954 the G3LCS was fitted with jampots at the rear and came with number plates despite its scrambles role

securely. Needless to say, the vice must be fitted with smooth jaws to avoid marking the castings.

Hand tools are best stored on a board so they are easy to reach, but keep files beneath the bench to avoid any chance of metal particles getting into the works. Your hand tools are likely to have been accumulated over the years and may be of a variable quality. Now is a good time to get ruthless with them and separate the good from the rest.

Spanner types are legion but the rules are to use only ones that fit and are made from a good steel. My preference is for combination spanners, open at one end with a ring at the other, both being of the same size, a set of $\frac{1}{4}$ in. drive sockets which give me feel on most motorcycle fixings, and a selection of $\frac{1}{2}$ in. drive sockets. Mine have been bought as needed to suit specific jobs so that, thanks to the changes from Whitworth to Unified to metric threads, a fairly full set is to hand. But it took many years to acquire and each of the big sockets was bought for a particular job.

The $\frac{1}{4}$ in. drive is thought light by many, but slimness is an asset in many situations. Often a nut may be slackened by a heavier tool and then run off with the smaller one which can tuck in better.

In addition to hand tools for taking things apart, you will need some for making things. It is at this point that you have to decide how much work you will attempt and what to farm out as the equipment becomes more specialized and expensive. Possession of a good electric drill is taken as read, and it is not too difficult to adapt this to a pillar drill or a bench grinder to sharpen drills. A flexible shaft will help with port work, but the next items come into another league.

There are two pieces of equipment to consider and their relative importance depends, to an extent, on the work you intend doing. If you will be making spacers, machining parts and working to a greater degree on the mechanics, then a lathe becomes essential. With a good set of tools and attachments, a wide range of possibilities opens up and parts can be made at a speed undreamed of. Should you intend to concentrate rather more on the cycle parts, then welding equipment is essential for you. Standard oxy-acetylene gear enables parts to be brazed, welded, filled, loosened, bent and re-formed. An alternative, which helps with the engine and a good deal of the cycle part work, is a butane torch. In all cases when using a mobile heat source, be careful where you point it and remember what items you have warmed up. A fire extinguisher of the correct type is a good investment.

For serious restoration work both a lathe and welding gear are really essential, although a great deal is possible without either. One area where both can help is in making special tools for working on the machine in general and the engine in particular.

A further piece of specialized equipment worth considering is a hydraulic press, which can be constructed using a car or lorry jack. Remember to disconnect the overstroke release, if it has one, as otherwise you can lock the press up solid and it will stay that way until a seal goes.

Also worth putting on your shopping list is an air compressor. It does not have to be new, and often it may be bought separately from the motor to drive it, but it can be very useful even if you have no intention of doing any paint spraying. What it will do is enable you to check oilways, pipe lines, carburettor jets and suchlike for obstructions. Also, an air-line will blast

Harry Louis checking for fuel while reporting the 1951 SSDT with a G9 modified to the form later seen as the CS model

your cleaning agent off the parts as they are done and can save lots of time drying with a cloth.

The equipment you decide to acquire will depend on many factors and relates to your earlier assessment of your abilities. There is no point in having more tools than you can handle, but do not confuse lack of confidence with this. If welding or machining is unfamiliar to you, read about them, consider attending an evening course at the local college, and above all practise before working on anything expensive or hard to replace.

Data

Just as important as tools for the workshop is data for

the mind. Before laying a tool on your AJS or Matchless, there is a great amount of information to be collected if you want the best results. Even if you are only after a good working machine you still need certain basic engine settings, while for a concours job the data needed is far more detailed.

In all cases, the first step is to establish what you have by checking engine and frame numbers for year and model type. The latter can be further checked against the machine specification and often this will

19

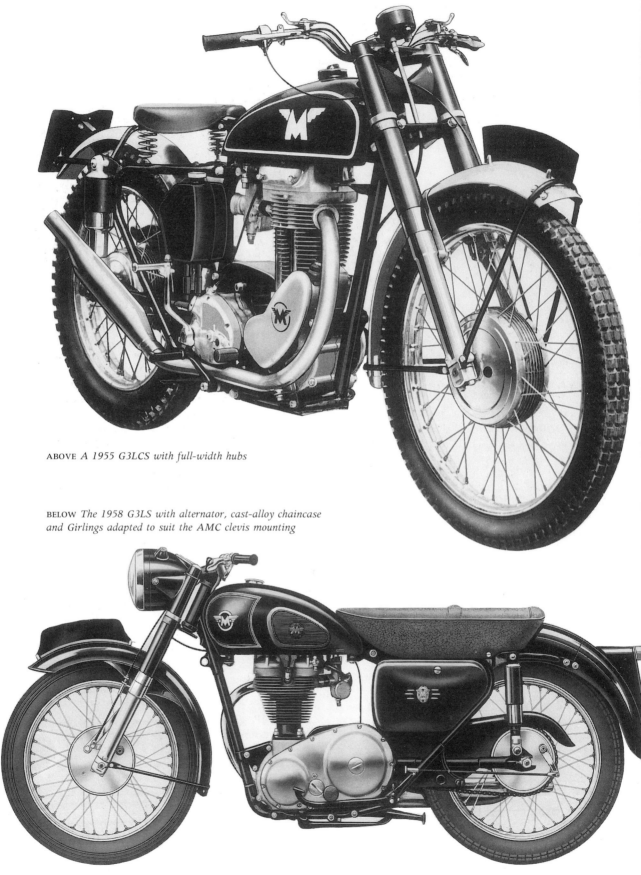

ABOVE *A 1955 G3LCS with full-width hubs*

BELOW *The 1958 G3LS with alternator, cast-alloy chaincase and Girlings adapted to suit the AMC clevis mounting*

Rigid-framed 1957 G80 flat track racer during a try out at Brands Hatch when it bit Vic Willoughby in a tender spot

reveal discrepancies. It is all too easy to switch engines around, so it is as well to check that the engine and frame numbers match and agree. All manner of changes can occur to a machine during its life and some may date from long before the classic machine revival.

Hybrids are a common problem to any make that stayed in production for a long time with few changes to basic dimensions. With the use of Norton parts in the 1960s, there can be further problems to sort out, as the Norton part for an AMC may not be quite the same as when used for the Norton. Specials constructed from AMC parts are also awkward and machines may often be a combination of AJS and Matchless details— this may, or may not, matter, but it is difficult to unravel.

It therefore pays to be wary and to check with the data, as the interest in original specification machines has inevitably led to some being built up from spares or parts from many sources. In other cases, items may not match due to an engine blow-up sometime in the past.

The magazine agony columns indicate that all this is a common happening with most makes, and so it is always something to be aware of and to check. For the machine to be a hybrid may be a good thing, rather than bad, for the changes may have been a worthwhile improvement. The important matter is knowing exactly what you do have.

Dating is complicated by the British industry's tradition of starting its model year in August or September. Like most confusion, it arose from good intentions and came about because the works

switched to making the new models when they returned from their annual holiday. Production was therefore well under way, with stocks in the warehouse or at the dealers, when the new models were announced in the press in the run-up to the Earls Court Show held in November.

With the maker's year out of step with the calendar, it is quite possible to find a machine first registered in October of the year *before* its model year. Further complication for the restorer lies in the changeover of parts which may not coincide with the start of a new model year. Often stocks of old parts would be used, where feasible, until run down before the new ones were phased in. In many cases the change is internal and out of sight, but some are on the outside and can cause real confusion.

The only answer is to work from the engine and frame numbers using the relevant parts book. This list is a most useful publication and is really essential for the restorer, along with a workshop or maintenance manual. In some ways the parts list is the more important for anyone striving for originality, as it lists every part used on the machine with its part number and quantity.

Other literature that will help, and which can be obtained from specialist book dealers, include the rider's handbook, in case it can add to the data in the manual, and a sales brochure, often the only indication of the colours of the machine and its component parts.

A marque history is well worth having as it will fill out the background, and I am biased to recommend *AJS & Matchless—the postwar models* as I wrote it. You should also be reading the specialist magazines, *Classic Bike*, *Classic Mechanics* and *The Classic Motor Cycle* to note addresses and articles that could be

useful to you. The addresses to take note of are any that look to be good and helpful, such as those close to you and the ones offering a special service likely to be needed. Plating, painting, wheel rebuilds and crankshaft regrinds are common needs, but you may also need someone to help with seat renovation, electrics or instruments. *Classic Bike* now publishes a supplier list in the autumn, usually in the October issue, and this is something worth keeping to hand.

Firms of this type are not listed here for two reasons. The first is the general need for them to be local. It is one thing to send a dynamo away for repair but quite another if you have 40 items for stove-enamelling. The second is that firms are built up of people and their expertise. A good reputation may be due to the owner ensuring it is so or the workforce being skilled, or a combination of the two. This can easily change if one or more men leave, so recent recommendation is the best guide.

It will also be most useful to join the AJS & Matchless Owners Club as they offer a unique combined experience. No other body has quite the same outlook and members are in the best position to carry out very real evaluation tests on machines, modifications and their effects. There is also the Vintage Motor Cycle Club in Britain (with others elsewhere), which offers a further source of data, a marque specialist, and from their work has come a transfer scheme now available to all. AMC owners are more fortunate than most in that their owners club has its own transfer scheme with the items based on factory replicas, and these are usually preferred by members. This is yet another reason to join this most useful organization.

Yet another source of information is the show in its various forms. This may be a straight exhibition which includes older machines, a classic machine show, a rally or a race meeting with events for older machines. All provide an opportunity to study other machines, talk to owners, gather information and find out where to get parts. Autojumbles, which are often combined with other events, can become an important part of the restorer's life for they offer the opportunity to seek out elusive spares, data and services. Local and

capabilities of both yourself and your equipment. Now you have to think again and decide how that happy dream of a concours win, sweet-running machine or whatever is to be reached.

In essence you have to decide whether to deal with the machine as a whole or by major parts. The first is usually quicker but requires more fortitude. Once apart, you will have a vast number of parts, all of which will need attention, and long before you get to the assembly stage you may have run out of interest. The alternative is to take a major unit and renovate that alone. It will take longer to complete the whole machine, but this method does reduce the storage space needed and you also feel that you are getting somewhere as each major lump is completed. Whichever way you go, you need notes, photographs and sketches in large numbers. If you are going to rely on photos, you will need to take plenty and they must be good close-ups. It is possible to do this with a very basic camera, but for the best results you really need a

ABOVE *The off-road style for the twins can be seen to advantage with this 1958 G11CS*

RIGHT *AMC entered the lightweight market with this 1958 G2 and a matching AJS*

not so local ones should be attended, with dates and venues to be found in the specialist press.

Work plan

This is the grand title for you tearing the engine out and apart in the first flush of enthusiasm. Unfortunately, come winter, this fades and the mix-up of parts you now have in various boxes, bags and tins becomes very unattractive. Before too long, another basket job hits the ad columns, which is both sad and unnecessary.

Before you pick up the first tool, have a long look at yourself, your facilities and the machine. *Think*, painful though it is. Make sure that you have decided what *you* want to do and that this is within the

Line drawing of the G12CSR in 1961 when it was a fast machine but hard on cranks, cam followers and petrol tanks

decent SLR which can focus down to three feet or less. Unless you can get that close, you just won't record the detail you need. Good lighting will also help to get good photos, and a wide-angle lens could be a useful asset.

Notes and sketches are a good alternative and mean that you can safely proceed without wondering if your film is going to develop satisfactorily. A pad of paper should be kept handy for rough notes in the workshop and it is a good idea to write them up cleanly the same day. It is all too easy, especially with cycle parts, to forget the order in which parts fit on to a stud, which way round a bolt goes, or even where the horn is fitted when you come to put things together months later. Plenty of labels and plastic storage bags will make life easier.

Even if the assembly you start with is wrong, it is useful to record it as a basis to work from. Do not think that you can remember it all, as you cannot; nor is it always obvious as to how the parts should be. Mudguard stays, in particular, can cause problems— often the apparently same part is used on both sides of the machine and can be fixed in four alternative ways in each position. Four? Yes, as it can be turned over or end for end, but only one way and one position will get it back where it came from. In theory this may not matter, if the stays are all the same, but in practice they always seem happier if replaced as they were. This no doubt arises because of small distortions that the parts have accommodated and if switched round they will have to begin again.

If you start with someone else's disaster as a basket case then the problem becomes more difficult as you will have to determine what each part is, where it goes and if it needs attention or was made in its present shape at the factory. A common difficulty with basket cases is rogue parts from another machine that have crept in and can give you hours of fun and frustration.

Lists

Some people live by lists, other abhor them, but in restoration they really are essential and should form part of your note-taking. Starting from a complete machine, parts can be listed as they are dismantled with notes as to whether they need to be repaired, treated or both. By working with a parts list missing items can be highlighted and a shopping list compiled. Consumables will go on this as well.

When starting with a basket case a parts list really is essential and one or more photocopies are well worth obtaining at the start. Using one as a master the parts can be checked off one by one down to the last nut, bolt and washer. What is left on the list at the end becomes the shopping list and any parts not identified are, or ought to be, rogue.

While checking the list you can begin to establish the work needed on the parts you have depending rather on how much you are short and how essential the missing items are. How you fulfil the shopping list depends on your aims, money and the items themselves. You may have a good selection of nuts and bolts that would be fine for the job even if not correct to concours standard. If your aim is a good working machine then use them and the same philosophy can apply to many other items.

RIGHT *A rather old-fashioned single in the form of this 1961 AJS 16 on test*

These can include parts from another machine which is no trouble for you if they are stamped BSA or Triumph but could be a small headache if marked AMC. If you have a late model they may belong—or they may not! A larger headache is the appearance of real AMC parts which happen to come from another model but are not compatible with yours.

You must also beware of parts that changed in detail over the years but remained very similar in appearance, and some pattern parts. Of the latter, some are very, very good but others can be awful. A side headache can be proprietary parts which were common to many English machines and some of which happened to fall into your basket. A handful of petrol taps might be useful but not if they all came from some other machine.

ABOVE *The 1962 31CSR with siamezed exhaust pipes, alloy guards and short dualseat*

OPPOSITE *Largest of the genuine AMC twins was this 1962 750 cc G15/45 which was built for the American market*

BELOW *The standard big twin was the G12 here seen in 1963 form which was the last year with the AMC forks and hubs*

At the end of this operation you will have dismantled the complete machine and listed all the parts that require your attention or their purchase. With this knowledge the restoration work will be easier to organize and the assembly straightforward to carry out.

Security

Classic motorcycles and their component parts are valuable and in some cases nearly irreplaceable. One professional restorer was quoted as saying, 'What man has made, man can make again', which is perfectly true, but only at a price.

Therefore security has become a point to bear in mind. This is especially true if you are forced to use a lock-up garage as your workshop and the necessary

BELOW *The final twins went further with the Norton 745 cc engine, as well as cycle parts for this 1967 AJS 33CSR with nice swept-back pipes*

ABOVE *By 1966 the singles were very long in the tooth and had Norton forks and hubs*

steps should be taken before the machine is on the premises. Avoid publicity as the word can quickly get about so don't leave the doors open if the premises face on to the street.

Working at home reduces the problem but may not remove it so again discretion is a good idea. It could also avoid an argument with the local council if a neighbour thinks you are using your home as a repair business.

A method used by some restorers to at least cut down their risk once a machine is partly dismantled is to store the parts in different areas of their home. This is a particularly useful way of protecting the smaller, more delicate, rather expensive and fairly universal items. These minor assemblies such as magneto, dynamo, speedometer and carburettor all lend themselves well to this arrangement and benefit from the household heating.

29

*Brothers John and Joe Disimones with their 1959 31CS and
some of the hardware they had won*

2 First steps

Clean machine

With your 'before' pictures safely taken, work can begin on your project but not in the workshop. The very first thing to be done is to take the machine outside and give it a good clean to remove dirt, grime, grease and oil. There are a number of cleaning agents to help with this task and the aim is to get the bulk of the dirt washed away and the machine dried before it enters the working area.

Transfers

While this chore is in hand, care must be taken not to damage the finish or any transfers as reference to them may be necessary. In fact, once the machine is clean and back in the workshop it is a good time to go round it and make notes as to the exact position of all the transfers with dimensions from fixed features.

If you are just overhauling the model then the transfers are unlikely to be of any major concern but for a full restoration they are. The position of the oil tank level, for instance, is a fixed dimension from some other point and for a concours job should be correct. The owners club transfers come with this information which is a help if your machine lacked the transfers in the first place or you forgot to measure where they were.

First removals

The initial steps are to remove the parts that are fragile and easily damaged or which impede access to the major items. The first step is the fuel tank but before touching it have a look at the control cables and note how they run. Are they to the left or right of the steering head and above or below the fixing lugs?

On some models you cannot remove the tank without taking the seat off first so if this is the case tackle it that way without forcing anything. If any of the bolts involved hold something else as well then you must note the order the parts are in, as well as which way round the bolts go.

Note also the run of the petrol pipes while the tank

and taps are in their correct location and watch the handlebars as you shift the tank. It is all too easy to catch the front of it on something and have the bars swing round and clout it to produce a dent or a nasty scratch.

Now get the machine up on the bike bench and make quite sure it is secure. If it is on a stand check that the feet cannot slide off the edge of the bench even when you lean on it with a tool. Check what will happen as you dismantle the machine. Most with a centre stand will keep their front wheel on the ground but if there is any doubt force a piece of wood under the back tyre to ensure stability. If the whole machine rocks back just as you try to lift the engine out, it can really put you off your stroke and cause you to drop something. Or worse still, if you dive to save the model and knock it over.

So aim for stability until you have the major heavy items out and then jack up the front and take the wheel out. Do it the other way round and you have too much mass balanced on too short a wheelbase for safety. Remember this for when you come to assemble.

With the bike up in the air and secure continue with the dismantling by removing the exhaust systems which may fall away or could stick. If the latter occurs don't tip the bike over while hauling on the pipes, just try to work them off a little at a time.

Tackle tight systems from the rear, a section at a time. Keep the pipe fixings tight and just remove the silencer bolts and clips. Work at the silencer to ease it back and off and then move on to the pipe, which should respond to the same treatment.

Now attend to the fragile items which start with the headlamp rim with its glass, reflector and bulb. Place something soft over the front mudguard so the assembly can rest while you disconnect the wires or pull out the bulb holders. Store with care and add the rear light lens and bulb.

Next is the speedometer, and rev-counter if fitted, noting which is to the left or right. Watch the bulb holder fitted in the back of the instrument and remove the bulb itself. Tie the parts so they stay together at the end of the wire and don't slide off into the main harness. The same trick is often worth doing with the

A 1954 AJS 16MS at the Paris Show with its new full-width front hub

instrument drive cable to restrain the knurled end fitting. A clothes peg can be used temporarily and the run of the cables must be noted.

Remove the carburettor(s) and float chamber and store but drain the petrol out first. If a complete strip is intended the slides could best be removed from the cables and kept with the carburettor until attention is turned to that item.

The wiring is next on the list along with the control cables for they may well be inexorably linked by clips and tape holding them to the frame. More notes are needed before they are released. Then disconnect the battery and remove it. Don't hide it as it will need immediate attention if it is to act as a case, or regular attention if it is to be used further.

The cables, suitably labelled, may come off first and the label should indicate which end is which if it is not obvious. The wiring is usually best detached working from the rear of the machine forward to the headlamp switch. Depending on the year of the machine it may be best to detach it from the switches and other electrical parts or it could be simpler to leave it joined and to take the parts off. Some don't leave you any choice, for example a dipswitch. More notes will be necessary, of course, but also check along the harness as you remove it for any points where it has been

rubbed or shows signs of damage. They are areas to do something about on assembly to prevent problems occurring.

It is likely that the rectifier will have been removed during this operation but not necessarily the regulator if one is fitted. It is fragile so take it off for storage.

With the delicate details and the tangled mass or mess of cables and wiring out of the way the machine will look a lot cleaner and easier to work on. You can now really see what you are doing and can get at it without fear that you may damage something both fragile and costly. This is no reason not to take care, of course.

Basket case

Where your AJS or Matchless has come in boxes you start your restoration with the assembly of shabby components. It is well worth cleaning the contents of each box as this will make them nicer to work on but nothing special is needed at this stage as they are going to need a lot more work and another, better, clean before the final assembly.

What you have to do is to build up your collection of parts, each checked off against the parts list, into a complete machine. There are three problems in doing this. First is that it may not all be there. If the missing items are mainly bolts and fixings then anything from stock can be pressed into temporary service but if you lack structural items it becomes more tricky.

Second, some parts may be damaged and ill fitting, even distorting other parts. Allowance must be made where this occurs. Finally, there are rogue parts which may throw you off course.

At this stage keep everything and in fact this is a sound move with any part from any older machine. No matter how tired or worn it may be, at some time you or someone else will want to use it because it is the best one available. If you don't use it yourself you may be able to swap it for something you do need and many a rebuild has been completed on this basis. Sometimes the swaps involve three or four people but usually all will finish up with the parts they need— often at little or no cost.

With a basket case you have to build the complete machine up as you get the parts. It is valid to leave out, say, the gearbox internals as their space is defined but beware of any assumption with the cycle parts. It is only too easy to think all is well, begin final finishing and then having to destroy that finish with further fitting work.

This is why a basket case always takes so much longer to complete and tries the worker's patience as it is ages before any progress at all seems to be made.

From this first assembly exercise, a list of missing parts and those needing attention should have been compiled. Once you are satisfied that it is all there and will all go together then you can continue along the same lines as someone fortunate enough to start with a complete machine.

You can now take it all apart again.

Restoration

This is another word for repair and is closely linked to service and maintenance. The philosophy is the same whether you have a 1947 single or a 1965 twin and the work involved and techniques used are similar or the same for both machines. The problems will vary enormously with no regard to the age of the machine and only spares availability will relate to years to any degree.

The essence of the job is that the machine is reduced totally to its component parts. That means studs out of castings, spokes from wheels, seat cover from frame and so on until you are down to a single piece of metal, rubber or plastic for just about any item. Ball races and rectifiers you do not dismantle if you want them to continue living but most assemblies will come down to individual pieces.

Once in pieces each of these have to be checked and then mended or replaced. This may be as simple as running a die down a thread or as complex as metal spraying followed by grinding to a very close tolerance. Again, it could be a specialist welding process plus a careful freehand cutting using a flexible drive followed by a machine operation.

K. G. Edwards on a G3LC at Beggars Roost in 1952

Replacement can be by a new spare or by an uprated part from a later machine which improves the performance. Or it can be by a modern component that does the job in a better way; tyres, shock absorbers and electronic ignition are just three examples.

After mending or replacement comes finishing when the outer coat goes on to the piece part and may be paint, plating or polish. In all cases they mirror the base material and reflect its preparation. You can then put it all together again.

Dismantle

There is a whole special technique to taking things apart and if you want to restore successfully you need to learn it. The first aspect is to soak parts in paraffin or penetrating fluid. If anything is stuck this is the opening move — and time. Let the fluid soak well in, give it another dose and come back days rather than hours later.

Try to move it. If there is any sign of a shift, you are winning; give it another soak, more time and bit by bit it will come. Rush it and it will snap.

Stubborn, well-rusted nuts and bolts holding cycle parts together call for another method. If they are too far gone for further use, if they hold solid sections and if the parts are none too strong don't try to undo them. You can easily do real damage to nuts, bolts, the major parts and your fingers, either with the spanners or the saw if you try that method. You will not be able to hold the fixing still to saw it and will inevitably damage the parts.

The answer is to just do them up. For once get out the $\frac{1}{2}$ in. drive socket and wind it on until the bolt goes bang. If it is largish, drill a hole up its centre first, but *never* try this on bolts fixed to tapped holes.

Timing cases often respond well to an impact driver but if you take that route two rules apply. First is that the blade must fit the screw and second is to hit it good and hard. A series of taps is no use, it has to be one good blow. One of the very best motorcycle men I have known told me once that this distinguished the pro from the amateur. The latter would tap at a puller to jump a taper apart and either shift nothing or damage parts. The pro would decide it was tight, select a four-pound club hammer and hit it once, good and square as direction is as important as the force behind the blow.

It always pays to think before playing the heavy hand as often parts will not give because you have not

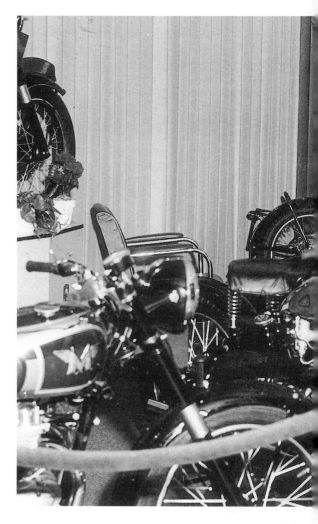

RIGHT *Line of AMC models and others at the 1950 New York Show held at Grand Central Palace*

BELOW *Early competition model for 1946 when little of this 16MC was altered from standard*

BELOW RIGHT *Rather nice 1966 31CSR hitched to a suitable chair while on test*

undone all you should have. Particular care is needed when dealing with castings or mouldings as both are brittle and respond in the same way if put under bending strain. They crack. So if it is stuck check against the parts list as this may indicate a screw you have missed, either because it is hidden down a dirty counter-bore or due to it assembling from the other side to the rest of the fixings.

Checking

At this point you really start to find out how much work you have let yourself in for. You need to go over each part to establish if it can still be used, if it needs mending and if it needs finishing. More lists I fear.

Whether a part can still be used will depend on what it is, its material and whether it is bent, cracked, broken or worn badly. If it is in any or all of these conditions, it will need mending or replacement. Bent parts will have to be straightened using heat and a press on occasion, cracked and broken ones may be welded and worn ones reclaimed.

It is while you are checking parts that you will find the bodges that have been done over the years to keep the machine running. Often these are the greatest problem and you are left thinking that if only the owners of the past had just repaired the model your troubles would be minimal.

RIGHT *This 1966 G80CS was the last of a long line but still preferred by some for off-road riding in Western USA*

BELOW *A 1951 G9 showing off its nice lines, good dualseat and poor primary chaincase*

Mending

You are thus left to return parts to their original standard and it can often take all your ingenuity to deal with the past horrors. Some of the worst concern studs and threaded holes, the former often broken off in the latter. Removal means making a drill bush, drilling into the stud and using an extractor to wind it out.

One thing with cover screws is that if all else fails you can drill the head off and by this means release the cover which will expose enough screw for it to be easily removed.

Threaded holes in castings or the frame are another source of problem and thread inserts can be one solution. Normally there is enough material available to accommodate them but for success the manufacturer's instructions must be followed carefully.

Mending also includes getting joint faces flat. To do this all the studs will need to be removed and it is worth checking round the hole that each screws into.

Often the metal will have pulled up a little so it needs to be counter-sunk and then the whole surface made flat. If you have to machine it keep it to a minimum, as modern gasket sealants can help a good deal in keeping oil where it should be.

Welding or heating equipment is often vital when dealing with the cycle parts which need to be warmed up before being straightened. It also allows holes to be filled up and redrilled where really needed so it is very handy for some rear mudguards. It is not unknown for several sets of holes to exist for various pillion pads of the past, all long gone so the holes need removal as well.

It is possible to take parts to a shop for welding as individual items but the need for a heat source in your own workshop may be emhpasized if some assembly is out of line. Getting everything straight really can call for the parts to be in place and this makes it difficult for the job to be taken elsewhere other than to a restoration specialist.

Finishing

Once you are satisfied that a part is correct and will assemble as required then it needs to be finished. This may be as simple as a coating of oil to prevent rust for engine and gearbox parts. Or it can be a complex sequence of plating, painting and lining for a tank.

Castings may be bead-blasted or polished, cycle parts are mainly painted, details are plated and in many cases parts will need to be masked to protect threads and holes.

The specialist electrical assemblies and others of the same delicacy all go through their own special processes as detailed later but their basic mechanics may need the same mending and finishing as everything else.

Then all you have to do is put it all together again.

The Rickman Metisse fitted with the Matchless single engine and superbly finished as always

Note

From now on I will assume you are either starting from a complete machine or have loosely hung your basket job together and have collected most of the major parts needed. This is to avoid needless repetition of this assumption together with the notes relevant to it and already mentioned.

3 The engine

Most people like to begin with the engine because it is of the greatest interest to them. It is also likely to be the easiest area to restore and the least boring.

The exact procedure you follow will depend on which model you have and on your working style. The first job is to take the engine, or engine unit, out of the frame and then to dismantle it. Before removing it a decision needs to be made about the large, tight nuts that are used in various places. The purist approach to large nuts is to use a suitable tool to hold the part they are attached to and undo them. However, this can be a problem in the number of special tools that may be needed and it may govern the sequence of operations.

At this stage all that is needed is for the nuts to be loosened and common practice is to do this with the engine in the frame and connected to the rear wheel and brake. With the machine in top gear, each nut is attacked in turn starting at the engine and working through the transmission to the rear wheel. A combination of jammed-on brake and clouted spanner will usually prevail unless the clutch slips.

This method means that the timing cover has to come off at what is really too early a stage so that the pinion and cam gear nuts can be slackened. The alternatives are less messy in their approach and enable parts to be dealt with as desired. The first is to use tools to hold parts still and a further option, given the equipment, is to use an impact spanner. If you do take the latter route, do ensure that all the parts will take the shock.

Engine types

There are three basic groups—singles, twins and light singles. All were built in more than one capacity but the construction of each stayed much the same throughout its life.

The singles began in two sizes for each marque with both based on a 93 mm stroke and iron head and barrel. The same units also served the competition models until 1950 when these became all-alloy. The road models were given an alloy head for 1951 and the next year the Matchless magneto moved ahead of the cylinder.

The next change came for 1956 when the 348 cc competition models were revised so the 1950 alloy engine went into a sprung frame for trials. For scrambles there were new 85.5 mm short-stroke, all-alloy engines in 348 cc and 497 cc capacities with integral pushrod tunnels cast into the cylinder. The trials 497 cc engine was dropped.

The road engines were fitted with alternators for 1958, therefore losing their magneto drive chain cover. In its place a small cover concealed the ignition points. The competition trio ran on for two years but the short-stroke 348 cc scrambler was dropped at the end of 1959. The enlarged scrambles engine used 89 × 96 mm dimensions to arrive at a 597 cc capacity.

The next change came for 1962 when the 93 mm stroke, 348 cc road engine was replaced by an 81 mm short-stroke one with integral pushrod tunnels. The competition engine retained its old form and 93 mm stroke while the two 497 cc models ran on as they were and the 597 cc single was dropped at the end of the year. It was 1964 before the next change when the two road models both adopted the 85.5 mm stroke and cylinders with integral pushrod tunnels. The competition 348 cc machine also went to the 85.5 mm stroke but still retained its magneto as did the 497 cc version. All engines adopted the Norton oil pump in place of the long-standing AMC type and in this form they remained until they went out of production.

The twins dated from 1949 in 498 cc size and were joined by the export 550 cc version for 1954 and the 593 cc versions for 1956. For 1958 CS and CSR versions of the larger model were built and the next year saw the 646 cc engine in these forms along with the 498 cc one also in standard and sports guise. The standard engines went to an alternator but the sports ones kept to the magneto.

The sports 498 cc engine did not continue for 1960 and the standard one went at the end of 1961. The 646 cc engine continued in both states of tune and during 1962 was joined by a small number stretched to 750 cc for export only. For that year the sports twin joined the standard one in fitting an alternator although it still clung to the magneto.

The 646 cc twin engines stayed in these two forms

Engine of the 1960 G80CS with its racing carburettor and oil tank on the left of the machine

up to their end in 1966 but were joined by the 745 cc Norton Atlas engine for 1965. This continued in use up to 1969.

The first 248 cc light single appeared in 1958 with semi-unit construction as the gearbox was strapped to the back of the crankcase. For 1959 a sports edition was used for the CS model and for 1960 the engine was enlarged to produce a 348 cc light single. For 1961 the sports version was used for the S model and in 1962 for the CSR. At the end of that year the S, CS and 350 models were dropped to be followed by the standard 250 during 1963. The CSR ran on to 1966 before it went as well.

Removing the engine

The exact procedure depends on the engine you have, the machine it is in, your strength and your lifting tackle. No engine is light which makes the task a job for two or three, preferably two with some form of lifting gear.

The solution often used is to remove some of the heavier parts while the engine is still in the frame as this can make the rest much easier to manage. The reverse is used on assembly which may not be as neat and tidy as building it up on the bench, but is at least an answer to the problem.

In all cases start by draining the oil tank, primary chaincase, gearbox and engine sump, replacing the plugs to stop the oil remnants dripping on you and the floor. During the first steps you will have detached the

40

control cables and wiring but if you left them for any reason, now is the time to do this job anyway. The dynamo, where fitted, can readily be removed but the other electrics can stay unless you plan to part-dismantle before engine removal.

Detach the main oil pipes between engine and oil tank plus the small one that feeds the rocker gear. Take care when undoing any fixings that hold these in case they stick to the pipe union and try to carry it round which will put a nasty kink in the pipe. You must hold the union to prevent this. Store the pipes with care so they do not get distorted.

Next deal with the primary transmission and, having removed the outer chaincase, undo the engine sprocket nut using a good fitting socket spanner and jarring it undone. The clutch is next and you undo the spring nuts to remove the plates.

Having taken these out you then have to undo the clutch centre nut and to hold the centre while you do this you either rely on the rear brake or a locking device. This can be an old clutch plate with a handle attached, one plate of each type bolted together to lock the centre to the drum or a scotch made from bent steel strip. This last is not recommended as it puts all the

Standard model G9 or G12 from 1960 with sombre paintwork which could be brightened with chrome or colour

load in one place. The centre is splined to the gearbox mainshaft and may slide off or may need an extractor. If it does, take care to apply the load evenly so as not to bend or crack anything.

The same applies to the engine sprocket and the alternator which have to come away before the inner chaincase can be removed. As this comes off, check and note carefully any spacers behind it as if these are not as they should be you can easily distort or crack the case on assembly. You may well have to return to this point on final assembly in case things have altered because of other work you have carried out on the parts. This is an important point on all models.

Now move on to the top half of the engine if you intend removing it at this stage and follow this by the timing side and gearbox internals as covered in more detail in their own sections.

This brings you to the point of the big heave and the exact sequence depends on the model, assistance and method chosen to support the engine weight. The general principle is to remove the engine torque stays, slacken all the fixings, slide out the minor ones and then support the weight on a box or a jack, or with a sling. Pull out each remaining bolt in turn to remove all distance pieces, noting where they came from. A diagram with their lengths will help. Then remove the bolts and lift out the engine.

A 1958 G11CSR with the sports specification and a higher performance than the standard model

Single dismantling

This may have begun in the frame but the essential tasks are the same whether there or on the bench. First, hold the engine in the vice by its front mountings and add a support at the rear if this is needed. Make quite certain it is secure and that the unit is held firmly. You can now take it apart but don't rush it and do observe as you go. It is well worth checking the valve timing before you remove anything in case the markings are missing or the assembly wrong. Use a degree disc clamped to the drive side of the crankshaft, set the valve gaps as

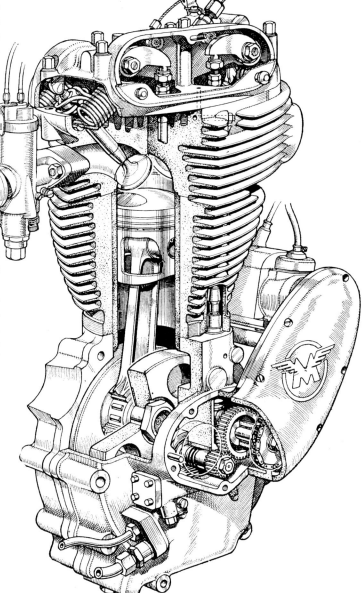

The Matchless scrambles engine with short-stroke and pushrod tunnels cast into the barrel for 1956

prescribed and make your notes. While you are at it and have the degree disc in place also check the ignition timing on full advance and retard.

The engine will come apart easily enough and on anything unknown the golden rule is to check everything, assume nothing, suspect the worst and take it all apart. It may seem less trouble to leave a crankshaft intact, but only full examination will show if it is really fit or about to fail.

These engines all follow a very similar pattern and should not give any problems of dismantling. Start at the top with the rocker box, once the crankshaft is set so both valves are shut, but keep the assembly as one for the time being to avoid losing any small details.

Next remove the cylinder head which will release the pushrod tubes unless these are part of the cylinder itself. This can come off next along with gaskets and any compression plates to leave the bottom half.

Remove the circlips and put in a bag labelled 'used'. Don't use them again but keep them in case you need a pattern when looking for new ones. The piston should be marked F for front on the inside and the pin should push out, but if it won't, warm the piston so the pin will slide out. Drifting is another method but requires two people as the piston must be supported during the operation.

Remove the outer timing cover, the drive to the magneto, or the points, and then the inner cover. As this comes away be careful that the cams do not come out of mesh until you have had a chance to check their mesh and the timing marks.

You can now lock the crankshaft by one of two methods. The first is with a good clean bar through the small-end plus supports placed across the crankcase mouth after it has been wiped clean. Second is by the use of an alloy bar placed between the flywheels to lock the rod against the crankcase.

The crankshaft timing gear is a taper fit and keyed to the shaft. It is held by a left-hand nut for most but

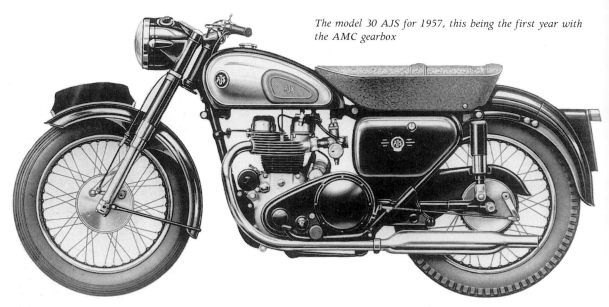

The model 30 AJS for 1957, this being the first year with the AMC gearbox

right-hand for the 1960 on CS and some other scrambles machines and this can be identified by the addition of a lock washer. The gear may come away if carefully levered or it may require a puller. The oil pump must come out before the crankcase is split and to do this the end plates need to be removed along with the location peg. The pump spindle can then emerge to the rear.

The crankcase bolts can next be removed and the cases parted for removal of the crankshaft assembly. Check for any distance pieces and note the order of parts.

The major parts are now ready for your attention.

Twin dismantling

Again begin at the top and take the rocker covers off. Remove the inlet manifold and head steady followed by each head in turn after its valves have been allowed to close.

The barrels follow, once the pushrods have been taken out and labelled, and then the pistons. The pins are likely to be tighter than on the single and so the piston could need to be warmed up. Mark the pistons L and R on the inside so they are not mixed up and also mark the cylinders so these do not get switched over.

The bottom half is dismantled by first removing the timing cover and then the plate carrying the two oil pumps. Follow this with the dynamo or alternator and magneto or points housing. A tool is needed to pull the

A 1952 model 18 AJS with rigid frame, Burman gearbox and saddle

ignition gear from the armature but the dynamo one can be left in place.

The camshaft gear nuts have left-hand threads and a simple drawbar puller is needed to remove the gears. Next to come away are the oil filter details, release valve and oil distributor. Follow this with the crankcase bolts which will allow the timing-side case to come away along with the camshafts and followers.

Finally, undo the nuts holding the centre web and withdraw the crankshaft. Its timing gear can stay in place if you wish and once more the parts await your attention.

Light singles dismantling

This engine is similar to the heavier and larger singles but with quite a number of detail differences including having the oil tank built into the right crankcase.

The work begins by removing the right outer cover and the whole of the primary transmission. This releases the inner chaincase which in turn allows the gearbox to be unstrapped from the back of the crankcase.

This leaves the basic engine and the top half as for the singles. The bottom half has a right inner cover which carries the points plate and retains the camshaft and its followers. Below is the outer part of the oil tank and the right crankcase half also carries the oil pump and its details.

These all need to come away first, after which the crankcase halves can be parted to release the crankshaft and the bearings and distance pieces associated with it. All are there for you to clean, mend and assemble.

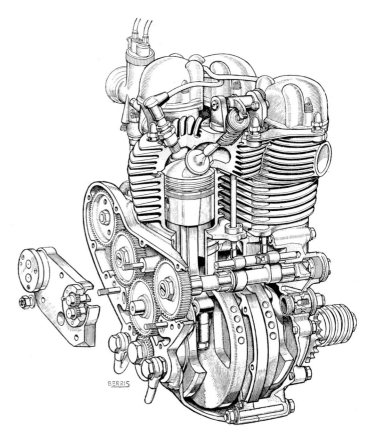

ABOVE *The smallest twin engine in 1956 but much as all the AMC units*

BELOW *The very sporting G15CSR of 1966 with Norton engine, forks and wheels*

45

Crankshaft

The singles had a built-up crankshaft with caged roller big-end while the AMC twins had a one-piece shaft with shell big-ends and a third, centre main bearing. The Norton twin engines had a built-up crankshaft and plain big-ends.

The light singles had the mainshafts keyed and pressed into the flywheels but the heavy singles retained them with nuts as well. Early models of the latter had a taper fit but this was changed for a parallel one to improve rigidity.

The singles crankpin was of two-part construction with a hardened sleeve pressed on to a tough crankpin. Due to this form of construction there were no radii at the corner between the pin and the sleeve shoulder and thus no clearance needed in the flywheel hole.

It is imperative to note that most replacement pins are made in one piece and therefore have a good radius at this point. The flywheel hole must be altered to give clearance for this or it will dig in on assembly before the parts are fully home. If left in this condition the pin can be guaranteed to break.

The crankshaft should be inspected for damage and big-end wear before it is dismantled and notes taken as to the exact position of each item. It is quite practical to undo the crankpin nuts using a close fitting socket, a decent-sized vice and a locking bar through the small-end. Before doing this, scribe a line

Off-road or street scrambler G12CS for the American market in 1961

across the wheel rims to assist with their re-alignment.

Inspection and the feel of the parts will show if they need replacement and a worn roller track will appear grey and matt instead of shiny. Where a new big-end is fitted you will probably have to lap out the rod liner to remove any distortion that occurs when it is pressed into place.

The twin crankshaft should have the connecting rods removed after the parts have been marked. As it is in one piece the only other job is to remove any sludge traps and check very thoroughly that these and all the oilways are totally clear. They must be unimpeded from entry to exit and the latter are the small holes in the crankpins themselves.

The crankpins must be inspected for wear and damage. It is feasible to remove light scores, marks and even surface rust with fine emery cloth but if they are worn they will need regrinding. A micrometer or vernier is an essential tool to have, but some idea of the degree of ovality can be gauged using callipers and feelers to detect variations.

If grinding is needed the reduction in diameter is in 0.010 in. steps from the nomimal to a maximum of 0.030 in. In all cases the finish and the end radii dimensions are very important and have a bearing on big-end life and crankshaft reliability.

The mainshafts also need to be inspected as they

must be a good fit in the main bearings and their threads in good condition. If there is any sign of trouble its cause must be located and remedied.

The crankpins are an area where metal spraying may be used for reclamation if there is no other solution. This is a process where minute metal particles are heated and directed on to the hot surface of the parent part so they fuse to it. When cool the part can then be ground back to the standard size. The process requires special equipment and a degree of skill to achieve the right result but it can save parts otherwise damaged beyond repair.

When assembling the crankshaft first recheck that everything is scrupulously clean including the nuts, bolts and your tools. Make sure you have everything laid out in the right order and then proceed with the job. The actual method depends on the crankshaft type but all except the one piece will need truing up once together. The singles will, with few exceptions, need a press to assemble them as well as when dismantling and the parts must be aligned before they are pushed together.

Make quite sure that all shafts are positioned and keyed so that no oil hole is blocked off and check this feature once the parts are together. Fit any locking washers or screws using Loctite to make sure these are secure.

In all cases it will then be necessary to check the alignment and for this you must have a dial gauge and some means of supporting the crankshaft. This may be by rollers for each mainshaft or with the drive side held in bearings and the reading taken on the timing one. The dial gauge will show the size and direction of the error which then has to be removed.

Methods include clamps, wedges, lead mallets and a lead block on the floor. Experience is needed to know exactly where to hit and how hard, but care and practice will get the assembly in line. The closer it is the better and recheck that the oilways are all clear right through to the big-end.

The twin crankshaft simply needs to have the rods fitted for the AMC type but the Norton one has to be assembled with studs, lock washers and dowels. The same rules on cleanliness, sludge traps and oil flow still apply.

Singles big-end

The same crankpin remained in use for many singles right up to 1963 with a part number change for 1951. It was joined by a stronger pin for the 1956 scrambles engines and this continued to be used in the 497 cc CS engine from 1960, after the 350 scrambler had been dropped. From 1964 only this type was fitted.

Associated with the original pin was a cage which carried three rows of ten $\frac{1}{4} \times \frac{1}{4}$ in. rollers while the 1956 pin had a single row of 14 $\frac{1}{4} \times \frac{1}{2}$ in. rollers. For 1962 this was changed to two rows of the smaller roller

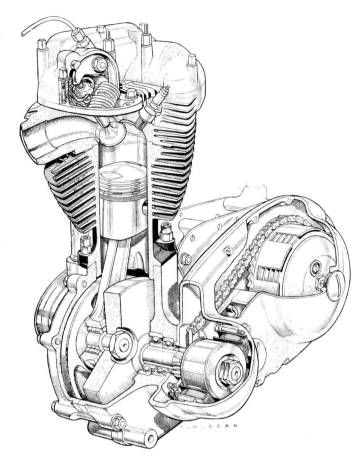

The heavy AMC single engine as built from 1958 with alternator electrics but much as in the past

for the CS model but reverted to the single row after 1963. The cage for this assembly was modified for 1960 so the original was not used for too long. The original roller was also listed plus 0.001 in. on diameter but this could only be used if the pin and rod liner were lapped to fit.

A pair of thrust washers went with the 1956 crankpin, used in that application only and revised for 1964. Thrust washers were also fitted up to 1950 and were in steel for that year only and bronze before then. The crankpin nuts were also made to suit the two crankpin types but while the 1945 one ran through to 1963, the 1956 type was revised a little for 1957 but then ran on till they went out of production. With it, from 1957, was a single location key.

The light singles had two types of big-end, each with its own pin, cage and either 20 or 28 rollers of the $\frac{1}{4} \times \frac{1}{4}$ in. size. The first went in the basic 250 model, the S and the CS for 1959–60. The second was used by the CS for 1961 on, the CSR and the 350. In either case the crankpin was located by a key and this and the second cage were common to the heavy singles post-1957 parts.

Standard model 31 in 1959 with rear rack for luggage

Thrust washers went on the second type only with those of the 1960 CS differing from the other years and models. The crankpin nuts came in three forms with one for the 250 and S models, one for the 350 and 1960 CS and one for the 1961 on CS and CSR. The one for the 350 was that used by the heavy singles for 1945–63.

Flywheels and mainshafts

Despite the 93 mm stroke which was common to so many of the singles there is an impressive list of changes for these parts. Right up to 1963 the 350 and 500 used different pairs even after the diameter became the same when the 350 engine number 8000 was built in 1948.

Prior to that point the 350 had wheels of $7\frac{3}{4}$ in., as for the 500, but balanced to a different piston weight. The next change came for 1951 when the crankpin thrust washers were no longer fitted and the wheels were altered to suit.

The existing drive-side wheel was retained for the competition models in 1954 but the road engines went to slimmer and lighter wheels. In both cases the timing side was new with the mainshaft hole altered to a parallel press fit in place of the earlier taper arrangement. It was still retained by a nut.

There were changes for 1956 with new drive-side wheels for all except the two scrambles engines which

altered to an 85.5 mm stroke. The latter had steel wheels with the mainshafts pressed into place without nuts as this design gave them greater support. A location key was added on the timing side of these engines only. The timing-side wheel of each scrambles engine was amended for 1957 and from then on there were fewer changes.

The 348 cc road engine stayed as it was until replaced by new wheels with an 81 mm stroke for 1962–3. The trials version with its 93 mm stroke stayed as it was till 1963 but the CS went at the end of 1959. The 497 cc road and CS engines ran on as they were till 1963 and from 1964 both sizes and all models had the same new wheels with press-fit mainshafts.

For the light singles there were five pairs of wheels with a 64.85 mm stroke for the 250s and 85.5 mm for the 350. The standard 250 had a cast-iron set for 1958–60 and another for 1961 on which were also fitted by the S model. The CS had one pair for 1960 and another for 1961 in steel and these went into the CSR as well.

The mainshafts went through a similar series of changes, especially on the timing side. This began with a taper fit in the flywheel and a single-start worm drive for the oil pump. This became a two-start drive for 1947, when the part was stamped 2S, and had an extra groove added within a year or so for improved strength and wear resistance.

For 1954 the design was changed to a parallel fit in the wheel and this item went on all engines from then till 1963, excluding the CS models. The latter adopted a press-fit shaft with locating key for 1954 and this was modified for 1957, replaced for 1960, but returned to the 1957 type for 1961–3.

On the drive side the original was used up to 1955 and a revised part for 1956 other than CS engines. These used a keyed, press-fit shaft which was revised for 1957 when it was shortened to suit the AMC gearbox. It was altered for 1960–3 and this part also went into the 1958 18CS. The road models used another shaft for the early part of 1956 prior to the adoption of the AMC gearbox and this part also went into the trials models from 1958 to 1963. The road ones adopted another for this period to suit the alternator fitted to them.

For 1964 the 350 competition machine had the driveshaft from the 1957 CS model while the rest of the range used the one from the 1960 model. On the timing side there was a new, pressed-in shaft which drove the Norton gear-type oil pump.

There were just two types of mainshaft used by the light singles with one for the standard, S, 350 and 1960 CS models and the other used by the last of these from 1961 and the CSR engines. One key served to locate these, all of which were a press fit in their wheels.

The nuts used by the heavy singles to retain the mainshafts were dissimilar at first. The one on the drive side remained the same part throughout but the one on the timing side changed for 1954. It was altered again for 1962 when it became the same item as the nut on the drive side but they were not used after 1963.

Two location keys were used on the drive-side shaft, were amended for 1950 and reverted to the original type from 1957 on. The timing side used the same key when it was pressed into the wheel but otherwise it was located using a jig at the works. It is thus essential that the parts are corectly aligned, if they are disturbed, otherwise the oil supply could be cut off and the valve timing incorrect.

Twin crankshaft

The original was first altered during 1951 when the centre main bearing had thrust washers added at AJS engine 7000 and Matchless engine 5966. For 1952 it was again altered when the crankcase release valve was fitted into the end of the drive side and early crankshafts could be modified by drilling a $\frac{1}{4}$ in. hole along through the drive-side mainshaft.

The crankshaft was amended in detail for 1953 when the big-end shells were altered and again for 1956 when it was joined by a similar part for the 593 cc engine. Both changed once more for 1957 when the AMC gearbox was adopted and for 1958 a second type appeared to suit the fitting of an alternator but for the 498 cc engine only.

The 646 cc crankshaft had a 79.3 mm stroke rather than the 72.8 mm of the others and was made in forms to suit the use of alternator or dynamo. From about 1960 its material was uprated from a high grade, alloy iron casting to nodular iron, which could withstand the power of the higher performance versions. The 745 cc Norton twin engines kept to one crankshaft type for the AMC application and were not affected by the changes introduced for the Commando. Thus, the later Commando part is not suitable for AMC engines as the primary drive and flywheel differ.

Connecting rods

The singles all had steel rods with a pressed-in liner for the big-end rollers to run in. The twins all had forged light-alloy rods with separate caps and replaceable shell bearings.

In all cases they must be handled with care and not

The sports G2S of 1961 which differed little from the standard 250 but did have dropped bars

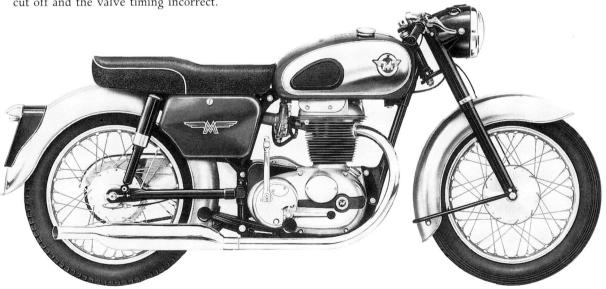

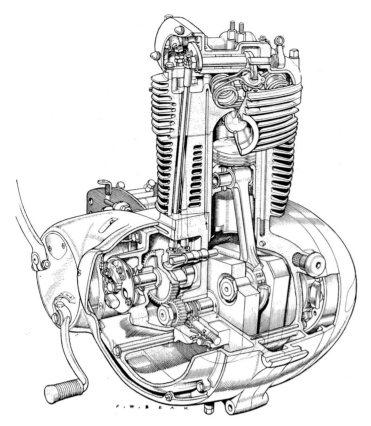

The 348 cc light single with unusual flywheel shape and built-in dry sump oil tank

and was joined by another for 1956 and the scrambles engine. The first remained in use till 1963 and the second till the end of the line. Each had its own liner to suit the roller track width which was $\frac{3}{4}$ in. and $\frac{1}{2}$ in. respectively.

The light singles were more complex with the original standard engine rod being used for the CS version for 1960. New rods appeared for 1961 with one for the standard and S engines and another stiffer one for the CS and CSR ones. The 350 had its own rod. The big-end liner for the 350 was common from 1961 while the 350 first had its own type and then used the one from the 1956 heavy single.

The twins had no real change at all with one rod serving up to 1959 and another joining it that year for the 646 cc engines. This only differed in that it had a chamfer on both rod and cap to allow it to swing within the crankcase of the 646 cc engine. Otherwise the rod was the same and early ones can be modified for use in the larger engine. The chamfer points out from the engine centre.

All the rod details of studs, trunnions and other items remained the same from start to finish. The only parts to vary were the big-end shells which were first altered for 1953, the top shell became a two-layer bearing and the bottom shell a three-layer one. From 1956 the latter was fitted in both positions. The Norton twins had a change for 1966 when the rod gained an oil hole which had to point away from the engine centre and the top shell was drilled to suit.

Small-end bush

If worn this can be pressed out using a new bush and this reamed to give a nice sliding fit on the pin. Avoid hand reaming, if possible, as a guided machine reamer will do a much better job. Check for oil holes.

Just one bush served all the heavy singles and another all the light ones. There were no bushes fitted to either the AMC or Norton twin engines.

Pistons

The first step in checking the condition of the piston is to see if the cylinder needs boring as if it does you will have to fit a new one anyway. If you plan to keep the existing one it will need to be closely inspected. It must be examined for cracks in the skirt or around the gudgeon pin bosses, while the ring grooves must be in good condition as must the pin holes and circlip grooves.

There are a number of pistons that were available for each engine size, some used as standard and others listed as options. On the singles the use of a compression plate was also common and these came in two thicknesses, one sometimes fitted as standard. This means that if there is any doubt the piston and compression ratio should be checked. The latter is

allowed to knock against other parts. This includes the crankcase mouth when working on the engine and all rods should be inspected carefully for any signs of damage which should be polished out. The rods may also be checked for alignment if there is any reason to suspect that they are not true and if there is any doubt about a rod it should not be used.

In general, AMC rods are robust but a snapped one will wreck an engine and is not worth the risk. Repair is by renewing the big-end liner and small-end bush as required and, for the twins, fitting new big-end nuts. On these engines also inspect the stud thread for any sign of distortion and replace it if there is any doubt. On Norton twin engines replace both the nut and bolt but first remove the sharp edge from the underside of the bolt head. This will stop it shaving a sliver of alloy from the rod which would then lodge under the head and pack down under running loads. Check that this has not happened in the past.

Rod types

The early singles had a rod with $7\frac{3}{8}$ in. centres but for 1947 this was reduced to one of $6\frac{7}{8}$ in. This remained in use for all engines with the triple-row roller big-end done by measuring the combustion chamber volume and doing a small sum. Also compare the valve head diameters with the cutaways in the piston crown to see if they are compatible as this provides further evidence as to the piston type to hand. The standard pistons are listed in an appendix.

If you replace the piston use a quality make and keep to the standard compression ratio for your model. Any attempt to raise this could bring a major disaster in its train as the middle-aged or old engine objects to the added loads. Should you find yourself with a sports engine fitted with an old cast-iron head use the old type ratio or the engine will overheat.

If you keep the existing piston expect to renew the rings, in which case you may need to remove the glaze from the bores with a specialist tool, or medium to coarse emery cloth. Check the gaps on the new rings and do fit the taper ones the right way up or you will have a plug oiling problem.

There were four types of gudgeon pin listed for the 348 cc singles with one for each of the 69, 72 and 74 mm bores. The fourth was for use with a high compression piston and was listed for the 69 mm bore for 1953–5. The 497 cc singles had one pin for each of the 82.5 and 86 mm bores while the light singles had one pin for each engine size.

The twins had one pin for the 498 cc engine and another for the 593 and 646 cc ones which shared a 72 mm bore. The latter pin was common with that of the 348 cc light single as were the circlips with one for the twins and light singles and another for all the other singles.

The pins should be checked for ridges and changed if not in really good condition. The clips should be changed as a matter of course. If they are of the Seeger type they should be fitted so that their sharper outer edge is away from the pin as this gives the best support against end thrust. Circlip pliers must always be used for dismantling or assembly.

Cylinder

This (or these in the case of the twins) needs to be checked for damage and wear as either may have occurred. Damage may be to the fins, the top or bottom mating surfaces or to the threads. Wear occurs in the bore. The cylinder may need to be finished to restore its appearance and both iron and alloy ones were used.

Damaged or broken fins may be repaired by welding or brazing but it is a tricky job to do. If a middle fin has gone you may have to cut others away to gain access and then refix them once the broken one is repaired. Be careful about heating the cylinder and let it cool slowly. Do all this work before any rebore or machining that may be needed.

Check the gasket surfaces for burrs and distortion. At the base these may only cause an oil leak but at the top could lead to a blown gasket which could mean burn damage to both head and barrel. If extensive, machining may be necessary to clean it up but this must be kept to a minimum. However, it must be done or the trouble will recur. If high-compression pistons are fitted it may be prudent to check the piston-to-valve clearance when you assemble the engine. Check that any oil feeds or drains are quite clear.

The Norton twin block has tapped holes in its top surface and these need to be inspected to ensure that the threads are in good condition and not pulling up around the holes. If poor it must be machined flat, the holes lightly countersunk and the threads cleaned up.

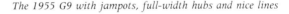

The 1955 G9 with jampots, full-width hubs and nice lines

Bore wear is best checked with a Mercer gauge which will provide exact measurements. An idea of the position can be gained by feeling the wear ridge at the top of the bore but judgement as well as an oily finger is needed. Alternative methods, if you don't possess a Mercer or an internal micrometer, are available. One is to use an internal bore gauge which can be set to the unworn diameter at the bottom of the bore and used with feelers to find the wear at the top. Internal calipers can do the same job but a more delicate touch is needed to get accurate results without measuring caliper spring. More homespun techniques are to use the piston and measure the skirt clearance at several points, or a piston ring and check its gap in the same way.

If the bore is worn it will have to be rebored but before this is done two other points need attention. First, you must establish whether it is on standard or oversize at the moment. This will indicate what you have to go out to. Second you *must* get the new pistons˙ before having the bores machined in case there is a supply problem.

Nearly all the cylinders can be taken out to plus 0.040 in. with one or two singles only having plus 0.020 in. pistons listed for them. Do not be tempted to go out too far or the cylinder spigot may be weakened below a safe level.

Finishing

When the cylinder is mechanically fit for use it needs to be finished. This process will have begun with the cleaning it received before work began but this now needs to be completed. It will need to be masked and bead- or sand-blasted to get an even matt finish and to get all the dirt out of the crevices between the fins.

It then needs to be painted either black or silver and stove-enamelling is preferable for obtaining the tough finish needed. An alternative is a modern air drying paint but to get between the fins a spray gun is needed. A trick that sometimes will work is to use a piece of felt, stiffened with wire, but a brush is most awkward to use for this job so is best forgotten.

Let the paint dry fully and then remove the masking and check carefully for blasting grit in all holes. If you have masked properly there won't be any but make certain.

Cylinder types

The first check on the cylinder is the bore size and for the singles, the next is whether it has integral pushrod tunnels or not. The material can also help as both iron and alloy barrels were used, and the method of retaining can also play its part.

The road 348 cc engines began with an iron barrel, separate pushrod tubes, a 69 mm bore and a base flange with four stud holes. An oil feed ran from the cylinder base to the rear wall of the bore to lubricate the thrust face of the piston.

From engine 8000, made during 1948, the cylinder was modified so it could fit the 497 cc engine crankcase which then became common. For 1949 the fins were made deeper and for 1956 the cylinder bore oil feed was deleted. The fins were extended further for 1958, when the magneto went, and the bottom flange altered to improve the appearance. The 1962 engine had integral pushrod tunnels and a 74 mm bore while the 1964 one had a 72 mm bore. Both were in cast iron.

The competition 348 cc engines went to an alloy barrel for 1950 with one for the AJS and another for the Matchless. This arose to cope with the fore and aft magneto mounting and from 1952 the AJS one became common. For 1956 it lost its oil feed to the bore.

The 72 mm bore scrambles engine of 1956–9 had integral pushrod tunnels and was in alloy. The 1964 trials one had the same bore and features.

The 497 cc single began much as the 348 cc one but with different barrels for AJS and Matchless. For 1948 the Matchless one went on both marques and in 1949 the fins were made deeper. Due to this there were once more two types for the two marques and the AJS one was altered for 1950.

For 1952 the compression plate was no longer used and one common cylinder was used by both makes and was $\frac{1}{8}$ in. longer than before. It lost its oil feed for 1956 and from 1958 no longer had its fins cut away, as before, to clear the magneto. For 1964 the original 82.5 mm bore was changed to 86 mm and the cylinder had integral pushrod tunnels, although it continued to be cast in iron.

The early competition models had the 82.5 mm bore and from 1950 were in alloy. There was one for each make until 1952 when the AJS one became common. From 1956 an alloy barrel with integral pushrod tunnels and 86 mm bore was used.

The twins had two separate, identical barrels which is why they need to be labelled left and right. The 498 cc cylinder had six fins and the original was altered for 1956 so it fitted a common crankcase with the 593 cc engine. The bores of these were 66 and 72 mm and only one cylinder was listed for the larger engine.

The smaller had one further change and this type was listed for 1960 onwards. The same thing happened with the 648 cc barrels with one for 1959, one for 1960–3 and another for 1964 onwards. All had more fins than the smaller barrels and the last was drilled for $\frac{3}{8}$ in. holding down studs while all the others managed with $\frac{5}{16}$ in.

The Norton twin had a cylinder block and this was revised for 1966 at engine 114870 when it lost its top spigots and just relied on the gasket to keep the hot gas within.

The light singles had a 70 mm bore for the 248 cc

A show Matchless single-cylinder engine of the type used for 1954–7 with auto-advance for the forward mounted magneto

engine and a 72 mm one for the 348 cc ones. One cylinder with eight fins served most of the smaller engines but the CSR models had their own which was finished in silver, although it was still cast in iron just like the rest. The 348 cc cylinder was longer and had eleven fins.

Compression plate

This is only to be found on the singles and was used to adjust the compression ratio of the older style of engine. It is a simple plate which locates under the cylinder, along with a second gasket, to raise it and the head and lower the ratio.

The plates used by 348 cc engines were always $\frac{1}{16}$ in. thick and those for the 497 cc ones were $\frac{1}{8}$ in.

Some competition engines could be fitted with two plates for trials use.

The road 500 had a plate fitted as standard up to 1951 but this was dispensed with for the following year when the barrel was lengthened. That plate was also fitted to the competition engine for 1949 only and was listed for the 1956 road engine as an option.

For 1950 the 497 cc competition engine had a new form of plate, as did the 348 cc version, fitted as standard but from 1954 they became an option. For that year and the next they were used to lower the ratio if a high compression piston was fitted but its ratio not needed. Prior to this the 348 cc competition engine had one plate for 1948 up to number 8000 and another for after that number and 1949.

The 348 cc road engine joined the 497 cc one in having an optional plate listed for 1956. Both were revised for 1957 and remained in use while the road machines kept to the old 69 mm and 82.5 mm bore dimensions.

ABOVE *Adjusting the tappets on a 1965 G15 engine*

Cylinder head

You may find this a victim of misguided enthusiasm with valve seats cut back due to years of keen but unnecessary valve grinding. Each owner may have done this 'to put the sparkle back' with the result that the valve heads are now well masked. The only answer will be an insert—a job for a specialist.

The first task with the head is to remove the valves and, on the twins, the rockers and to clean it thoroughly. If iron this can be done using a caustic soda solution but *never* use this for aluminium parts. These can be done in a hot household detergent. After immersion in either case the head must be well washed with hot water, dried off and the iron or steel items oiled or greased to prevent rust.

Inspect the valve guides. If they are worn or cracked they must be replaced and this is best done with the head evenly heated. Unless the valve seat has been damaged the fitting of new guides is normally the only occasion when the seats need cutting. Even then a *light* cut only is needed followed by a minimum of valve grinding with the valves it is intended to fit.

Check the plug thread and fit an insert if it is in poor condition. Check all the other holes and fit inserts if required. Inspect the head joint area for any signs of gas leakage and deal with this. On Norton engines examine the exhaust port threads of the big twins as these are susceptible to damage if the pipe nuts have not been kept tight. Certain engines do have locking washers but in some cases the gasket compresses so

BELOW *The sports 31CSR from 1965 with AMC engine on Norton wheels*

the nut loosens, although the tabs on the washers prevent it coming undone. In this state it can rattle enough to knock the port threads out and then reclamation is the only cure. This can be done by sleeving, or with a thread insert which will make it better than new. The only repair considered by the works was a Helicoil insert. Keeping the nuts tight will prevent any re-occurrence.

Check that any oil drain holes from the head are clear and remove any obstruction found. Also, on Norton twins, check that there is no flash in the pushrod tunnel that could touch the rods. This has been known to occur and needs to be filed away.

Once the features of the head have been repaired it can be finished either in natural or by painting as for the cylinder.

Cylinder-head types

The singles' heads all followed a similar pattern whether for road or competition use, or 348 cc or 497 cc capacity. The first were in cast iron with coil-valve springs but all types followed a very similar pattern. The originals were offered in either bronze or light alloy as an option for the competition models in 1948 but that was the only year this occurred and also the last year of coil springs.

The engines changed to hairpin valve springs on all models for 1949 and for 1950 the competition engines had light alloy heads. These were altered to a die-cast type for 1951 and alloy heads were also fitted to the road engines that year. The next change came for all in 1954 when the inlet ports were enlarged.

The head was next altered for 1956 when the pushrod tubes were shortened and located into the underside of the head rather than higher up and thus the two cutouts in the three lower fins went. At the same time the exhaust-valve guide gained a locating circlip and the scrambles engines a change in cylinder bore as well. These had a larger inlet valve for 1957 and a modified inlet tract for 1959. On the 497 cc engine there was a new combustion chamber form for 1960 and this change applied to the road 497 cc head as well. This was revised for 1964 to suit the change to the 86 mm bore while the competition head was revised at the same time.

The road 348 cc engine had a head change for 1962 to suit the 74 mm bore and this part remained in use when the bore changed to 72 mm in 1964. The competition engine had a new head for the one year (1964) it was listed with the 72 mm bore.

All the twins had light-alloy heads which were handed left and right. The original types served the AJS to the end of 1952 but only to Matchless engine number 5966 built during 1951. From then to the end of the next year a different pair of heads were used. This variation continued briefly during 1953 when the original rocker cover fixing was altered from four

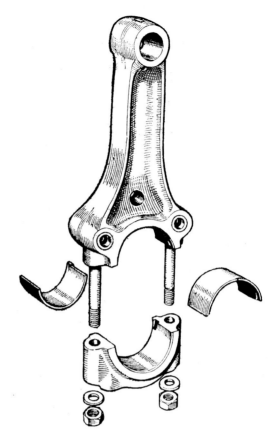

· The alloy connecting rod from the AMC twin engine with its shells and trunnion stud fixing

to two screws. At first there was a pair of heads for each marque but after engine number 15000 the AJS fitted the Matchless part. Both continued with it for 1954 and had a revised pair for 1955.

The 593 cc engine appeared in 1956 with a new pair of heads which were also fitted to the 498 cc engine and resulted in a raised compression ratio for that unit. Both changed for 1957 with a bigger inlet valve going into the 593 cc part. The next detail change for the 498 cc engine came in 1959 when the 646 cc version was introduced.

For 1960 both engine sizes had cylinder heads with an extra fin beneath the exhaust port area and this fin carried three small diagonal fins. The head for the 646 cc engine was altered once more for 1964. The Norton head was altered during 1966 to remove the head recess for the block spigot.

Several cylinder heads were used by the light singles with the original head serving the standard and S models up to 1961 and the CS for 1959. The latter had a revised head with larger inlet for 1960 and a further increase for 1961. It was this last head that went on the standard and S models for 1962 onwards.

The CSR models had their own head with big inlet valve and port and longer inlet tract while the fin

The Matchless G12 with AMC engine but Norton forks and wheels for 1964

edges were polished to add style. The 348 cc engines had their own head to suit the larger capacity and bore.

Cylinder-head fixings

The original post-war singles had the head held to the barrel by four bolts. On the 348 cc engine there were two lengths but the 497 cc one used four of one of these. For 1949 the 348 cc type followed suit and this

arrangement continued for the standard engines right through to 1963.

For the all-alloy engines built from 1950 there was a different arrangement with sleeve nuts screwed to studs in the crankcase. One type served all years. The

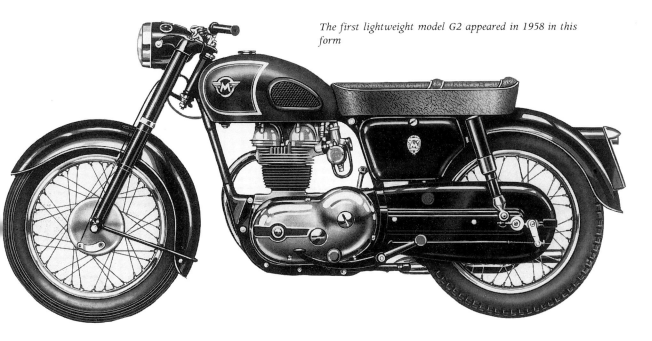

The first lightweight model G2 appeared in 1958 in this form

The 1958 model 20 AJS twin with cast-alloy chaincase but still with dynamo and magneto

same type of fixing went on the light singles but the sleeve nuts, although common to all models and years, were a different part. These models also had an extra bolt near the pushrod tunnel.

Each twin cylinder head was held by four nuts screwed to crankcase studs with spacers between head and nuts. The original nuts were of the domed type but for 1953 became plain. They were changed for 1962 and again for 1964 when the size altered from $\frac{5}{16}$ to $\frac{3}{8}$ in. The spacer was only fitted up to the end of 1959.

Gaskets

The singles with iron barrels had a head gasket for each engine size at first but from 1949 shared one part. This was used for the 348 cc engine up to 1961 and the 497 cc one to 1963 after which there was once more a gasket for each capacity. None of the all-alloy competition engines had a head gasket.

The singles had a base gasket, for the cylinder, for each engine size up to 348 cc number 8000 built in 1948, after which the 497 cc one became common. It was changed for 1957 to match the revised shape of the bottom flange and for 1962 there was again one for each road engine size.

The competition engines had one base gasket for 1950–63 and another used only on the CS engines from 1963 on. This one went on all engines, both road and competition, from 1964. One rocker-box gasket was used for the coil-valve-spring models and a second for all with hairpins. This was therefore used from 1949 to 1969.

The twins had a change to the head and base gaskets for 1956 and another for the head one for 1960. Both then changed for 1964 to suit the increase in stud size. Two rocker-cover gasket types were used, one with four screw holes and a second with only two from 1953 on.

The light singles had one base and one rocker-box gasket for all years and models. The head gasket was altered for 1960 and the type in use for the year served all the engines.

Inlet manifold and spacers

These were all cast in light alloy and are often polished. They should be examined for damage, flatness of the mounting faces both in and out, and for the condition of the holes, whether threaded or plain. Where twin carburettors are fitted to separate tracts connected by a balance tube, this, and its fitting, should be checked for leaks.

All standard AMC twins had a single carburettor and a one into two manifold. It was first altered for 1953 when the outer face had a recess machined in it for an O ring to act as a seal. It reverted to the original

type for both 498 and 593 cc engines in 1956 but the larger had a new part for 1957. The 498 cc one changed for 1959 and was joined by a new part for the 646 cc engine. For 1960 both engine sizes fitted a common manifold and this type continued in use from then on.

The 745 cc Norton engines had two separate inlet tracts with a thick and a thin spacer for each. These parts were used for all years while the AMC twins had one spacer for 498 and 593 cc engines from 1957 on and another for 646 cc ones.

The singles normally only had a spacer between the carburettor and the cylinder head except for the 497 cc CS engines from 1958 onwards. These had a manifold and the one part served all years.

The spacers came in a variety of bore sizes but most were $\frac{3}{4}$ in. thick. The ones used by the singles are listed in an appendix and the one used by the last road models also went on the 250 CSR engines. The other light singles had other spacers with one for the 350 and another for the other 250s.

Valves

These should be replaced unless in very good condition, especially the exhaust which has a hard time. Grind the new valves in lightly without taking too much off the valve seat.

The 348 cc and 497 cc singles seldom used the same pair of valves and this applied for 1945–8 when coil springs were fitted. There were two new pairs for the hairpin springs in 1949 and on the road models these remained in use till 1961 for the 348 cc engine and till 1959 for the 497 cc one. After these two dates a new, common inlet valve was used by both engine sizes but

Matchless G9 from 1951 with jampots and the shapely megaphone silencers

the exhausts differed.

The 348 cc competition engine had a new exhaust valve for 1955 and the trials version ran on with this pair to 1963. For 1964 it fitted the same pair as the road engine. The 497 cc competition engine continued with the road engine valves up to the end of 1956.

For 1957 the two CS engines had new pairs of valve of which the inlets were changed for 1959, the last year of the 348 cc version. For 1960 the 497 cc CS changed to the valve pair also new for the road 497 cc engine that year and stayed with these from then on.

The twins had one pair of valves for the 498 cc engine which also went into the 593 cc one for 1956 only. The larger engine had new inlet valves for 1957 and there was also a new pair for the 498 cc one for 1960–1. The 646 cc twin was listed with the valves from the 1957 593 cc engine for 1959 but with another pair from 1960. The 745 cc Norton engine had the valves lengthened by 0.1 in. at engine 125871, built in 1968, so this point must be watched for.

The light singles had two different inlet and exhaust valves over the years in various combinations. The original pair were used by the standard model until the exhaust alone was changed for 1961 onwards. This combination also served the CS models. A larger inlet went in the CSR along with the final exhaust while the 348 cc engine began with the larger inlet and the original exhaust. It changed to the CSR format for 1961.

Valve guides

These should be removed or replaced from alloy heads with these heated and, except for the early engines with coil springs, the inlet and exhaust guides differ. Most are pressed into a dimension but some later singles and all twins and light singles have a circlip on one or both guides for location.

The original type was replaced by a new pair to suit the hairpin valve springs for 1949 and these were revised for 1954 when high lift cams were fitted. The exhaust changed for 1956 when a circlip was added to it for location and this pair served the road 348 cc engine to 1961, the road 497 cc one to 1959 and the trials 348 cc one to 1963.

They were also used by the CS engines for 1956 but for 1957 these had a new exhaust guide. For 1959 a new pair was listed for the CS engines and for 1960 another inlet was used in these, also with a circlip location groove. These guides were also listed for the road 497 cc engine from 1960 onwards, the road 348 cc from 1962 and the 348 cc competition for 1964.

The twins had one pair of guides up to 1958 with a revised exhaust for 1959 and new guides for 1960 onwards to suit a revised head design. All types were circlip located. Norton twin guides were common to both valves and one part served all the years in question.

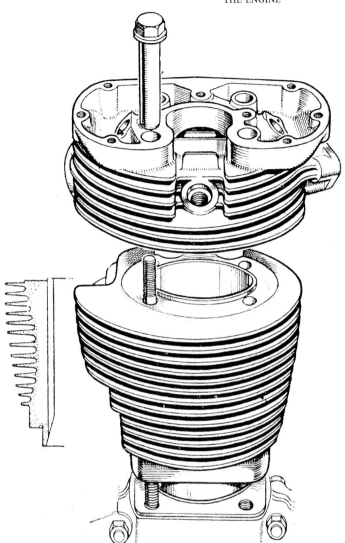

The light-alloy head and barrel introduced on the competition models for 1950

The light singles had one inlet guide type and two exhaust, all with circlips. The first exhaust went into the standard engine to 1960 and the 348 cc one for that year, while all other years and engines used the other guide.

Valve springs

These should be replaced as a matter or course. All models have two springs, with coils for the twins, early singles and late light singles, and hairpins for all others.

The singles had a change to their dual-coil springs for 1948 before altering to hairpins for 1949. These had their prongs lengthened for 1952 and this type remained in use up to 1963 on at least one engine. For 1957 there was a new spring pair for the CS engines which were changed for 1958. A further pair were

Engine of the 1961 model 8 with its extra fins, but otherwise much as the 250 on the outside

and the parts also need to be checked for any sign of collar collapse or collet pull through.

Caps were only fitted to the singles with coil springs and thus up to 1948, as were the spring cups. These were changed to seatings for the hairpins which were blocks fitted round the guides with side holes for the valve spring prongs. When these were lengthened for 1952 the seating became an open tray which was amended slightly for 1957 and used in that form from then on. The pre 1952 hairpins must not be used with the open trays as they could come adrift which would not be nice.

The collars for the singles were one for the coil springs, another for the hairpins for 1949 and a third introduced in 1959 for the CS inlet valve. The last later went on the road 348 cc engine for 1962 and all engines from 1964.

One set of collets was in use on the singles from 1945 to 1963 but another appeared for the 1959 CS inlet. The latter went on both CS valves for 1960, and also the road 497 cc engine, but only their inlets for 1961 when another collet appeared for their exhausts. This pair went on the road 348 cc for 1962 and was used on all from 1964.

On the AMC twins one type of seat, collar and collet served up to 1959 with another set for 1960 onwards. The Norton twin had its own set of details which were common to all years and included heat resisting washers.

The light singles used the seat and collar from the post 1957 single but their own collets. The first type was used on all inlet valves and the original exhaust but an alternative set went on the exhaust of the CS engine. This was then used for all engines from 1961 until the change to coil springs for 1965.

Rocker-box details

Considering the number of detail parts involved, there were not too many changes in this area. The basic design for each engine type stayed the same for all years and models.

On the singles the rocker box carried the rockers and was first changed for 1949 when the valve springs became hairpins and the lifter mechanism was moved up to the box. A modified type came in for the 1950 alloy engines and both were changed again for 1955 and 1962.

The side cover and its fillet were changed for 1949 and a second side cover added for the alloy engines of 1950 onwards. The bushes for the rocker spindles were the same for all years but the spindles were altered once. The original stayed in use to 1961 and the revised type was used from 1960.

The detachable spindle arms were changed for 1949 and up to 1953 the valve and tappet arms were common to both inlet and exhaust. Both were modified for 1955 and used in this form from then on.

used from 1960 on the CS engines, from 1962 for the road 348 cc engine and for all engines from 1964 onwards.

The twins had one pair of coil springs for 1949–57 and 1959 with a different inner listed for 1958. A new pair were used with the modified head from 1960. The light singles had one hairpin pair for the standard 248 and 348 cc engines and another for the CS and CSR ones. For 1965 the CSR was fitted with coil-valve springs.

Valve detail parts

These comprise caps, cups, seatings, collars and collets with some common to a number of engines. All need to be cleaned and inspected for any signs of damage or cracks. Replacement is the only answer if there is any

At the tappet end the one part served after the 1949 change until 1962 when another for the inlet side joined it. The associated sleeves and washers that went with the spindles and arms were common for all years while three metering plugs were added to the rocker box for 1956. Once the valve lifter parts had moved up to the rocker box they remained as they were, except for a change to the spring for 1962.

The light singles were constructed very much as the heavy ones with some common parts. Three box types were used with that of the 348 cc engine having a valve lifter, using the heavy single parts. The CSR type was polished and the original served the other models. Inside, the details were common to all models and years.

The twins differed in having the rockers supported in posts cast on the cylinder head and enclosed by small covers. The rocker spindles were eccentric so were turned and clamped to set the valve gaps while the rockers were one piece. There were few changes.

The rockers had oil grooves added for 1955 and the spindles were changed for that year but reverted to the original parts for 1956 onwards. The clamping parts were the same for all years but the rocker bushes

altered for 1956. In place of two of the same for each rocker there was one original and one new. From 1952 a rocker spindle bush was also used.

The covers began with four bolts to hold them in place but this changed for 1953 to two bolts each. This type remained in use but was joined by another for 1958–62. This went on the standard and de luxe engines while the 1953 type continued on the CS and CSR versions and from 1963 on the 646 cc standard one.

For all engines the rocker box and covers need to be checked, as for other alloy parts, for cracks, damage or poor mating surfaces. They will need to be repaired as necessary and the details inspected in a similar fashion. To do this properly you will need to dismantle all the parts but mark the rocker arms and spindles on the singles so all the parts return to their original places.

Rocker-box oil pipes

One assembly was used on the singles and ran from the front oil-pump plate to the rocker box. It may need to be annealed by heating and then being allowed to cool while it should run in a smooth line.

The ends must connect without straining the pipe and any repair is best done with silver solder if possible, or ordinary solder if not. Flux-cored solder

The 1963 AJS 31CSR with its siamezed pipes and other sporting features

Cutaway Matchless show engine from 1951 with hairpin valve springs, magneto drive and other features in view

will not be adequate and it must be remembered that the pipe is subject to oil-pump pressure and not return line suction.

Tappets and guides

Tappets are only found in the singles and need to be examined for wear and their fit in the guide. The guides should not be disturbed unless this is necessary and if so the crankcase should be heated first. Note the position of the guide and don't forget to remove the guide screws if these are fitted.

In the immediate post-war years the inlet and exhaust tappets and guides differed from each other and there was a pair for each engine size. For this period the exhaust parts were machined to suit the valve lifter and a collar was fitted to the exhaust.

This continued up to 348 cc engine 8000 and to the end of 1948. For 1949, and the hairpin valves, the tappet and guide, as used up to then on the inlet side of the 497 cc engine, was used for all engines and sizes. There were new guides for the CS engines for 1956 and those were held in place with guide screws. The tappets on the CS engines were changed for 1958 and the guides the next year. Both changed again for 1962 while the 1949 type continued on the other models up to 1963. For 1964 there were new parts for all engines with only the guide screw continuing from before.

Cam followers

These were used by the twins and the light singles, the twins being known for wearing theirs rather too quickly.

The twin followers were lengthened a little for 1953 and retained this form from then on. There was a modification for 1962 and a change of material for the next year. This last type was in forged steel with stellite pads and can be used in all engines back to 1953. The spindle they oscillated on was common to all years but the spacer changed for 1955. Both types were given as $1\frac{19}{64}$ in. long but the first had a flat machined along its length which was left off the second.

On the light singles all the details were common to all years and models.

Pushrods

Check these for straightness by rolling them on a flat surface such as a sheet of glass. Examine the ends for cracks and their security to the centre section while all threads and details must be in good order.

On the singles the valve gap adjuster was at the top of the pushrod and this part was common to all years. In the immediate post-war era there was one pair of pushrods for each engine size and these were altered for 1949. For 1950 there were new items for the competition versions of each capacity and for 1951 these parts went into all engines.

There were new parts again for 1952 but with one for all touring engines and the other for all competition ones. The first also went in the 348 cc competition engine for 1953 and from 1957 was only used in this engine size but not for the CS version. It returned for use in the road 497 cc engine in 1960–1 and was then used only in the 348 cc competition motor for 1962–3.

The second part only served the 497 cc competition engine for 1953–5, the CS version only for 1956 and this, the 348 cc CS and 497 cc road engines for 1957–9. It stayed in the CS for 1960–2. Another pushrod served the big CS for 1957–9 with a further one for

Rocker-box view of a 1961 model 14 engine

1963. The road engines each had new pushrods for 1962–3 and there was another new pair for 1964 onwards.

The twins had a change of pushrods for 1953 and another for 1960 with a different part serving the 646 cc engines. Note that in Norton engines there was a change in length during 1968 at engine 125871 when they were shortened. The light singles kept to the heavy single design with an adjuster and had two part types, one for each engine size.

Pushrod covers

These, and their seals, only occur on the singles as the other engines had tunnels in head and barrel to accommodate them. This also applied to some of the

heavy singles as well. Be careful that you have the correct seals and washers, which are essential, to match the barrel and compression plate in use as there is a good deal of variation possible.

The early engines had pushrod covers for each capacity but from engine 8000 in 1948, the 348 cc used the same part as the 497 cc. The tube was shortened for 1956 but otherwise continued in use up to 1963.

Camshaft

The singles and twins each had two camshafts while the light singles only had one. On the singles, one cam was used to drive the magneto or points, but in the twins, both ends of both camshafts drove something. The light singles camshaft drove the points cam.

In all cases the cams and bearing need to be checked for wear while there should be no obvious damage in any area. Note that in addition to the standard

This de luxe version of the 1961 model 31 had the chrome tank panels as standard

camshafts there were others with high lift cams or for racing. If there is any doubt as to what you have it is best to check the timing it gives.

Generally it is best to run the parts specified for your engine and set these to their correct timing. Always make sure there is ample clearance for the cams themselves and all the rest of the valve gear even at full lift.

There were a good number of cams used in the singles and in all cases one of the pair had to drive the ignition. As the early Matchless engines had the magneto behind the cylinder, unlike the AJS and the 1952-onwards Matchless, there had to be two drive arrangements. This was achieved by switching the cams over so the one with the shaft extension for the magneto drive sprocket was in the right place.

The gear wheels were suitably marked to allow for this but be careful in case the marks are not fully original. If in doubt, check the timing. Work to the book figure and remember that while the figures were usually common to both engine sizes for any one type this was not always so. For a period the inlet differed from one to the other although a common cam was fitted.

There were fewer camshafts for the twins with changes for 1955 and 1959 but the last type can be fitted to all engines. Just to make sure you check there were two other camshaft pairs, one for a race kit and the other for the G45 road racing engine. One single camshaft served all versions and years of the light singles.

Camshaft bushes

There were not many changes in this area. For the singles there were three of one type and one of another which went in the timing cover for the shaft extended to drive the magneto. This stayed in use for some engines right up to 1963. For the 1958 road engines the odd man out was changed to suit the points drive camshaft and was revised once more for 1964.

The camshaft bushes may be used to control the camshaft end float which will give rise to an irritating rattle if excessive. To check this the camshafts should be assembled to the timing-side crankcase and the timing cover added complete with its gasket. The end float can then be checked by inserting a finger through the mainshaft bush and any adjustment made by first heating the timing cover and then moving the bush. The result should be re-checked to make certain it is as required.

The situation was simpler on the twins as each camshaft was supported by one plain bush in the drive-side crankcase and two flanged ones in the timing side. This applied to all models and years and the light singles were similar with one pair of bushes for all.

Timing-side drive

All engines had gear drive to the camshafts and there were few changes to any of the layouts. The greatest came on the road singles for 1958 when they went from magneto to coil ignition.

The singles had a change of crankshaft pinion for 1964 and the addition of adjustment shims for the exhaust camshaft from 1951. These made it easier to set the camshaft end float but this is best restricted by moving the bushes as described above. One crankshaft gear key served all models and a left-hand thread nut most of them. This was altered for 1964 but a few engines had a right-hand thread nut. These were CS units built in 1960–1 and where this nut type was used a tab washer was also fitted to lock it.

Matters were simpler on the twins and the first change was for 1951 when the crankshaft pinion was made shorter and a spacer added. The only other change was for 1955 when the shaft for the intermediate gear was enlarged with corresponding changes for the gear and its bush. The light singles were even simpler with no changes over the years.

The magneto drive on the singles was the same for all engines fitted with that form of ignition other than the chain length and auto-advance. The chain was longer for the Matchless up to 1951 when the magneto was aft of the cylinder but from 1952 both marques had the same length. An auto-advance mechanism was built into the magneto sprocket of the road 497 cc engines for 1954 and went on to the 348 cc ones the next year.

Prior to then the two sprockets looked to be the same but are not and it is quite easy to switch them round and upset the chain line. This can be avoided by loosely fitting the sprockets and checking the

alignment with a straight edge across them before the chain is added.

The dynamo on the singles was unusual in that it was driven by chain from the left end of the crankshaft. The driven sprocket and its nut were altered for 1957 when the drive chain increased its length by one link. It had also lengthened for 1949.

On the twins the magneto and dynamo were both gear driven from the timing gears. The magneto went behind the crankcase and the dynamo was clamped to its front. All engines fitted with these components had the same detail parts and where they were not used there was a distributor mounted in place of the magneto and driven in the same way.

The Norton twin engines had their own unusual drive system which combined both gears and chains. It must be carefully marked to ensure correct timing on assembly and equal care is needed when dealing with the nut on the end of the camshaft. This is because the engine has to be locked to hold the parts and the spanner load passes down the chain to the intermediate gear and sprocket. As the cover has to be removed to give access, this is thus not fully supported. A slave, cut-away cover is one answer and a steady pull on the spanner is another.

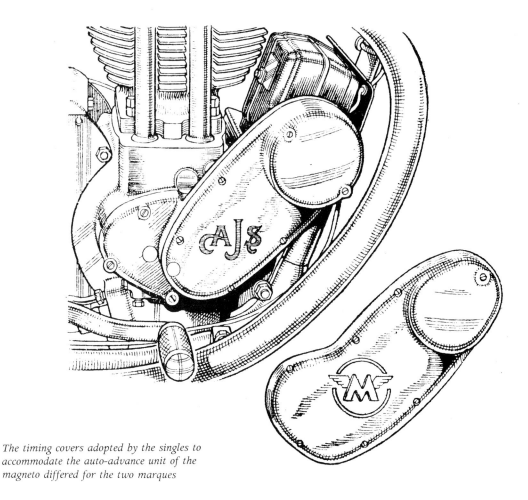

The timing covers adopted by the singles to accommodate the auto-advance unit of the magneto differed for the two marques

On the light singles the points cam was on the end of the camshaft so there were no drives as above.

In all cases the detail parts need to be cleaned and inspected for wear or damage. Timing marks should always be noted and the correct pullers used to remove gears or sprockets from shafts. These are always cheaper than damaged parts. If one gear in a train is worn it is likely that the rest have suffered so the full set is best changed. If only one is renewed it will soon wear to match the existing ones.

Timing covers

These need to be inspected for damage, cracks, flatness, clear oilways, thread condition and for any bushes or oil seals. Most owners polish to a high degree as well to highlight the marque monogram usually inscribed on the cover.

The singles had an inner and outer cover throughout the years with the first enclosing the cam gears and fitted with bushes to support their shafts. The outer enclosed the magneto drive chain at first and, from 1958, the points mechanism of the road engines.

Timing covers for the twins were always different and marked with the make name as on this 1949 model 20

Except for this last engine type, there were always different inner covers for the two marques. At first this was simply because of the different directions the two magneto drives ran in. The AJS inner was altered a little for 1949 when the valve lifter no longer had to tuck in behind it and this part remained in use up to 1962.

The Matchless inner cover altered for 1952 but the part was not the same as for the AJS. This was formed so the casting formed the rear of the chain drive enclosure and extended to the rear as the cover for the inlet cam area. The Matchless one differed in that while it extended in the same way, and had similar location and fixing, it required the outer cover to fully enclose the end of the inlet cam spindle. This type continued in use till 1963 and for that last year went on the AJS as well, but from 1964 one part did serve both marques.

The road models changed to coil ignition for 1958 with a much smaller casting which was common to both marques. This was altered for 1964 onwards.

The outer covers began as a simple form held by six screws and one part was used on AJS engines with a manual advance magneto up to 1962. The early Matchless part was equally simple and at first may have been made in cast iron to enable the firm to use up its wartime stocks. By 1947 it was in the more usual

Near the end of the line, the AJS model 33 looked like this in 1967

light alloy and was next altered for 1952. In its new form it extended over the whole of the timing case and so differed from the AJS part. It was fitted to the AJS for 1963 to match the inner cover but there was a revised cover common to both for 1964.

On the road models there were two new outer covers for 1954, one for each marque, and these had a bulge in the upper end to accommodate the auto-advance mechanism. These parts were first used on the 497 cc engines and then on the 348 cc ones from 1955. For 1958 both sizes changed to the smaller points housing with a common, simple lid but from 1961 this came with a marque emblem motif set in it.

On the twins there was a timing cover for each marque for all years. The first change came during 1951 at AJS 7000 and Matchless 5966 engine numbers when the dynamo draw stud was extended through the cover. This allowed the dynamo to be removed without disturbing the cover.

The next change was for 1956 when the 593 cc engine appeared and the relief valve went. These covers were used up till 1959, other than for the standard models of that year which were fitted with alternators. For that year only they used the original 1949 covers but from 1960 there were new covers for both marques and to suit the fitment of dynamo or alternator to the engines. From 1962 only the 646 cc twin with alternator was made and there was a new pair of covers. These were changed once more for 1963 on to accommodate wider oil-pump gears.

The light singles had a main cover that ran back to encompass the gearbox and simulate unit construction. The standard engines had a small round marque motif in the casting and one part served all years. Another was used for the CS model while the CSR had no motif and was polished to suit its sports machine role.

67

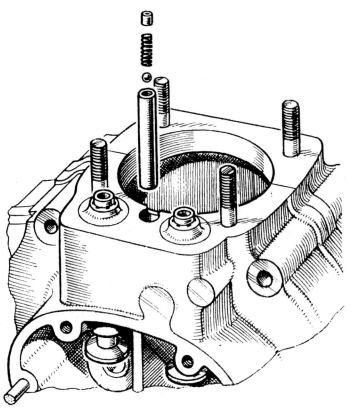

Before 1956 the singles had a ball valve set in the top of the crankcase to control the oil feed to the cylinder wall

Under the main cover went a housing for the points plate and the camshaft bearing with all models fitting the same part. On the outside of the main casting went a points cover with a polished one for the CSR engines and another for all the others.

Crankcase

The case halves will need cleaning well and checking for damage, cracks, poor threads and obstructed oilways. To remove or refit main bearings the case around them should be evenly heated after which they should drop out. If you have to knock the case on to a wood plank, first check for dowels to make sure you don't drive them into the case. To check the case temperature the usual way is to spit on the bearing housing. If it spits back it is ready. A temperature around 200°C (gas Mk 5 or 6) is usually needed and the drive side could have to go hotter still before the bearing will drop out. Don't use an oxy-acetylene torch or drill punch holes in the cases.

A ball or roller race must be completely cleaned before checking and if in doubt renew. In fact, expect to renew on a restoration as the cost is small compared to the trauma of changing them later.

The main bearings may benefit if held in place by

Loctite and replacements must be wiped clean before being dropped into place in a hot case. Don't forget any washers, shields or circlips involved with the mains.

Crankcase types

There are many of these with changes occurring nearly every year to one half or the other so great care and attention to detail is needed to ensure that you have a matching pair of the correct year. The drive side should have the model and engine numbers stamped on it which should make that side easy, but the timing one is less so.

The singles began with one crankcase assembly for each engine size and the timing side of these were altered for 1947 to suit changes in the oiling system. They changed again for 1948 for the same reason and from engine 8000, built that year, the 348 cc engine went over to the 497 cc crankcase so common parts were used.

The timing side was altered for 1949 with the removal of the hole for the valve lifter and there were two pairs of cases for 1950. One was for the road engines where a round marque badge appeared on the drive side while the other was for the all-alloy competition units. For these the normal short $\frac{3}{8}$ in. barrel studs were changed for long through studs of the same diameter but with a $\frac{7}{16}$ in. thread at the crankcase end.

The marque badges went for 1951 so the road engines used the 1949 cases while the competition ones began with the parts used for 1950. During the year at engines 16MC-1205, 18C-1092, G3LC-1203 and G80C-1050 there was a change to the timing-side case when the mainshaft bush became a flanged bush. This new case continued for 1952 when the road engine timing side had the same change but both drive sides continued. In fact the drive side bearing housing bore had been modified during 1951 to provide a tight fit on the bearing nearest to the engine sprocket and a slight interference on the inner race.

There were new crankcase pairs for 1954 when the timing-side mainshaft was increased in diameter and again for 1955 when the flange on the timing-side bush was enlarged and the drive side became supported by two different size ball races. For 1956 the cases were altered to remove the cylinder wall oil feed and to accommodate a new magnetic drain plug with a new pair added for the short-stroke CS engines. The drive sides were all amended for 1957 when the AMC gearbox came in and so was the timing side for the CS.

The alternator appeared on the road engines for 1958 so the drive side had to be altered to suit and the next changes came for 1960 when a duplex frame took over the job of supporting the cases. The road 348 cc engine had new cases for 1962 when the short-stroke

The standard G12 of 1959 with its alternator and coil ignition could still have the two-tone tank option

was adopted and there were more new cases for 1964. One pair of these was for the 348 cc competition engine and the other for the rest of the singles range.

The original twin crankcases were altered during 1951 at AJS 7000 and Matchless 5966 engine numbers when the centre web was altered and the crankcase oil deflector was deleted. At the same time a thrust washer was added to the centre bearing and this change only affected the timing-side case. Both cases changed for 1952 when the timed breather was replaced and the exit pipe removed.

For 1953 the cam followers were lengthened which altered the cases to move the pivot point and leave the follower cup where it was. The cases were amended again for 1954 and once more for 1955 when the intermediate gear spindle in the timing gear was enlarged.

For 1956 there were new cases for the 593 cc engine and these had a magnetic sump plug to remove the ferrous debris from the oil. At the same time the pressure relief valve was discarded and the rocker oil feed was modified via the top front crankcase bolt. The oil filter was amended for 1957 when only the drive-side case was changed.

Further changes occurred for 1958 when an alloy primary chaincase was fitted and the badges set in the drive-side cases were deleted. For 1959 the drive side of the standard twins was altered to take an alternator. The pressure release valve was located in the base of the crankcase filter area for 1960 when the fabric filter was replaced by a metal gauze type.

For 1961 there were further lubrication alterations but the position simplified for 1963 by which time only 646 cc crankcases were required and only the

The G3LS in its 1959 form representing the traditional English single

timing side altered. The cases were altered once more for 1964 when the cylinder studs changed.

The light singles had their own series of crankcase changes over the years. On the standard and S models the drive-side case was changed for 1961 but the timing side was common to all years and this combination was also used by the CSR engines. The CS engines also changed the timing side for 1961 as did the 348 cc but in both cases the crankcases differed from the standard parts and the timing sides were common to all years.

Centre web

This was only used by the twins and the original was amended during 1951 for the engine numbers given above. The revised part served all models and years from then on.

Main bearings

Most singles had a bush on the timing side and two ball races for the drive but not for the earliest post-war engines. These differed and had a plain bush with a $\frac{7}{8}$ in. bore roller race inboard of it on the timing side although the drive one did have the two ball races, $1 \times 2\frac{1}{4} \times \frac{5}{8}$ in., plus a washer and a collar between them.

During 1947 the timing-side roller began to be omitted and in this case the bush was made longer to compensate. This bush, plus a locating peg, became standard for 1948 while the drive side continued as it was. This area fitted Skefko races as standard and in 1949 it became necessary to use Hoffman as an alternative when a different washer had to go between the two bearings. This part was used up to 1954 and also had to be used if there was one bearing of each make, but the collar remained the same.

The timing-side bush for the competition engines became a flanged bush during 1951 at engines 16MC-1205, 18C-1092, G3LC-1203 and G80C-1050 and this part went into all engines for 1952. It was changed for 1954 when the timing-side mainshaft was increased in diameter and again for 1955. For that year the drive-side inner race was changed to one of $1 \times 2\frac{1}{2} \times \frac{3}{4}$ in. dimensions and the crankcase housing to a stepped bore. A new spacing washer appeared between the new race and the one old race remaining and this arrangement continued from then on for all engines.

On the timing side the 1955 flanged bush remained in use for most engines up to 1963 along with its peg but the CS engines for 1956 were different. They had a plain bush, which was amended for 1957, and an inboard roller race. This arrangement also continued till 1963. For 1964 there was a new plain bush and roller race which was used for all engines.

The twins had a much simpler time. The two outer ball races, each $1\frac{3}{8} \times 3 \times \frac{11}{16}$ in., were the same for all years and models. The centre main began with each half of the bearing and thrust washers in one piece but this awkward construction was dropped at AJS 7000 and Matchless 5966 engines during 1951. From that point the bearing was a simple pair of shells flanked on each side by a split thrust washer.

The light singles has a plain bush on the timing side with the same location peg as the heavy singles. On the drive side went two ball races, $\frac{7}{8} \times 2 \times \frac{9}{16}$ in., but for 1961 on one of these was changed to a roller race.

The Norton twin engines had a roller on the drive side and a ball race on the timing, both being the same $30 \times 72 \times 19$ mm size.

Assembly

In general this should be done as set out in the manual with any amendments to acknowledge the use of modern sealants and fitting compounds. The sequence of locking up the major nuts may also be varied as long as none are left loose.

Slow and steady is the guiding rule so make sure everything is as it should be at one stage before moving on to the next.

Begin by laying out the first parts to be assembled and check that your tools are nice and clean. Put the crankshaft together and fit the mains. Make quite sure there is nothing trapped behind the outer race when you do this or the bearing may tilt and the crankshaft

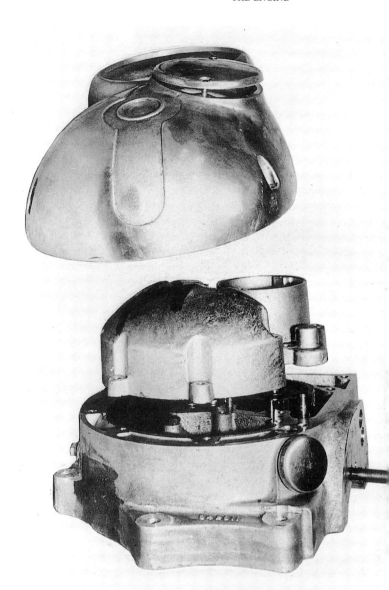

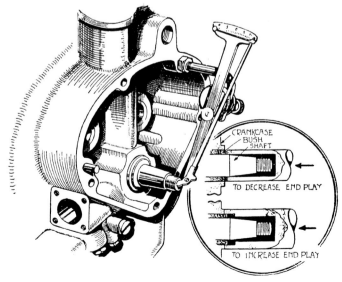

ABOVE RIGHT *The bottom half castings for the light singles showing the oil tank bolted to the right case and the outer cover that concealed it*

RIGHT *Setting the crankshaft end float of a single by moving the right-side bush to give the correct figure*

71

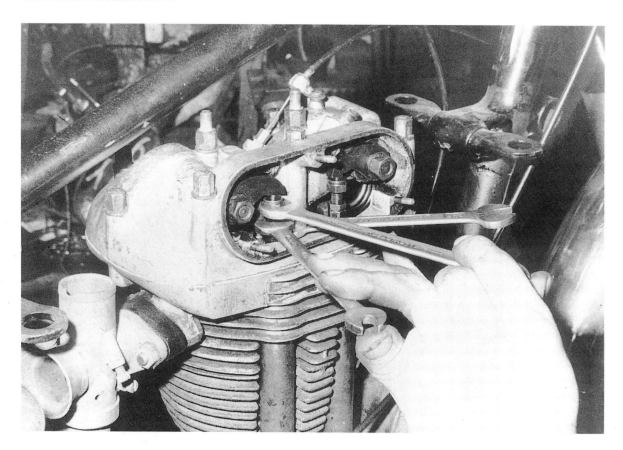

ABOVE *The G11 of 1958 continued the Matchless line in both engine and cycle parts*

ABOVE LEFT *Setting the valve gaps on an AMC single with access to the tops of the pushrods via the rocker-box side cover*

BELOW LEFT *The points of any engine need setting before the timing is checked and on this 1962 G2CSR they are at least easy to get at*

fail to rotate freely. Check on the camshaft bushes in the heavy singles and adjust the end float of the camshafts while you still have the crankcase halves apart.

Fit the crankshaft, camshafts on twins and other details to the crankcase. If in any doubt fit the other case half, bolt up and check that all is well. If it is, undo and proceed, if it is not, find out why.

Continue with the timing gears, set the valve timing and follow on with the oil pumps and valves to complete the timing side. Make quite sure the camshaft nuts are tight before fitting the cover.

The piston may need to be warmed before fitting to allow the pin to slide home and the clips must fit securely into their recesses. Don't drop them into the crankcase! Add the barrel and then the assembled head along with the pushrods if needed at this stage. Check the ignition timing once the magneto or points are in place and add the covers. Complete the top assembly and adjust the tappets.

During assembly you should have lubricated the parts as you went along and charged the crankshaft with oil. This should look after the bearing surfaces while you deal with the rest of the machine. Don't seal it completely if you have to store it any length of time and do turn it over occasionally.

The above applies to most engines but all assemble with much the same techniques. The details may vary but the same basis of slow, careful assembly using clean tools will ensure that the parts go as they should and the resulting engine runs smoothly, reliably and without leaking oil at every seam.

4 Transmission

This covers all the mechanical parts from the engine crankshaft to the rear wheel sprocket so it takes in two chains, four sprockets, a clutch and a set of gears. Included with the gears is the kickstart mechanism, and ancillary to them are the gearchange mechanism, clutch lift and gearbox shell.

Attention

Articles on the restoration of a machine often state that the owner has not stripped the gearbox but is using it as found. In many cases it is apparent that the box history is not known and this practice must be condemned.

Unless you check you cannot be certain that a gear tooth is not about to fail or an errant part about to jam the gears. In the timescale of a restoration the period spent on inspecting the gears is minimal and even on a straight rebuild the time will be well spent if, as a result, you make sure the box is not going to lock up on you.

AMC transmission

All models had a four-speed gearbox with footchange and on all both this pedal and the kickstart lever went on the right. All the heavy singles and twins had a separate gearbox while the light singles had the assembly strapped to the rear of the crankcase to give the appearance of unit construction.

Both primary and final drives were by chain and most models had a single strand primary. Exceptions were some of the light singles which fitted a duplex one but all models had a multi-plate clutch.

Engine sprocket

Up to 1956 the singles and twins had a range of sprockets which incorporated a shock absorber but for 1957 this item was moved to the clutch centre. The singles sprockets had the dynamo one incorporated in them and up to 1948 this had 17 teeth. This number rose to 21 for 1949 on but from 1958 only the competition models had the dynamo sprocket as the

road ones had moved on to an alternator.

The light singles had the clutch shock absorber. All sprockets need to be checked for the condition of their teeth and their fit to the crankshaft. If in good condition continue to use but if doubtful change along with the chain.

In nearly all cases the machine gearing was adjusted by changing the engine sprocket and for the singles a range from 15 to 21 teeth was available up to 1956. It extended to 23 teeth with the new sprockets the next year and remained so to 1963, after which it was reduced a little from 17 to 23 teeth.

The twins began with 19 to 21 teeth and extended this to 18 teeth in 1953. The new sprockets for 1957 ranged from 18 to 22 teeth with 23 added for 1959 and 24 for 1963. The Norton engines had their own sprocket type with 21 to 23 teeth.

On the light singles the matter was complicated by the three chain types fitted and the outcome was parts as needed. The $\frac{3}{8}$ in. single sprocket was available with 21 or 22 teeth, the duplex one with 22 teeth and the $\frac{1}{2}$ in. pitch one with 17 teeth.

Shock absorber—engine

This design was only used on machines fitted with Burman gearboxes and thus up to 1956. With it the engine sprocket ran free on the crankshaft to which a slider was splined. This and the sprocket had matching cam ramps and were held together by a spring. Thus, when the sprocket turned relative to the crankshaft, the ramps forced the slider along the splines against the spring to provide the absorbing effect.

The parts remained common for all years and included different springs for the 348 and 497 cc single engines. There was an attempt to make the spring from the larger engine common to both during 1948 but this was not continued with except for 1956. The springs from the singles were listed on the twins at first with the 348 cc one going on the Matchless and the 497 cc one on the AJS. The parts were amended for 1951 and all, other than the early springs, differed from those fitted on the singles.

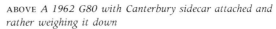

ABOVE *A 1962 G80 with Canterbury sidecar attached and rather weighing it down*

BELOW *The G2CS of 1961 with battery ignition despite the scrambles specification*

Shock absorber—clutch

This was built into the clutch centre and comprised a spider with three vanes which lay inside the centre and its vanes. Drive and rebound rubbers went between the vanes and plates held the assembly together.

It should be checked and the rubbers renewed if they seem at all soft or perished. Get them out by compressing the wide ones so the narrow ones can be picked out and reverse this on assembly.

This spider and the outer plate were altered for 1962 to suit the CSR clutch and this type then became the standard fit the next year. The rubbers were common to all models including the light singles.

Primary chain

Expect to renew this unless you find it in perfect condition. The singles and twins fitted chain of 0.5 in. pitch × 0.335 in. roller diameter × 0.305 in. between inner plates, more commonly known as $\frac{1}{2} \times \frac{5}{16}$ in. The number of links for the singles ranged from 65 to 69 and for the twins from 66 to 69.

The light singles began with 0.375 × 0.250 × 0.225 in. single strand chain with 73 links and this was used by the standard and S models. The CS used 0.50 × 0.335 × 0.205 in. chain, that is narrower than on the heavy singles, and with 55 links. The 348 cc engine used $\frac{3}{8}$ in. duplex with 72 links and the same dimensions as the single strand chain. This duplex

Tool for holding the clutch centre while its nut is attended to and which is well worth having

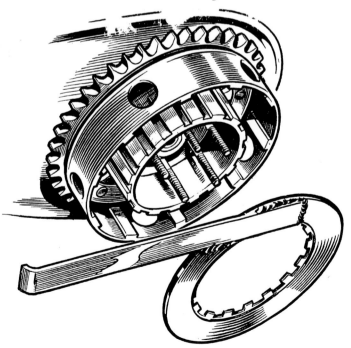

chain, of the same length, was also used by all CSR engines and the standard, S and CS models from engine 12128 on, built late in 1962.

Primary-chain tension

On all AMC machines this is set by moving the gearbox relative to the engine. Generally, the box pivots about its lower mounting but on the light singles it rotates against the crankcase. As the mainshaft is offset from the box centre this action alters the drive centres and the chain tension. In general, follow the handbook and first set the chain too tight and then loosen it off to the right measurement.

Clutch

There were two clutches used on AMC machines, one for the Burman gearbox and the other for the AMC one used from 1957. Both were multi-plate and each design stayed much the same while in use although there were detail changes.

For the Burman the most noticeable of these was from four to five springs in 1950 for the 348 cc competition models, all 497 cc singles and the twins which used five from their start in late 1948. From 1951 the five-spring clutch was used on all models until the AMC one took over.

The clutch parts should all be cleaned and examined for wear or damage. Normal wear points are the tongues of the plates and the slots in the drum, the hub rollers or bearing and the springs which may tire. Plates should be checked for flatness and the clutch nuts for the locking nib under the head.

For most parts replacement is the normal course of action and do this with hub rollers, but only if necessary. Fit a new lock washer where applicable and new compression springs if they are much below their free length.

The clutch springs on all models must be adjusted so that the pressure plate lifts squarely and turns truly. If it does not the clutch will drag and spoil the gearchange. It is for the same reason that the plates must be able to slide sideways in the slots and which, in turn, must be free of burrs or notches.

Clutch hub

This fits on to a spline on the gearbox mainshaft and was a single part on Burman boxes while the AMC type carried the shock absorber in its centre. In either case it was retained by the mainshaft nut with a lock washer.

Two centres were listed for the Burman clutch, one each for the four- and five-plate types at first. These all had four springs and from 1949 on the twins and 1950 for the singles the five-plate one changed to five

The G9 in 1951 form with panniers and bags typical of the time

springs as did the four-plate one for 1951. There were two centres listed for the AMC clutch and the spider changed in 1962 for the CSR models and then became the standard fitment. The rest of the AMC hub stayed the same for all models and years other than the outer cover plate and its screws, which also changed for 1962.

The light singles used their own set of parts at first although one or two details became common in later years. The clutch centre has to match the mainshaft used as four of these exist along with two centres.

Sprocket, drum and bearing

The first two are assembled into one item that runs on the last. The sprocket teeth need to be checked for wear along with the drum slots and the bearing.

The Burman clutches all used the same race, rollers and thrust washers to form the bearing for all models and years. The drum and sprocket were altered for 1951 when the drum gained drive tongues in place of the earlier slots and for all years was listed in two forms to suit four- and five-plate clutches. The drum was also amended for 1948.

The AMC clutch had the sprocket and drum riveted together and the part was also a friction plate. Up to 1959 the friction came from inserts but during that year a part with bonded on pads was introduced and was used on all models from 1960. Once again the

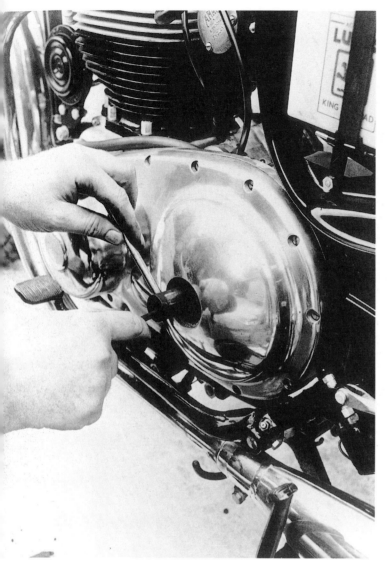

Adjusting the clutch centre screw via the chaincase plug on a 1965 G15

bearing details were common to all models and had caged rather than crowded rollers.

The light singles were similar but without inserts in the clutch drum. There were drum and sprocket assemblies to suit the three primary chain sizes used but otherwise the detail parts served all models.

Springs, cups, studs and nuts

On the Burman box these four details were the same for all models and years. The number used was four of each up to 1949 and for the 1950 road 348 cc models. For the 1950 348 cc competition, all 497 cc singles and all twins including those for 1949, five were used and this was standard from 1951–6.

The AMC clutch had three sets of parts and the cup, nut and stud nut were common to all models right through to 1969. The springs and studs were altered for the CSR models in 1962 and the parts were used by all from the following year.

The light singles used the original spring, cup, nut and stud nut common to the rest of the range. The studs varied with one for the standard models up to 1961. It then changed to one used by the CS models up to that point and this stud also went into the CSR models. Meanwhile the CS changed for 1962 to the stud fitted to all 348 cc models. None of these studs were common to those used by the other models.

Plates

These may be friction, plain, back or pressure and the numbers of the first two depend on the power to be transmitted. Both internal and external splines for both friction and plain plates were used at different times so some care is needed to establish the correct items for any one year and model.

The Burman box began with a clutch with four friction plates for the 348 cc models and five for the 497 cc ones. There were the same number of thin plain plates, one thick plain plate and one pressure plate with holes for four springs. For the twins in 1949 a five-spring pressure plate was introduced and used with the five-plate clutch. For 1950 this combination also went on all the 497 cc singles and the 348 cc competition single while the smaller road singles continued as they were. In the first case the plain plates were all the same, without the thick one, although this continued for the smaller road model.

For 1951 all models adopted the five-spring clutch and a new friction plate. Up to then the plate had external ears to transmit the drive but for 1951 these were moved to the drum and the plates had small recesses cut into them. In 1952 the pressure plate was altered to add an adjuster screw, as the lift mechanism was of a new design, and all except the 348 cc road model had six plain plates as for the year before. From 1954 a new material was used for the friction plates and the plain plates were all the same for all models. Quantities were four and five or five and six of each.

The road 348 cc model continued to be the odd man out when the AMC clutch came in for 1957 as it had its own pressure plate and three friction and four plain plates compared with the four and five used by the other models. As the clutch drum had inserts there was also a back plate. This design had drive tags on the outside of the friction plates.

The design continued in use to 1959 but from that year a bonded insert type also began to be used and this had the friction plates splined on the inside. There were also new plain back and pressure plates to suit and a single-sided, bonded friction plate which reduced the number of plain plates to three or four. For 1962 a five-plate clutch with its own pressure

plate was introduced for the CSR models and in time became the standard fit.

The light singles mainly used parts from the other models with two, three or four plates for the standard, CS or 348 cc models. From 1962 the standard and CSR models had three plates and the CS and 348 cc ones had four plates. Initially there were two types of single-sided friction plate but from 1962 only the one common to the other models. There was also a shouldered plate introduced for the 348 cc model in 1961.

The plain plates were as the other models as was the early pressure plate but this differed for the 348 cc model and used the five-plate CSR type from 1962 for the CS and 348 cc models. The backing plates were special to the model series.

Clutch mechanism

This is the system that connects the clutch cable movement to the pressure plate via the pushrod and it lives under the outer gearbox cover. Four designs were used, two in Burman boxes, one in the AMC and one for the light singles.

ABOVE *The infamous AMC pressed-steel chaincase in 1953 form but still enclosing the dynamo drive as well as the primary one*

BELOW *The cast-alloy chaincase used by the singles in 1958 had the alternator stator located in the outer half*

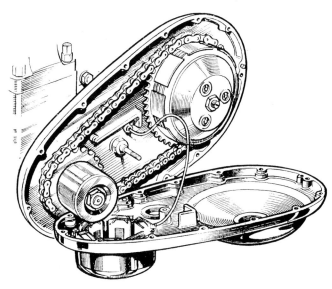

All are easy to dismantle and the parts need to be checked for wear or damage. Make sure the pushrod is quite straight or the clutch will feel very heavy. Lubricate the mechanism load points on assembly so the action is smooth and easy. To assist this check all details for their finish, and polish if necessary so it can work more easily.

The early post-war models used the pre-war design with a lever to move the pushrod and a threaded support for this lever to provide the adjustment. For 1952 the gearbox was improved and the clutch mechanism changed to a three-ball ramp type with an adjuster in the clutch pressure plate. This last item remained in use for the AMC box adopted for 1957 but this had a lever with a cam form which worked against a roller to move the pushrod.

This last design was used from then on for all singles and twins but not the light singles. They had a simpler arrangement with a lever working the pushrod but they retained the adjuster in the pressure plate.

With either AMC type the lever body is clamped in place with a lock ring. It is important that the body and cable are in line when the ring is tightened or the clutch will feel heavy.

The early models had a choice of pushrods with one $9\frac{7}{8}$ in. long being used for all four-plate clutches up to 1956. The five-plate began with a $10\frac{1}{8}$ in. rod and changed this to $10\frac{3}{16}$ in. for 1952. The AMC box had its own rod which did not alter until 1966. In addition the pre-1952 and AMC boxes had clutch rods of $\frac{1}{4}$ in. diameter while the B52 type was of $\frac{5}{16}$ in.

BELOW *Nice alloy chaincase with two access plugs on a 1962 G12CSR with its alternator*

Road and competition singles in use at the 1947 TT with Harry Louis on the left and Jock West with him

Chaincase

After the war AMC continued with their pressed-steel chaincase which few owners could ever keep oil-tight and it remained in use right up to 1964. In 1958 it was joined by a cast-alloy case for the road models and this was finally used by all. All the light singles had a cast-alloy case.

Whether cast or pressed they need to be cleaned and carefully inspected for cracks, damage, poor threads, irregular joint faces or distortion. Be very careful to check on all the distance pieces that go behind the inner case and make sure they fill the gap they are supposed to without straining the case.

The steel case is very prone to leaks and most are due either to distortion of the inner due to poor mounting or distortion of the seal faces. It may be possible to rectify this with some thought and a little panel beating. The rubber-band seal can be shortened

as long as the join is at the top and silicone rubber sealant can be the solution to many ills. When assembling the pressed-steel case remember that the footrest nut can affect the seal joint as it is tightened, so this point must be watched for.

Chaincase types

The two halves of the steel case were modified for 1947 and at the same time the band screw was lengthened to give owners a better chance of joining the two ends round the seal. The next change was for 1949 when the frame was altered and the chain line widened for which a new inner case half appeared, although the outer stayed as it was.

There was a revised inspection cap for 1949 and this also went on the twin-cylinder models which had their own inner case without provision for the dynamo drive. The cap itself was to remain in use to 1964 for all the steel cases. The competition models received a new case outer for 1950 as the footrests were mounted directly to the frame on these models. For 1951 there was a new rubber sealing band with a revised cross-section and the competition type outer case became the standard fit for all models.

For 1952 there was another new outer with a small inspection plate which gave access to the adjuster in the clutch pressure plate. There was a new, endless, synthetic rubber sealing band for 1953 and a new metal outer band to go with it. At the same time the inner case of the twins was modified.

There were further changes for 1954 when the outer case was fitted with a large dome to give access to the whole clutch. This replaced the small cover of 1952 and at the same time a new inner with a sliding seal was used on the competition models.

The next alterations were for 1956 when new frames were introduced and there were new inner cases for singles, twins and competition models. In addition the clamp screw was made even longer. The inner and outer cases changed again for 1957 and the AMC gearbox and the competition one no longer had a sliding seal listed for it but the model alone had a new outer.

All the road models went over to a cast-alloy chaincase for 1958. At the same time the singles changed to alternator electrics so the outer for them had a larger boss into which the stator bolted. The twins kept to their dynamos so they only had a small dome over the end of the crankshaft and their inner differed from that of the singles.

One common part was the inspection cover of which two were used, one for access to the chain and the other for the clutch adjuster. The first was also used to replenish the case oil.

The standard twins soon went over to alternator electrics and copied the singles in chaincase style but with their own inner and outer halves. The two halves

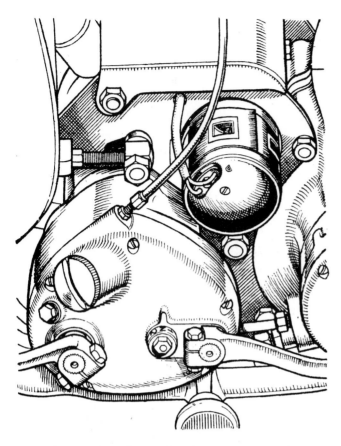

The Burman gearbox as adopted for 1952 with smaller end cover than the earlier type

Gearbox

All models had a four-speed gearbox with positive stop gearchange and the gear and kickstart pedals on the right. Two Burman, one AMC and one light AMC designs were used with detail changes over the years. The light single box had many parts in common with the Norton Jubilee series which could be useful to know when searching for spares.

In all cases dismantling is straightforward and best done with the box clamped in a vice by its bottom lug. Check on the change mechanism and the selectors as you go and don't muddle the parts. The selector forks may be the same part but will prefer to remain with the gears they have run in with. Be careful to keep the gears, washers, bushes and circlips in order to ensure they go back where they came from. During assembly check this and make sure that the operation of the box and its gear selection is exactly as it should be.

Gears

Inspect these carefully for any signs of wear or damage to the teeth and the driving dogs and splines. Replacement is usually the only answer if things are bad, although it is possible to build up and machine or grind them back to original if the dogs are worn. This is not easy to get right and is very specialized.

The gears changed over the years, so if parts are needed it is most important that they match. It is good practice to replace them in pairs as an old gear can easily wear out a new one. Consult the parts lists and check the numbers of teeth on the existing gears before shopping. Also note the form of the gear to assist in identification.

The 1945 set of gears was for the Burman CP box and was joined the next year by a wider ratio version for competition use. For the CS models of 1951 another form, the BA, was used but only for that one year. Both standard and competition types were revised into the B52 for 1952, again with normal and wide ratios. Two other forms of this box were used, one for trials from 1954 on and another for scrambles for 1954 only.

For 1957 all models changed to the AMC gearbox, first described in May 1956, and this came with standard or trial ratios. The internal ratios of both were altered for 1960 and these boxes served all models from then on.

The light singles had their own gearbox with a standard one used up to 1964 and another from then on. The CS models for 1960–2 had a version of the first standard box with a higher first gear. There were a number of changes incorporated in all boxes for 1961 to improve the engagement and to stop gears jumping out of mesh.

for the de luxe and sports models continued as these machines kept their dynamos. For 1960 the CS models also changed to the alloy case and remained with it. The 348 cc competition model had a new inner steel case for 1964 but that was the last year it was produced.

By 1961 the de luxe twins had the alternator type chaincase as did the CSR ones for 1962 so only these cases were produced then. The road singles carried on with their 1958 type while the CS used their outer and its own inner as before. The twins ran on with the alternator case halves with a change to the inner for 1965 and another for 1966. The inspection caps stayed as they were to the end.

The light singles used the same inspection cap but had their own series of chaincase halves. The inner was common to all standard, S, CS and 348 cc models with another for the CSR ones. The outers differed and at first carried a round badge in a common part. This practice continued for the 348 cc engine which had its own outer case but not the CSR or 1962 on standard or CS engines. These had smooth outers without badges and, for the CSR, were polished as well.

The 1966 model 33 with the AMC gearbox which also went on the Norton range so there was not too much AJS left in this machine

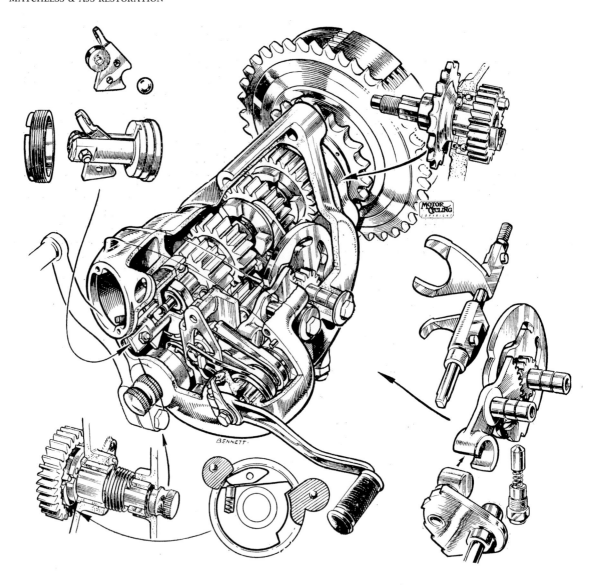

The AMC gearbox adopted by them and Norton from May 1956 and a development of the earlier Norton type

Shafts

These need to be inspected for damaged splines, poor threads and the condition of bearing surfaces. Replacement is the normal course of action if all is not as it should be and, as with the gears, care is needed to make sure the correct part is obtained and that it will work with the other items.

The Burman boxes had a change to both main- and layshafts for 1948 when a bush was added to the mainshaft third gear. The original mainshaft stayed in the competition box for 1950 but the second one was used for 1951 except for the machines with the BA box

which had its own shafts. All models had new shafts for the B52 box while the layshaft for the competition models differed from standard from 1954. The AMC box had one mainshaft for all years and one layshaft except in 1957. For that year alone there was another used in the CS models only.

The light singles were more complex as there were four mainshaft types although only one layshaft was used. The type can be checked by the dimension from the outer end of the clutch hub spline to the edge of the first gear. The original shaft was used in the 248 cc models up to engine 9974 and in 10064 to 10128 and had a 3.850 in. dimension. From then on another with a 3.751 in. dimension was used. The 348 cc engine had its own shaft and up to engine 3757 the dimension was 4.102 in. and after it this became 4.003 in. The clutch centre must match the mainshaft in use with one for the early shafts and another for the later pair.

Bushes and bearings

Ball races need to be completely cleaned before they are checked and if there is any doubt about their condition they should be renewed. Some play is normal for ball races but there must be no rough spots. Bushes must be renewed if worn.

The 1945 and B52 gearboxes used up to 1956 had a sleeve gear race whose dimensions were given as $1\frac{9}{32}$ in. $\times$ 62 $\times$ 16 mm which made it a non-standard size while the mainshaft race was 17 $\times$ 40 $\times$ 12 mm and thus more normal. The BA box of 1951, and used by the CS models only, increased these sizes to 35 $\times$ 72 $\times$ 17 mm and 20 $\times$ 52 $\times$ 15 mm. The sleeve gear had two bushes to support the mainshaft and two more carried the layshaft. The mainshaft third gear was bushed from 1948 and the layshaft first and second ones from 1952. There were also other bushes for the gear selector mechanism.

It was all change for 1957, and the AMC box, in which the sleeve-gear end of the layshaft was also mounted in a ball race. The sleeve-gear race was $1\frac{1}{4}$ $\times$ $2\frac{1}{2}$ $\times$ $\frac{5}{8}$ in., the mainshaft one $\frac{5}{8}$ $\times$ $1\frac{9}{16}$ $\times$ $\frac{7}{16}$ in. and the layshaft 17 $\times$ 40 $\times$ 12 mm. The sleeve-gear, mainshaft second, layshaft third and layshaft first gears were all bushed and there were other bushes for the selector mechanism and the kickstart axle.

The light single had a sleeve-gear roller bearing 25 $\times$ 52 $\times$ 15 mm and a mainshaft ball race $\frac{1}{2}$ $\times$ $1\frac{5}{16}$ $\times$ $\frac{3}{8}$ in. dimensions. These served all models and years along with bushes for the layshaft, sleeve gear, layshaft first gear, change mechanism and kickstart.

At MIRA in 1958 when Vic Willoughby crammed over 103 miles into the hour riding a G11CSR

Over the rocks with a 1957 G3LC which had become more specialized to suit its trials work

Shell and covers

All models had an inner and outer cover with some form of access to the clutch cable. The gearbox shell of the singles and twins was very much in the tradition of the English machine but that of the light singles was circular to fit against the crankcase rear. All parts need to be checked over as for any other alloy part for cracks, damaged threads and joint faces.

The original shell served up to 1951 when it was joined by another for the BA box. A new shell came in for the B52 gearbox of 1952 and for 1954 a version of this with an inspection hole was added. This was used from then on until 1956. The AMC box had its own shell and this was not altered until 1966. An alternative was listed for the CS singles in 1958 and remained in use for those models only. Note that the Norton gearbox shell is not the same as that used on AMC models although very similar. Norton ones are marked N or NA and AMC ones M.

The inner and outer covers were altered for 1948 when other details were modified and the outer changed again the next year while the inner stayed as

ABOVE *The 1959 model 31 AJS twin with alternator within its case*

BELOW *The gearbox used in the lightweight AMC models with the gears high in the shell and thus insistent on their full 3 pints of lubricant*

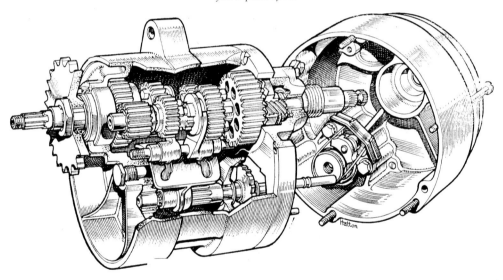

it was until 1951. For that year, covers for the BA box were also listed but there were new ones for the B52 box in 1952. The outer remained as introduced but the inner was amended for 1954 when there were other detail changes.

The AMC box covers had the outer revised for 1958 and both changed in 1962 at singles engine 133896 and twin X8252. The CS singles had their own inner cover but changed to the 1962 type for 1964.

The light singles differed from the other models with their circular shell and inner and outer covers to match. Thanks to the shape the gearbox *must* have three pints of oil in it or the gears run dry and wear rapidly.

Gearchange mechanism

This starts with the rubber on the gear pedal and runs through to the selector forks which move the gears. There are a number of wear points that need to be checked and the fork sides are one possible area. The various springs need to be changed if tired and the whole mechanism must operate smoothly.

The first Burman gearbox had a mechanism which was modified a little for 1948 and fully revamped for 1952. In either case there were few changes and these in detail only. The AMC box had even fewer alterations although the return spring changed for 1962. The other alteration concerned the camplate for

The G80 in 1948 when it still had the old type Burman gearbox and the dynamo tucked under the magneto and very hard to service

the CSR models which was changed in 1966 and continued along with the standard part.

The gear pedal of the Burman boxes altered for 1948, 1952 and 1954 and a rubber did not appear until 1948. It was modified for the next year and stayed in use in that form to 1956. The AMC box changed its pedal for 1958 and the next year another was added for the 348 cc competition models. Both stayed in use from then on with one pedal rubber type. One extra pedal appeared in 1966 for the CSR models and was used for that year and the next.

On the light singles the gearchange mechanism had a few detail changes over the years. The stop plate and plunger changed for 1960 and the return spring for 1962. It used its own gear pedal but the rubber came from the other models.

Kickstarter

Various systems were used by AMC for the kickstarter and the Burman gearboxes had a quadrant to mesh with a gear on the end of the mainshaft. This gear turned the shaft via a face ratchet and the design served all models up to 1956. The road machine had a rigid kickstart pedal and the competition models a folding one.

The AMC box had a mechanism with a pawl mounted at the inner end of the kickstart axle to drive a ratchet cut within the first gear pinion on the layshaft. The axle and its return spring were altered for 1962 but otherwise the parts stayed as they were for all models.

A fixed pedal was used up to 1964 and a folding one served the competition models with a detail change for 1958. It then went on the CS and CSR twins as well as the singles and continued on all models from 1965. From 1966 it was fitted with a pedal rubber.

The light singles had a different design with a quick thread cut on the inner end of the kickstart axle. This turned in a nut which then engaged with the layshaft first gear via a face ratchet to turn the engine over. All models had a folding pedal and this was amended for the road machines for 1961. The CS models were fitted with a longer pedal from 1960 and this went on all machines from 1962.

In most cases the return spring will need replacement and the ratchet parts should be closely examined for wear. Change if worn as it is painful if the mechanism slips as you try to start the engine. Also, be careful of pattern kickstart levers which may foul the exhaust pipe. If the machine is in pieces a check can be made by placing old and new parts side by side with their inner faces on a flat surface. Inspection should show if they are not the same. Note that the pedal must swing well clear of the pipe to allow for bending under load.

Gearbox sprocket

Expect to renew this. Check for worn or damaged teeth, tired splines that don't fit the sleeve gear well and a rough oil-seal surface or distance piece. Fit a new oil seal unless the existing one is perfect, which I doubt. There was one type each for the CP Burman, B52 Burman, AMC and light single gearboxes.

For many years the singles and twins fitted a 16-tooth gearbox sprocket, again with one type each for the CP, BA, B52 and AMC boxes. One with 17 teeth was listed for the last of these in 1958 but was not a standard fit until 1960 and then only for the CSR models. It was joined by one with 19 teeth for 1966. The light singles began with 19 teeth but also used 17 and 18 over the years. The 1965 gearbox had a different spline for the sleeve gear so the sprocket also changed and must match.

The nut and lock washer followed the same sequence with changes for 1952 and 1957. The BA box had its own parts and a water deflector was introduced for the competition models in 1950. This fitted under the nut and was modified for 1952. The light singles had their own set of parts and in all cases it is important that the correct spacers and washers are fitted in order to maintain the chain line.

Rear chain

Bound to need renewal on any rebuild. The singles and twins had chain with 0.625 in. pitch × 0.400 roller diameter × 0.380 in. between inner plates and better known as $\frac{5}{8} \times \frac{3}{8}$ in. Chain lengths vary from 90 links for early competition models to 104 for the G85CS. Except for these, all fall in the range 94 to 99 links. The light singles used chain of 0.50 × 0.335 × 0.305 in. dimensions with 123 to 124 links for the road models and 131 to 133 for the CS machines.

Assembly

This is a straightforward job but the details need to be checked as you go along. Bearings should be held in place with Loctite as an added security and joint faces can be sealed with the traditional gasket or a silicone rubber compound. As always, use the latter sparingly.

Work to the manual and check each stage for correct operation. Make certain you have the selector forks in the correct position and engaged in the proper cam track. Double-check the gear selection as a mistake can be traumatic on the road. Do make sure you have the gears with small shoulders the correct way round so the shoulder is against the adjacent bearing which gives a working clearance between the teeth and the bearing outer race. If you leave the main nuts until you have the machine assembled so you can use the brake to hold the shaft, make sure you cannot forget to do them up by some means or other.

A 1957 Matchless single for the army being tested over the rough by a factory man

Remember to fill the gearbox and primary chaincase with oil before using the machine. In the light singles you *must* make sure you have enough oil as the first pint will not even reach the gears due to the shape of the box. Thus they would run dry and soon wear if the full amount (three pints) is not used. Note that more light single boxes are worn out due to not having enough oil in them than from normal wear and tear. Keep an eye on the level to make sure you don't suffer from this problem. After the rebuild a tie-on label on the filler or the gear pedal may help to remind you about the oil.

5 Carburettor and exhaust

These are two areas that can give the restorer considerable problems unless the parts are simply replaced. The difficulties arise as the first wears and the second corrodes all the time the machine is in use, so their condition changes continuously. Both affect the performance of the machine, especially the carburettor, and both are important to the final appearance of the model.

All AMC machines had Amal carburettors and the standard models used type 76 and 89 ones to 1954, Monoblocs from 1955 to 1966 and Concentrics from 1967. Both TT and GP carburettors were used on the competition models.

A variety of exhaust systems were fitted over the years with the most common being a separate exhaust pipe and silencer mounted low down on one or both sides. Siamezed pipes were fitted as standard to some twins for some years with the silencer low down on the right but in all these cases a normal twin silencer system was also offered as an option. In the same way the siamezed system was often an option for some twins with the normal system.

The Amal number system

Amal stamped all carburettor bodies with a number sequence that was their method of stock control. This was the build standard and up to the late Concentrics was unique as to the internal settings of the instrument. Thus if *any* setting was changed the assembly received a new part number and was stored accordingly. In this manner they could easily check that they delivered the correct unit to their many customers who, in turn, could readily check them into their stores and in time out again on to the correct machines.

The type 6 carburettors were stamped with the basic type number followed by one or two letters, an oblique line and a further three-digit mark. The type number is 275 for units up to $\frac{7}{8}$ in. bore, 76 or 276 for those of $\frac{15}{16}$ to $1\frac{1}{16}$ in. and 289 for $1\frac{1}{8}$ in. or over. The letters give the build standard of the settings while the final series indicates the float chamber which goes with the unit.

Monobloc carburettors have no need for the last mark and are stamped with the type number followed by a one-, two- or three-digit build standard number. The first can be 375, 376 or 389 with the same size limits as the type 6. The Concentric carburettors used the same system for the 600 and 900 series and the units were numbered R or L for right- or left-hand, followed by a six or nine plus the bore in mm, to give 626 or 928, for example, with the build standard to finish.

The effect of this system can be seen in the carburettor settings list. The Monobloc and Concentric were also used in pairs to make a twin carburettor installation and the two inlet tracts were connected by a short piece of flexible pipe.

A perfectionist would seek to fit a carburettor with the correct number stamped on it but otherwise there is no obstacle to just changing the settings to the correct ones for the machine in question. Note that the data given is from Amal data and is sometimes at variance with the parts list and other published information. A carburation check to confirm the settings is always a good idea once all else has been correctly set.

Amal restoration

The instrument has to be taken apart and checked over. New fibre washers, float needle and seating are normal practice and a new needle and jet may not come amiss. Checking the mounting flange for flatness, its holes for clearance and all the internal passages for obstructions is also usual with any rebuild. Pilot-screw damage is common.

The problems arise from body and slide wear plus doubtful threads, especially the one for the top ring. Most of the other threads can be repaired or reclaimed with an insert, even in some cases by a thread change with a new mating part made from scratch. The top ring, or mixing chamber cap, is more tricky and often the chamber thread will be found to be damaged or worn away to a taper. It is possible to cut it deeper and make a new ring but it is a tricky engineering job needing good equipment.

Twin carburettors with an amount of downdraught on the 745 cc Norton engine of the 1965 G15CSR

The wear problem can be dealt with by sleeving the body, and again this is a tricky job which must be done to a high level of precision. As with all carburettor work it must be tackled with a delicate touch as the parts are fragile and easy to break.

If you can find replacement parts it will be easier than repairing an old carburettor and the notes about Amal numbering should help. The units were handed so you must check that you have the correct item for your model and also note the positions of throttle stop and air screw.

Chambers and their floats require normal inspection but usually it is only the needle and its seating that wear. Make sure the float in a Monobloc can move freely on its pivot as a tight spot can cause confusion. Check all floats for leaks.

Assemble the instrument with care and make sure the petrol feed area is as it should be. It is well worth connecting this up to a tank and checking that it holds a level and does not flood. Better to find out before it goes back on to the machine and drips all over the magneto.

The finish of the earlier Amal bodies was in a silver-grey paint specially developed to resist petrol. This is no longer available as no one is prepared to order the required large quantity so a problem exists. Do not be tempted to use any other paint without a trial first as it may react with the fuel to produce a dreadful mess that is more a sludge than anything and a full clean out will then be needed. Better to go for bead-blasting which gives a very similar result but do check every passage afterwards in case it was not correctly masked.

Petrol pipes

The early machines used copper tubing and brass-end fittings to form their pipes but from 1954 began to use flexible pipes. From 1955 all machines, including the light singles from 1958, used a tee piece and suitable lengths of pipe.

At first, there were two pipes listed for the singles with one for each capacity. Each joined the two halves of the tank with a single feed to the float chamber. The detail design was altered for 1949 and also produced in another layout for the twins which differed in the placement of taps and chamber.

For 1950 the competition models added a flexible joint in the feed to the chamber so that pipe was split. The road singles pipe was altered for 1952 but for 1953 copied the competition one with a flexible joint in the chamber feed.

Short tubes and flexible pipes were used by all for 1954 and the next year the range turned to petrol taps with built-in outlet pipes. These matched the float chamber connection on the Monoblocs adopted that year so only pipes and a tee piece were needed. This arrangement was used from then on with just variations of pipe length as needed.

All need to be treated with some suspicion as they can age and may then leak. Replacement is essential on safety grounds. The pipe and any end fittings need to be inspected regardless of type or age. The pipe for cracks or wear spots and the fittings for the way they seat and seal plus the condition of the nut threads. Old pipes can take a set and be very stiff so they pull on the tap or carburettor while the nuts may distort or stretch so they don't spin on as they should.

If new pipes are needed and total originality is not required then modern black neoprene is to be recommended as it has a long life and holds on to the fittings well, even without any clips. It also remains very flexible even in cold weather which is a good

The first post-war models such as this 1946 16M used the older Amal with separate float chamber

point. When making up pipes ensure they are long enough not to pull at the ends or kink, that they lie naturally and avoid vertical loops which can cause air locks.

Air filter

The element should be cleaned, renewed or washed, dried and re-oiled according to type while the body needs to be repaired and finished as any other sheet steel component. The hose connecting the filter to the carburettor must be carefully checked for cracks which could cause air leaks. If the filter is removed this will weaken the mixture so a carburation check is essential.

For all models the filter was an optional fitting and either attached directly to an adaptor on the carburettor or went between the oil tank and battery. They were listed from 1949 for singles and 1951 for twins and used by both touring and competition models. Their application to the 1960 497 cc CS singles caused that model to move its oil tank to make room for the filter.

The singles had a drum-shaped cleaner with adaptors for the two capacities but the twins had a slimmer part with rounded ends. The singles changed to this shape for 1955 and had the mountings revised for 1956 with both these parts also being used on the twins.

There was also a special cleaner for the 348 cc trials model in 1955 and another for the CS models in 1957, which was amended for 1958. For 1959 the cleaner for

the tourers was modified and joined by a new version for the CS and CSR models while the 348 cc competition machine continued with its 1955 part.

This last stayed on the 1960 models but there were new cleaners for the tourers, the twins and a special one for the 497 cc CS singles. This tucked in on the right to be in line with the big carburettor, which forced the oil tank to move out of the way.

There was a new cleaner for the 348 cc road model for 1962 and revised ones for most models for 1963 and changes for some for 1964. The machines with Norton twin engines had their own filter as did the light singles.

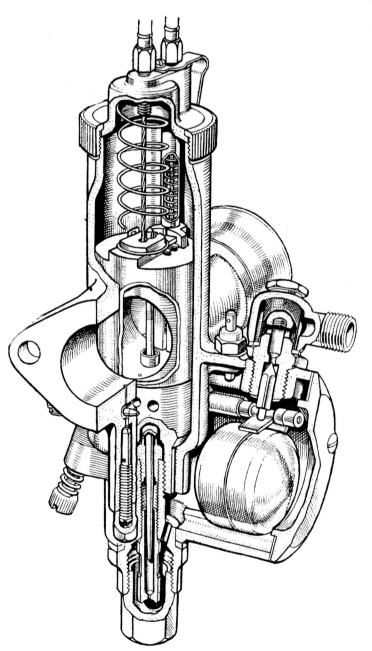

Exhaust system

This comprises the pipes and silencers plus the clips, brackets and stays which hold them to the machine. The parts are steel, chrome-plated, and this finish often suffers from both heat and corrosion which detracts greatly from the machine's appearance.

Fortunately replacement with pattern parts is possible for these popular models and it is worth paying a sensible price for the items rather than looking for the cheapest. The pipes and silencers are an important facet of the looks of the model so well worth getting right for the sake of a little extra money. Quality parts will also fit better and last longer. A further important aspect of this for AMC models is that in many cases the end of the original exhaust pipe was extended into the silencer with pepper-pot drilling and blanked-off end. This played a considerable part in the silencing and if let off, as it often is with pattern pipes, the machine is likely to be rather noisy instead of nice and quiet. Best avoided if possible to help with the MoT test and to avoid painful talks with the law.

If the pipes, clips and brackets are in good order it may be feasible to clean and polish them for further use. Before the final polish they should be checked for their fit to the machine mounting-points and to the cylinder head. All the machines with AMC engines have push-in pipes and for these you may need to swell the pipe to ensure that it is a snug fit in the port. Heat plus a wooden wedge may be needed to do this.

The Norton twin engines clamp the pipes with nuts screwed into the exhaust ports and in all cases the pipe must fit squarely into the port and the nut must be able to run in true into the threads without trying to damage them. If any parts are distorted real care may be needed to get everything back into line.

The brackets and clips should be easy to repair and refinish, if this is needed, as most are simple parts. The correct nuts, bolts and washers, plus any special parts used with the clips should be checked and refurbished as necessary.

The silencer body is much more of a problem if you wish to re-use it and it is not in good condition. Often the thin outer shell will have corroded from the inside which makes repair a skilled metal-working job. A further problem is the plating, for firms that undertake such work will not want to put a dirty silencer in their tank and it is just about impossible to clean it fully.

Thus the existing silencer can only really be used if in good order and the practical alternative has to be a pattern part unless you are lucky enough to locate an unused original.

Amal Monobloc carburettor adopted by much of the British industry in 1955

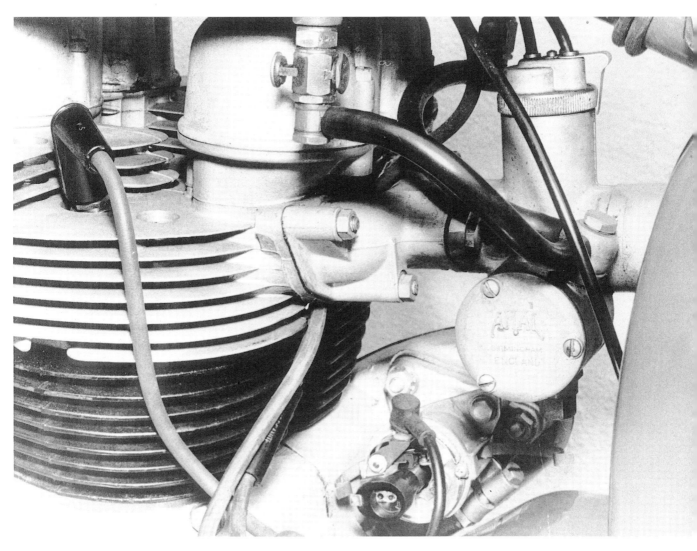

A 1962 G12 with Monobloc showing the side cover to the float chamber, feed pipe and petrol tap

Exhaust-pipe types

There are a good few of these and it is important to get the correct one or you could have problems with fit and alignment. The singles began with a pipe for each capacity and that of the 348 cc model ran above the right footrest and the 497 cc one ran below. The larger one alone had a separate baffle as the smaller was integral.

These two were joined by two with tilted ends for the competition models and for 1947 the pipe for the road 348 cc model was altered so it ran below the footrest as for the larger machine. The road pipes both changed for 1949, when they were also fitted to the spring-frame models, and the competition ones were joined by straight-through pipes for scrambles use.

The 348 cc road models stayed with their existing pipe for 1950 but with different pipes for AJS and Matchless for that year alone. The larger machine had the choice of the old pipe or a new one with integral baffle and the separate baffle was not listed after that year. There were new pipes and optional straight-through pipes for the competition models.

There were a total of six pipes listed for 1951 with one each for road, competition and CS models in both engine sizes. There were also two pipe extensions for the off-road models to be used in place of the stock silencer. The 348 cc extension became common for 1952 when all except the 348 cc road pipes were changed.

Only the competition ones altered for 1953, none for 1954 and the CS pipes for 1955 but only the extension continued for 1956 and only for the 348 cc engines. The 497 CS went back to the 1951 type and there were four new pipes. These served the road 348 cc, road 497 cc, competition 348 cc and CS 497 cc and a baffle re-appeared for the competition 348 cc

The AJS model 18CS as built for 1961–2

models. All except this, the extensions and the road 497 cc pipe changed for 1957 but for 1958 there was only a new baffle for the 497 cc CS models.

For 1959 there was a new pipe for the 348 cc competition models and for 1960 one for the 497 cc CS models and this was changed for 1962. That year the 348 cc road model also had a new pipe and this changed again for both 1963 and 1964 on. The road 497 cc pipe also changed for these two years as did the competition 348 cc and 497 cc CS ones for 1964.

The twins had one pair of pipes which did not change until 1955 when their fixing stud became a welded-on lug. A second pair appeared for the 593 cc engine for 1956 and both had a baffle up to then but not later. For 1957 one pair served both capacities and these had a perforated extension into the silencer. They continued for 1958 and were joined by siamezed pipes for the CS version.

There were four pairs of pipes for 1959 with the 1957 pair continuing on the road 498 cc models and the siamezed pair on the same sized CS and CSR ones.

There were new pipes for the 646 cc machines and again one served the standard models and the other was siamezed and for the CS and CSR versions. All the siamezed systems had the silencer low down on the right.

It was down to three pairs of pipes for 1960 as the smaller sports twins were dropped from the range but all the pipes were new with a pair each for the 498 cc and 646 cc tourers and a siamezed pair for the CS and CSR versions. The right pipe of the siamezed pair was altered for 1961 and this had been listed as one of a siamezed option for the early 646 cc standard models. In the same way a normal pair of pipes was available for the CS and CSR models from 1959 and this practice continued on to the end of the AMC twins.

The standard twins continued with two pipes and had new ones for 1963 while the left siameze one for the CSR stayed as the 1960 type but the right one was new for 1963.

The Norton engines had their own pipes made in two styles. For all the standard models and the G15CS the pipes ran low down on each side to separate silencers. The CSR machines differed and had swept-

fitted to both. Thus, only the larger road models had a different part once again.

This situation continued until 1955 when there was a new silencer shape other than for the competition models which kept what they had. The new shape came in four forms to suit the 348 and 497 cc models in rigid or sprung frames. For 1956 the rigid pair went but the sprung pair continued. The old competition silencer stayed with the 348 cc models but the 497 cc CS ones reverted to the one used by them in 1951.

The competition models had new silencers for 1957 with one each for the trials and two sizes of scrambles models while the road machines stayed as they were, as they did till 1959. The two CS models had new silencers for 1958 as did the 348 cc trials models for 1959.

BELOW *The 1965 G15 with its Monobloc carburettor*

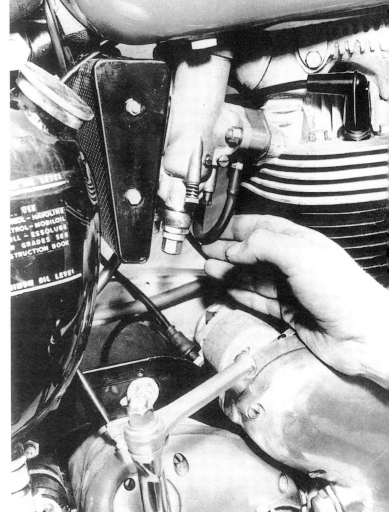

back pipes on each side which gave the models a very nice line. All had the same gasket and retaining nut, which must be kept tight.

The light singles had their own series of pipes, all similar with the silencer low on the right. One pipe was used on the standard models and the S for 1961. The latter used the CSR pipe for 1962 and this went on the super sports model up to 1965. For 1966 the CSR had a pipe which swept back in the manner of the sports twins. The 348 cc models had their own pipe and the CS machines an open pipe which was amended for 1961.

Silencer types

The singles began with a tubular silencer for each capacity with these joined by a common one for the competition models. These were changed to a type with offset ends to improve ground clearance for 1950 and one part served the 497 cc road models and the other the rest of the singles range. The first was used for the 497 cc CS model in 1951 while the last went on the smaller CS machine, but for 1952 this silencer was

There were new silencers for the 1960 road models with one each for the 348 and 497 cc machines plus yet another for the 348 cc trials machine. The CS machines were no longer fitted with a silencer although one remained available as an option for a few years. There was a new silencer for the 348 cc road model for 1962 which was changed for 1963 as was that of the 497 cc road machine.

The twins had their own silencers and for most years these fitted to the Matchless were of a megaphone shape which suited the machine very well. The AJS had the usual tubular type but they all differed from those fitted to the singles.

The first two pairs were changed for 1955 when the mounting was altered from a stud to a lug and next for 1960 when the clamp to the pipe was amended. Another silencer was listed for the 593 cc CS versions of 1958 with siamezed pipes, an alternative was used on either side when the optional dual-exhaust system was fitted. For the CS, and later CSR, models the Matchless was fitted with a tubular silencer and not the usual megaphone.

There were two further pairs of silencers for 1959 to suit the 646 cc engines and both those and the 498 cc ones were changed for 1960. There was also a single silencer for the sports twins of either make plus the optional pair used when the two-pipe system was

ABOVE The standard twin-pipe exhaust system as used by the 1966 G12 with silencers without tail pipes

ABOVE RIGHT Swept-back pipes of the 1965 G15CSR which gave it such a lovely line

BELOW RIGHT The silencer used by much of the range in the 1960s and here seen on a model 16 or 18 from 1962

fitted. From 1959, options were listed so that any twin, whether tourer or sports, could be fitted with dual exhausts or a siamezed system.

For 1963, a new silencer shape without a tail pipe was adopted which saw the end of the Matchless megaphone. The right-side standard silencer was also used by the CSR models in this instance and the same parts were used by all the 745 cc twins except the CS model. These had their own parts.

The light singles had a silencer for each of the standard, CS and 348 cc models with the first going on to the S and CSR machines. From 1964 the last of these fitted a silencer type without tail pipe.

Don't forget that the whole system must fit the machine without stress or strain to avoid fracture or parts coming adrift.

ABOVE *AJS model 16 for 1960 with new duplex frame but same rather old engine*

BELOW *A 1961 Matchless G80CS showing off its nice big carburettor along with air filter and open exhaust*

6 Lubrication

All AMC models have a dry-sump lubrication system and all except the light singles have a separate oil tank usually mounted on the right side of the machine beneath the saddle or front of the dualseat. Exceptions were the CS singles from 1960 which had the tank on the left or central, and the light singles. These had the tank incorporated within the right crankcase half, beneath the timing cover.

The singles had a reciprocating and rotating oil pump driven by a worm on the crankshaft up to 1963 and a duplex gear pump from then on. The light singles kept to their version of the original pump throughout the years while the AMC twins had two separate gear pumps. The Norton twins had a duplex gear pump.

Only the twins had a pressure relief valve but all models had filters to protect the pumps. The rockers were pressure lubricated on all models other than Norton twins built before engine 116371 in 1966. These had a take-off from the return line. A variety of breather systems were used on the different engine series.

Oil pump

This should run for long periods with little wear as it works in oil but a likely problem point is the pin that registers in the groove in the pump plunger. This must be the correct type, in perfect condition and properly located into the groove.

The gear type pumps can sometimes be reclaimed by lapping the parts so the gears turn smoothly without end play. After this attention all parts must be well cleaned before assembly.

The pump used on the singles had changes to its plunger and guide screw for 1947 and 1948 to tie in with the alterations to the timing-side mainshaft and its oil-pump drive worm. It is vital that the parts are not mismatched as the original type had a single-start worm drive and the 1947 one a two-start drive when the parts were stamped 2S. Otherwise the same parts were used for all models up to 1963. For 1964 on, all fitted the Norton duplex gear pump, still driven from the timing-side mainshaft.

The two gear pumps on the twins had most of their detail parts amended for 1952 and again a decade later for 1962 when the gears were widened to increase the pump outputs. The duplex gear pump fitted to the Norton engines was similar but not the same as that fitted in the singles. The light singles had their own set of reciprocating parts which served all models and years.

Pressure-release valve

This is only to be found on the twins as the singles took the pump output into the engine without this control on pressure. They could do this with mainly roller and ball bearings as pump volume was, if anything, more important than pressure in these engines.

The twins with plain big-ends required oil at pressure and had this limited by a valve. At first this went into the crankcase next to the oil-feed connection, the forward one of the two, from below. This arrangement was used up to early 1952, after which the valve went into the face of the timing crankcase near the feed pump.

The valve was not fitted at all for 1956–9 but reappeared for 1960, set in the base of the crankcase filter compartment. It was modified for 1964 in respect of its detail parts. The Norton twin engines had the pressure relief valve assembly screwed into the rear of the timing cover.

In all cases the valve seldom gives any trouble but make sure it cuts off cleanly and that the spring is not tired. It is possible to check the oil pressure by removing the screwed cap at the left end of the filter chamber just ahead of the exhaust camshaft. A pressure gauge can then be attached and when cold at idle it may read up to 140 psi, which is the valve blow-off pressure. When hot the pressure at idle should be 20 to 40 psi and it should rise as the engine speed increases.

Filters

The singles began with a filter in the oil tank on the return line plus another for the feed pipe. The twins copied this arrangement although with a different feed pipe filter up to 1955. For the next year all models had new oil tanks and these simply had the earlier twin type filter for the feed pipe. At the same time all engines adopted a common magnetic filter as a sump plug and this arrangement continued with a filter alteration for 1964.

The light singles had one filter set in the left side of the engine. This dealt with the scavenged oil before it was returned to the oil tank.

The twins had a filter set across the front of the crankcase with a blow-off valve at one end in case it should be blocked. The filter went into the lubrication system between the feed oil pump and before a non-return valve which led on to the engine supply. The original was a close-grained felt but for 1960 this was changed for a fine metal gauze. For 1962 it altered again to add felt fabric round the metal gauze and this type also fitted the 1960–1 engines. For 1964 it was replaced by the original 1949 filter which then remained in use.

Machines fitted with Norton twin engines retained the usual AMC oil-tank filter and added one in the engine sump. The latter was housed in a body which screwed into the underside of the crankcase and the same part was used in all models.

It is feasible to repair mesh filters but if this is attempted there are two provisos. Firstly, don't restrict the oil flow and secondly don't reduce the degree of filtration. Thus, do not replace fine gauze with wide mesh or the reverse. Also make sure the seatings and other details are in order.

Rocker-box oiling

This was done under pressure by AMC with an external pipe on the singles and internal drillings for the twins and light singles. The singles of all types had an adjustable needle valve in the rocker box to control the oil supply to the inlet valve stem and the same part

right exhaust was neither metered or plugged and the plugs had flats machined on them to give the required restriction.

From 1954 the plugs were altered to have holes drilled in them in place of the flats and four were used as the missing one had caused some confusion. For 1955 the rockers were grooved to direct oil to the pushrod ends but prior to then there was an oil hole drilled in the rocker posts.

The four plugs were left out for 1959 but returned in 1961 at engine X4706 for the 646 cc engine and went on all 498 cc twins.

The Norton twins began with a feed from the oil return line which could be a little marginal. The solution was to fit a restrictor in the return line upstream of the tee to improve the rocker feed. From engine 116372 in 1966 the feed was taken from the pressure side of the system with a banjo-bolt connection in the rear of the timing chest.

In all cases with an external pipe this must be really secure if under pressure and all joints and fittings able to withstand the loads on them.

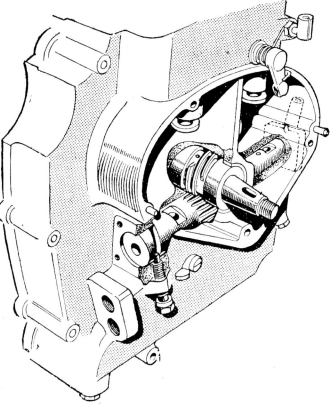

served all models and years.

The arrangements for the twins were not so simple and the oil diverted from the main engine supply went first to a distributor bush driven by the left end of the exhaust camshaft. This gave an intermittent feed to the cylinder heads via a series of internal drillings.

Up to 1954 the bush had a $\frac{3}{64}$ in. hole drilled in it, but for early 1955 engines it was replaced by a metering jet. During the year the bush returned and according to the AMC service bulletin it came with a $\frac{1}{16}$ in. hole. From then on just one part number is quoted for this item but for 1956 the workshop manual gives the bush hole as $\frac{1}{32}$ in. At the same time the bush was required to supply oil to the camshaft tunnels as well as the valve gear and two metering jets were used to control this. For 1957 the manual gives the bush hole as $\frac{3}{64}$ in. and for 1958 states that it had a flat machined on it in place of the hole.

This was not the end of the control on the rocker oiling for there were usually metering plugs in the cylinder heads. At first there were three of these with one for each left rocker and one for the right inlet. The

ABOVE *The mainshafts with worms for the singles with, from the left, up to 1946, a two-start for 1947–53, a modified version of 2, shouldered 1954-onwards pin and a stronger version of 4 used from 1960 onwards*

BELOW LEFT *The oil-pump shafts for the single with, from the left, up to 1946, 1947 only and from 1948 on and not much to tell the difference between the lot*

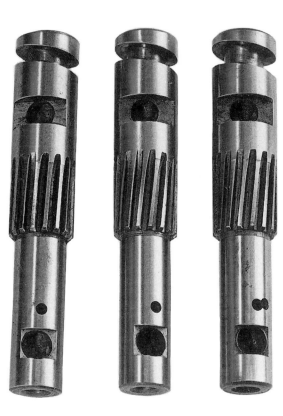

Cylinder-wall feed

This was provided on the singles up to the end of 1955 with internal drillings. On the twins a $\frac{3}{32}$ in. hole was added in the cylinder spigot aperture for 1960 on the drive side. At the same time a number of engines (X1994 to X2619) were fitted with a cylinder which had a hole drilled in the spigot. These must be fitted on the timing side, or the drive-side cylinder will receive too much oil.

Oil pipes

The main ones were the feed and return that connected the oil tank to the engine but there were also the rocker-box pipes, breathers and vent pipes. All need to be inspected for any signs of cracks or leaks. Check any flexible pipes carefully as their material may deteriorate and either swell up or break away and could block the pipe. Also check for any loose area that could flap about and stop the flow once this begins but which would leave the pipe clear when inspected. A rare fault maybe, but confusing and expensive if it happens.

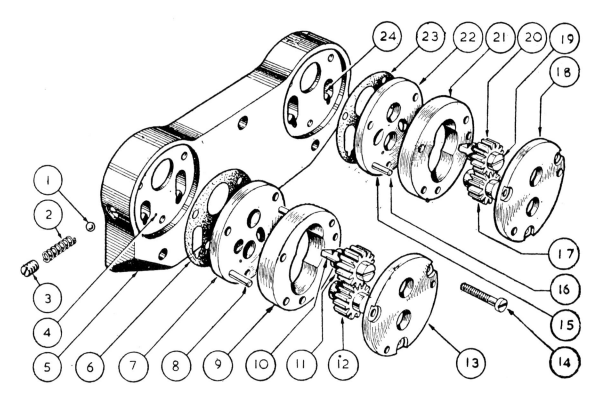

ABOVE *The two oil pumps of the twin-cylinder engine with their mounting plate as used by that engine for many years*

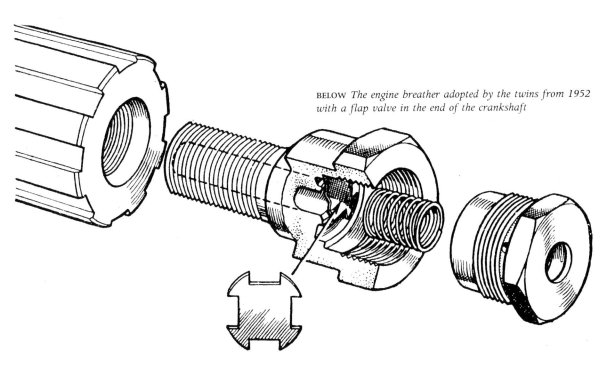

BELOW *The engine breather adopted by the twins from 1952 with a flap valve in the end of the crankshaft*

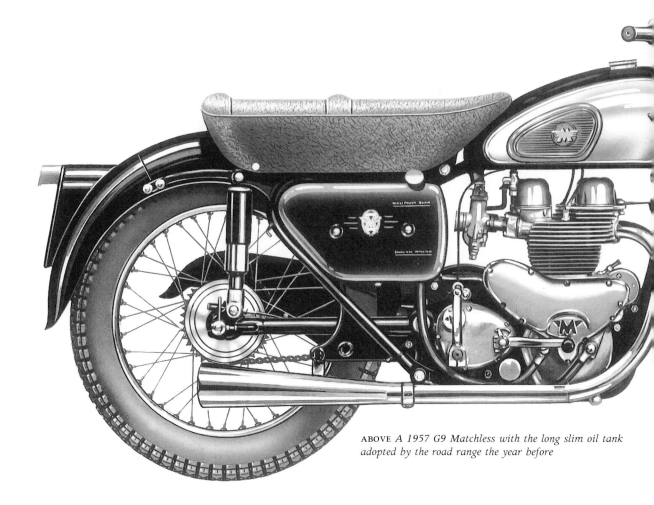

ABOVE *A 1957 G9 Matchless with the long slim oil tank adopted by the road range the year before*

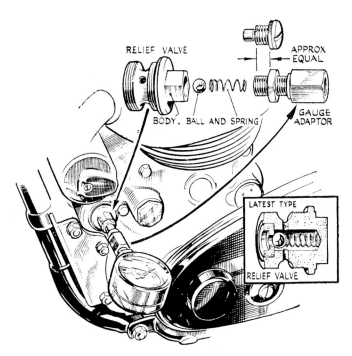

LEFT *Oil system details of the twin, including a pressure gauge used for testing only*

Breather system

This is an area that seems to give owners a headache if it has any problems. Perhaps the snag is that it consists largely of holes and as such cannot appear on a parts list.

The singles had a flap valve fitted into a boss behind the drive-side main bearing housing in the left crankcase and this arrangement served all models and years using the same parts. The light singles had a timed breather on the drive-side mainshaft with a rotor revolving within a stator. This last was amended for 1961 together with some other detail parts.

The twins began with a timed breather driven by the left end of the inlet camshaft. For 1952 this was changed to a flap valve fitted into the end of the drive side of the crankshaft and exhausting into the primary chaincase. Both steel and plastic board diaphragms were used over the years, with a sealed assembly being adopted for 1959. This came in two forms to suit

106

confined atmosphere. Whatever it is, you have to get it all out. It may take every solvent and detergent you have but the tank must be clean both inside and out.

Only then can it be checked over. Look for cracks and split seams which will need to be welded up. Oil tanks are prone to this due to the combination of heat and vibration. Thus the mounting system and the actual fastenings need to be inspected to ensure they are not straining the tank or themselves. Correct as necessary. Also inspect all the pipe or union threads and any washer seating faces that may need cleaning up. If this has to be done it is worth fitting the parts and checking that paraffin won't seep through the joint even if you have to clean it out again. Better than finding an oil leak later.

Check the fit of the tank cap and its washer. Examine the breather and froth tower or any other ancillary feature.

Oil-tank types

There were a good number of these for both singles and twins over the years but with some common use from 1952. The singles began with a tank with an angled filler cap and this went on both marques. It was altered in detail for 1947 and joined the next year by a similar part for the competition models.

The tank was redesigned for 1949 with a bayonet-type cap, more capacity and a near vertical orifice. There continued to be one each for the road and competition models with the latter changing again for 1950. The tank for the twins appeared for 1949 and was similar to that of the singles other than in the feed line filter fitting.

The twin tank was amended for 1951 when the touring singles tank also went on the sprung competition models. There were four revised tanks for 1952 with one each for the rigid, competition, sprung and CS singles. The sprung one was also fitted to the twins. All four changed for 1954 when the return line and tank filter were moved to the outer tank half to improve access for filter changes. The tank mounting for all except the competition models changed for 1955 so there were three more revised tanks with the sprung road singles and twins continuing to fit the same part.

With the end of rigid frames for 1956 the road models changed to a new style of long, thin oil tank for singles and twins. The latter also had a tank cover so the tank itself had two threaded inserts welded into its side for the attachment screws. The singles did without this so their tank side was plain, other than for the transfer that distinguished which marque the tank went on. There was also a new tank for the competition models, including the CS ones, similar to the earlier type but without the return line filter fitted into the top.

The road model tank changed for 1957 with the

machines with dynamo or alternator electrics and from 1962 only the latter was listed. Norton twin engines had a timed breather disc driven by the left end of the camshaft.

Any timed breather can cause trouble if it jams or breaks. If this happens, either the engine breathes all the time and loses oil rapidly or cannot breath at all so the pressure generated leads to oil leaks. The latter trouble will also occur if the breather pipe is blocked in any way.

On all engines good breathing is as important as good joints in cutting out oil leaks so it is vital that all the parts do their job correctly including all the holes within the engine that contribute to the system.

Oil tank

This container usually sits in the same place but comes in various shapes and sizes. Leaving aside the finish, which is covered later, the tank needs to be cleaned and inspected. On a running model the first part is, or should be, no problem, but an unknown tank can be full of horrors. Oil tanks seem able to harbour more dirt, sludge, spiders and unknown substances than even the underside of mudguards; maybe it's the

The 1951 AJS 16M with its old style oil tank and basic dry-sump system

addition of ribs on the tank side and an array of tanks were listed to cover the various sizes, types and makes with their transfers. The competition models kept to the 1956 tank but the CS changed to the long, thin road type. For 1958 this was set more into the machine, while the rest of the tanks continued as they were.

The tank form continued in use but was listed in many colours for 1959 while the CS and CSR tanks were of a larger capacity than the others and had a breather tower. The competition models changed to a new tank in the old style to suit their revised frame.

There was another range of tanks for 1960 in various colours but still with the ribs as before. The covers remained for the twins only. The competition model continued as it was but the CS singles had a new

tank fitted on the left side of the machine to give room for a GP carburettor and a massive air filter.

This arrangement continued with the standard machines all having tanks with a breather tower for 1962. Most were altered to a more rounded shape for 1963 although the CS singles and CSR twins kept the older style for that year and the next. For 1965 the CSR twins changed to the rounded shape and kept that from then on. The next year the G85CS appeared and had its central light-alloy tank fitted under the carburettor and between the rear engine plates.

The light singles avoided all this as their tank was part of the engine. The outer casting which bolted to the right crankcase to form it was common to all models and years.

A 1961 model 14 with dry-sump oil system but with the tank built into the engine under the timing-side cover

Rear-chain lubrication

There was no provision for this so it has to be done the hard way by removing it and treating it off the machine. Some owners prefer to regularly oil the chain on its inner run while on the machine and this is easier to do although still tedious.

Engine-oil grade

An area of myths and folklore, over which owners argue well into the night. In the beginning there were straight oils that were thick or thin. They had no additives and did not last very long. The grade of oil was classed by an SAE number, usually 20, 30, 40, or 50 and the rider changed to a thinner one for the winter and back again in the summer.

Then additives were put in the oil to prevent oxidation, inhibit rust, improve the load level and much more to give monogrades. These still needed to be changed to suit the season but lasted longer and are especially suited to all ball-and-roller engines and many motorcycle engines are that kind.

Finally, there came multigrades which combined the merits of thick oil for hot running with thin oil for easy starting, even in winter. These had an unfortunate time when first introduced but those days are long gone and modern quality multigrades are excellent for engines with plain bearings. Without them cold starting would be very difficult indeed.

AMC recommended SAE 50 in summer and SAE 30 in winter for many years and most owners prefer to keep to a monograde, especially for the singles. The twins with their plain bearings are better candidates for a multigrade, although the factory recommendation remained as for the singles. A good 20/50 multigrade is better than a poor monograde but the additives don't last so long in a high temperature, high specific output engine so the oil change periods must not be extended. The light singles were the same as the heavy ones.

Many readers may disagree with the above and, as always, the choice is theirs but it does seem that a good monograde is to be preferred in these engines.

Transmission-oil grades

Monogrades are more usual in these areas which are not subject to the same temperature range as the engine. The primary chaincase takes engine oil in all cases.

The gearbox began with grease but then moved on to an SAE 50 oil for many years. With more power and heavier loads on the gears this is best changed to an EP90 gear oil. This has a similar viscosity to the engine oil grade but is better able to cope with the stresses involved. It is to be recommended for all models.

Do not forget that the light singles *must* have three pints of oil in the gearbox!

First of the 1956 G3LC models with works rider Bob
Manns seated on it and about to test it

7 Electrics

This is an area which gives many owners considerable difficulties and even some very skilled engine fitters will admit that it is a big mystery to them. The problem stems in part from the fact that you never see the substance, only its effects. Also, like an oil leak, it can spread all over the place so easily without any obvious evidence as to where it came from.

If you intend to carry out a restoration you have to accept that you must wrestle with the subject or it could defeat you. Fortunately, real electrical faults are rare, despite what you may think, as nearly all troubles are caused by mechanical failures in some way or other. Most can be cured by correct assembly and settings. Remember the need to comply with current, local legislation.

Helpful points to remember are as follows. The system has two sides, one dealing with charging and the other with use. Although they may connect in operation and control they can be thought of as two distinct areas and dealt with accordingly. The most common fault is a poor earth, which is simply a poor connection for the return of the current rather than its supply. Also very common is a poor connection in the supply leads. Finally, buy the tools for the job, which means lighter spanners or wrenches, smaller screwdrivers, pliers, cutters, electrician's soldering iron and a small meter. The last does not have to be anything special as continuity checks will be its main job, but it will help a great deal. An old ammeter, preferably with centre zero, and reading 15 amps or so, is also worth having to check current flow in and out of the battery. Even if the machine has one it is not always convenient to use, so a meter with leads can be better.

AMC electrical systems

After the war AMC continued in their traditional way to fit separate magneto and dynamo units rather than the mag-dyno favoured by other makers. This continued on the twins when they were introduced so that up to 1957 all models used this system.

For 1958 the road singles changed to an alternator and coil ignition which they kept to from then on. The competition singles continued with their magnetos and on the trials model the dynamo was available up to 1963. From 1960 the 497 cc CS models had the option of an alternator if they were fitted with lights but stayed with the magneto for ignition.

The twins continued with their magnetos on all models to 1958 and for all except the standard build for 1959–61. These last ones changed to coil ignition with a distributor mounted in place of the magneto. This arrangement continued for the 646 cc models from 1962 onwards with coil ignition for the standard twins and magneto for the CSR versions. The 745 cc Norton engines differed and had a magneto in either build form. During 1967 most twins changed to a coil and capacitor system and this continued for the final years. The standard 498 and 646 cc twins first fitted an alternator for 1959 when the other versions kept to their dynamo. This continued until 1962 when all models had the alternator.

The light singles had a Wipac alternator and coil ignition for all road models and the CS from 1961 on. The earlier CS machines had an energy transfer system.

The electrical system began as 6-volt with negative earth but changed to positive earth for 1952. The twins went to a 12-volt system for 1964 onwards but stayed with the positive earth while the singles kept to 6-volts. With the 12-volts came a zener diode to give better control than the switching used by the earlier system.

Magneto types

The singles fitted a basic chain-driven N1 magneto to both marques and all models. It was platform mounted and rotated anti-clockwise, as viewed from the driven end. From 1950 the competition versions fitted the NR1 and from 1957 the NC1, which remained in use for them from then on.

The road singles changed to a rotating magnet SR1 magneto with auto-advance and this alteration went on to the 497 cc models for 1954 and the 348 cc ones the next year. Both stayed in use to 1957.

The twins began with a gear-driven K2F magneto, flange mounted and also rotated anti-clockwise. This

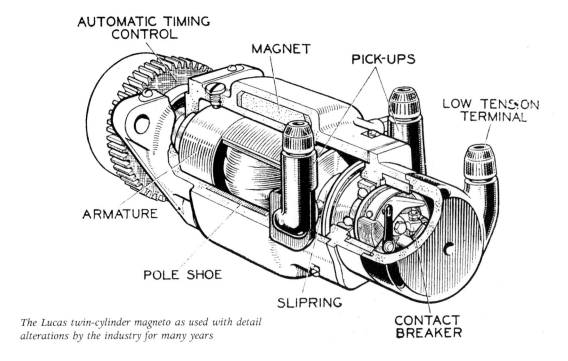

AUTOMATIC TIMING CONTROL · MAGNET · PICK-UPS · LOW TENSION TERMINAL · ARMATURE · POLE SHOE · SLIPRING · CONTACT BREAKER

The Lucas twin-cylinder magneto as used with detail alterations by the industry for many years

went on all twins right the way through to 1966, other than the standard models, including the Norton engines. During 1967 these went over to a coil and capacitor system so they, too, changed to a distributor in place of the magneto.

Magneto service

This concerns itself with the points gap, which is 0.012 in., and the brushes. There are several of the latter, for in addition to the high-tension lead pick-ups in one or both sides of the body there is a brush in the rear of the points plate on face cam magnetos and an earth brush. In many cases there is also one in the cap for the earthing lead and if the magneto fails to work this is one time when a connection to earth is not wanted so disconnect it. In use, it takes the low tension side to earth to kill the magneto and an intermittent fault in the line or the button can be a trial to deal with.

Lucas magnetos have safety gap screws and these *must* be removed before any real dismantling is done as otherwise the slip ring will be damaged. All brushes need to be examined for cracks and checked for free movement in their holders and their general good condition. If worn they should be replaced. Note that on occasion a brush or gap screw may be masked by a label, so care must always be exercised.

Tested as a de luxe model but with an alternator and distributor this 1961 G12 has to be a standard model fitted with the optional chrome tank panels

Magneto renovation

There is not a great deal more that can be done with a magneto other than to clean it and maybe replace the bearings. Dismantling is straightforward but mark parts first as often they could be reversed. Once apart, the details can be cleaned and inspected, especially for any cracks that could leak the high-tension current to earth.

It is a fairly skilled job to replace and set up magneto bearings and even more tricky to change a condenser or rewind an armature. Unless you are really competent in this work it should be sent to a specialist. This is especially true if the magneto has lost some of its magnetism and is therefore sparking poorly, if at all. Magnetizing equipment is complex and expensive so not really a practical proposition for any other than the professional.

Grease the bearings on assembly which should give no problems. Do make sure that all the little insulating washers and bushes are in the right place. More ignition systems fail to work after a rebuild for this reason than any other. Fit the leads, clamp the magneto in the vice, earth the plug or plugs to it and give it a spin (anti-clockwise, of course). Check that the earthing connection does its job.

Dynamo type and drive

Like the magnetos, the dynamos were driven in an anti-clockwise direction and by chain on the singles and gear on the twins. Thanks to the chain drive from the left end of the crankshaft the singles dynamo was not one commonly used by other makes and neither was its armature.

The early singles fitted an E3AR dynamo but changed to an E3N for 1951 on. In either case it was most awkward to remove and involved disturbing the primary chaincase to release the drive chain of which there were three lengths over the years. Up until 1951 it also meant removing either the clutch and inner case or the gearbox cover, but the smaller Burman gearbox fitted for 1952 improved matters slightly.

This arose because AMC chose to clamp the dynamo in the engine plates behind the crankcase. Access was poor on the AJS and non-existent on the early Matchless where the magneto sat directly above the dynamo. It only improved to the AJS level when the

AJS always had the magneto ahead of the engine on their post-war singles as shown by this 1945 model 18

magneto moved and could not compare with the ease of removing a mag-dyno unit.

The twins were better as the dynamo was a gear-driven E3L clamped to the front of the crankcase. It was also held by a draw stud to the timing chest and the nut for this on early engines was inside the cover, which thus had to be removed to release the dynamo. From AJS 7000 and Matchless 5966 engines it was extended through the cover so the dynamo became easy to remove. The drive gear was common to all engines and small enough to pass through the hole in the timing chest.

Dynamo testing

This can begin on the machine by disconnecting the leads to the dynamo. Then join the two terminals, D and F, and connect a voltmeter from the join to the dynamo body. Run the machine so the dynamo speed is up to 1000 rpm and look for the voltage reading to rise smoothly and quickly to 10 volts. Don't run the dynamo faster in an attempt to push the volts value up. If there is no reading at all look to the brush gear, if

it is about 0.5 volts the field winding is suspect and if between 1.5 and 2 volts then the armature winding is the likely culprit.

For any further work the dynamo will need to be dismantled.

Dynamo service

Mark parts before taking them apart and proceed with some delicacy as some items are rather brittle. Clean all the connections to reduce contact resistance and check that all wires are in good order and not frayed in any way. Examine the brushes and replace if worn down to about $\frac{5}{16}$ in. Make sure the brushes, whether old or renewed, can move freely in their boxes and that the brush springs are strong enough to hold them in contact with the commutator. Ensure that the brush connections are not transposed during assembly.

The commutator will need cleaning and if burnt may need machining to restore it to true round. Should this be needed remove the minimum of material and be prepared to undercut the segments. Also examine the wire connections to the segments for any signs of overheating which may indicate problems in the armature. Clean out all the carbon dust as it can short out the insulated wires.

Armature rewinds and field coil replacement are best left to specialists. The first requires special equipment but the second can be attempted with fewer facilities. There are two problems to overcome. First, is the single fixing screw which must be tight and, second, is ensuring the new coil is really home in the body. Service departments used a special driver for the first problem and an expander for the second but both can be overcome in the home workshop.

Grease the ball races but not too much or it will be all over the commutator. Reassemble with care to ensure everything goes back where it came from.

The finished result can be tested off the engine by connecting it to a battery so that it becomes an electric motor. This is done by joining the F and D terminals and connecting the join and the dynamo body to a 6-volt battery. The body connection is to the normally earthed terminal and if all is well the armature will revolve. This is not as good a test as that with a voltmeter but is useful if the engine is by now apart and not to be available for some while.

Regulator unit

This is also known as the compensated voltage control unit or cvc and may be referred to as the automatic voltage control or avc. This is not to be confused with the later cvc used for cars where the initials stand for current voltage control and the unit has three coils in its assembly under the cover.

The motorcycle cvc is simpler with just one control coil plus the cut-out under the lid. It has fewer connections than most cars with just four terminals in a row and these are usually connected to wires which plug in and are held by a strip secured by two screws. The wires are positioned by this strip and the screws are of different sizes to prevent a reversal of the connections.

All the twins fitted the MCR2 regulator from their start in 1949 but the singles had to wait until 1951 before changing from the older MCR1. This differed from the MCR2 as in that, the control resistor became a carbon disc fitted to the main frame behind the coils. It can be recognized by a swelling in the back of the cover, put there to clear it. On these two models the terminals were labelled FADE but for 1958 on the twins and 1959 on the singles the unit was changed to a RB108 which had its connectors in the order FAED.

The cvc is a delicate electro-mechanical assembly and must be treated as such. It can be set up and adjusted by the owner but this must be done precisely or the system will not work as it should. Really no different to valve clearances or ignition timing.

Regulator function

Two jobs are done inside the cvc unit. The regulator side switches a resistor into series with the field coil to reduce the field current and thus the generated output. It is in a state of vibration while doing this. The cut-out is simply a switch which disconnects the battery from the dynamo when needed to prevent it trying to motor the latter which would discharge the battery.

The confusion with the unit usually arises because the theoretical circuit diagram, practical wiring

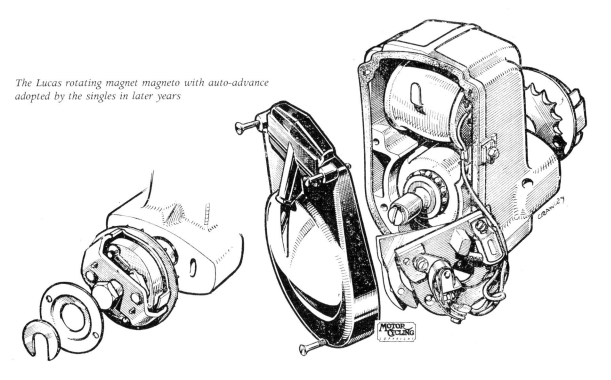

The Lucas rotating magnet magneto with auto-advance adopted by the singles in later years

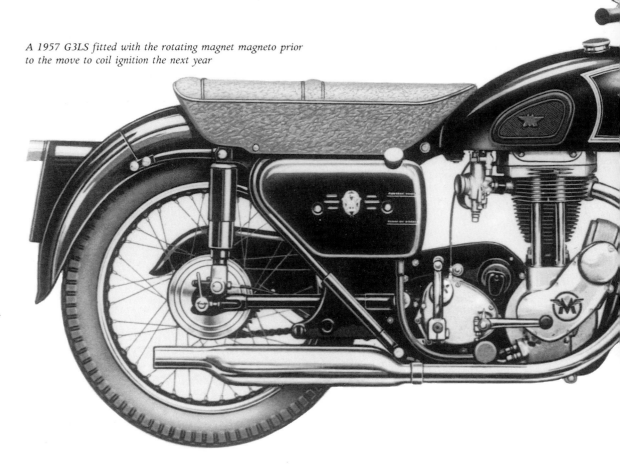

A 1957 G3LS fitted with the rotating magnet magneto prior to the move to coil ignition the next year

diagram and the unit all look completely different. Further confusion arises in that the internal frame is used as part of the electric circuit but is not an earth. In truth, it connects via the cut-out points to the battery supply line so it is insulated from the mounting frame.

Regulator service

If you decide to work on the cvc, trace out the electrical circuit first so you know where each part fits into the scheme of things. It will then be much easier to check each item for continuity or open circuit using your meter. In most cases the only problem will be the mechanical aspects of the contacts, their cleanliness and their adjustment. With those dealt with, the circuits are most likely to function as they should.

Looking at the coils, the one on the left is the regulator, which has a few turns of heavy gauge wire about its middle. The first adjustments are by moving the armature, which is the bent steel part pulled by the coil magnetism and carrying one of the contacts. The next adjustment is made by bending the fixed contact on the MCR units and finally, with an adjuster screw at the rear.

Air gaps are required between the vertical leg of the armature that carries the contact and the frame, also between the horizontal leg and the bobbin core on the MCR. The first should be 0.015 in. on the MCR1 and 0.020 in. on the MCR2. The second figure is 0.020 in. for both but with a tolerance of plus 0.005 in. on the MCR1 and minus 0.008 in. on the MCR2. On the MCR2, with the armature held against the bobbin core, the points gap should be between 0.006 and 0.017 in.

The RB108 has a different method of adjustment. The armature screws are undone, a feeler gauge of 0.021 in. is put between the armature and the bobbin and the screws are done up. The contacts are then adjusted so they just touch with the feeler gauge still in place.

The remaining adjustments are made with the cvc wired to the machine. Put card between the cut-out points and disconnect lead from A terminal. Insert the voltmeter between D and E and run the dynamo at about 3000 rpm. At 20°C the reading should be 8.0 to 8.4 volts and can be adjusted with the screw at the rear. If the temperature rises, deduct 0.2 volts for every 10°C and if it falls add it. Then run the dynamo at about 4500 rpm when the reading should not

exceed 8.9 volts. Do all this quickly or errors will occur, so if in doubt do it in steps.

Cut-out setting

For the MCR2 the armature-to-frame air gap should be 0.014 in. and to the bobbin core 0.011 to 0.015 in. With these two gaps held correct by gauges, press the armature down on them and check that the gap between armature and stop plate arm is 0.030 to 0.034 in. Bend the arm to adjust. Then place a 0.025 in. gauge between armature shim and core face and check that the contact gap is between 0.002 to 0.006 in. Bend the fixed contact bracket to adjust.

The RB108 is set by pressing the armature down to the core face and checking the gap between its stop arm and its tongue which should be 0.025 to 0.040 in. Bend the stop arm to adjust. Then adjust the fixed contact blade to give a blade deflection of 0.010 to 0.020 in. when the armature is pressed firmly down on the core face.

Cut-out checking

This is done on the machine, and a full test covers both cut-in and -out. For the first, connect an ammeter in the lead from dynamo D to cvc D and a voltmeter between there and E. Gradually bring the engine speed up and watch for the voltmeter pointer to flick back as the points close. This should occur at 6.3 to 6.7 volts and is adjusted by the screw, which increases the setting when turned clockwise. The ammeter should

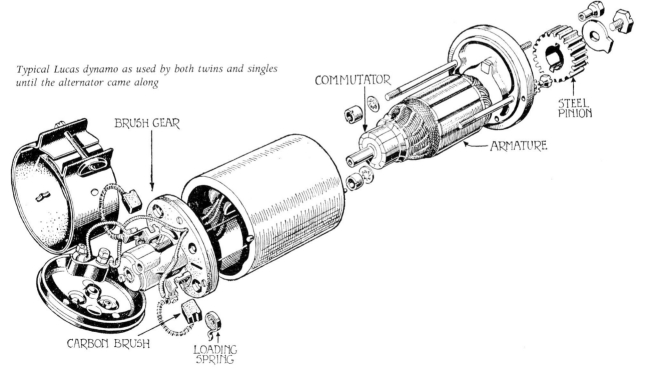

Typical Lucas dynamo as used by both twins and singles until the alternator came along

BRUSH GEAR

COMMUTATOR

STEEL PINION

ARMATURE

CARBON BRUSH

LOADING SPRING

show a charge when the points close. When the engine stops the ammeter discharge reading is taken and should be between 3 and 5 amps when the contacts open.

The cut-out check is done by detaching lead A from the cvc and connecting a voltmeter between terminals A and E. Run the dynamo up to 3000 rpm and then let its speed die slowly away. The voltage should be between 4.8 and 5.5 volts when the contacts open and the reading drops to zero.

Regulator oddments

The resistance used in the cvc, which is placed in the field circuit, can be measured if you have a good meter. The value for a carbon one is 36–45 ohms while the wire wound type of the MCR1 is 27–33 ohms.

If your machine has the short E3 dynamo fitted in error it ought to have a MCR1 cvc. If this is not available the MCR2 listed under part number 37144A should be used.

You can see the machine without a battery as long as the cvc is working correctly. This may not be fully legal in some way but can be useful in an emergency. However, if the battery is in circuit it must be topped up or the control is fooled into providing excess current which can ruin battery, dynamo and cvc.

The contact points do get dirty and may need cleaning. If they do they will definitely need resetting.

Should the dynamo polarity have reversed itself, which does happen, just hold the cut-out points together for a second or two and then pull them apart.

A 1947 G3L with inaccessible dynamo tucked under the magneto with chain drive within the chaincase

Do make sure that dynamo D is connected to cvc D and F to F. Although the dynamo leads are held by a kidney-shaped plate and the cvc one is non-reversible, they could have been switched at some time. Detach and check by meter as they often run out of sight on the machine.

Modern regulators

By using modern electronic components the problems of the electro-mechanical cvc can be removed with solid state devices. This is electronic engineering, quite outside most people's knowledge, but specialist suppliers make it easy for the rest of us.

A unit is available to replace the cvc and is one waterproof box which does the same job and enables the machine to convert to 12 volts. Battery and bulbs also need changing, but not the horn, and the change boosts output so better lights can be fitted. The new assembly is small enough to tuck out of sight so the alteration is not at all obvious for owners who wish to keep up appearances.

While this change departs from total originality, it is to be recommended for any machine used on a regular basis in modern traffic where good lights are essential. The move to 12 volts not only greatly improves the electrical efficiency of the system but also allows halogen lights to be used to give a further bonus.

Alternator

AMC adopted the alternator on the singles for 1958 and some of the twins for 1959 and with it came the advantages of no touching parts to wear and other delights. Unfortunately, these included control problems and boiled batteries so all was not quite as good as it might have been. In time, the zener diode came along and with it arrived better control and 12-volt systems, but not until 1964.

The 1958 and 1959 machines were fitted with a Lucas RM15 unit and this was changed to a RM19 for 1964. The light singles used Wipac alternators with a standard one for the road models and energy transfer for the CS for 1959–60.

Alternator checking

There is not a great deal that can be done other than cleaning and inspection. Check that the rotor has been running clear of the coil poles and look at the wiring for any damage. Use a meter to check continuity and insulation, establishing which coils are connected together and how the wires attach to them. Compare this with your wiring diagram and keep notes on this aspect, which may help a good deal when sorting out the connections to the rectifier.

Make sure the rotor is a good fit on the crankshaft. If it is not, it is possible to machine it to locate on a made-up spacer against the engine sprocket and with care and ingenuity to achieve a better design than the original. This will also allow a damaged crankshaft

end to be overcome by using other means to hold the rotor true.

It is possible for the rotor centre to become loose within the assembly and this can give rise to a nasty knocking noise in the engine. A cure is to machine away the alloy side enough to allow the core to come out and then to refit it using a Loctite gap filler.

Rectifier

Early alternators had their output turned into direct current by massive selenium-plate rectifiers. The original boxes soon became a smaller set of four plates on a single central bolt and, in time, this assembly was replaced by a similar silicon-diode rectifier.

All the four-plate types give full wave rectification and the centre stud is one of the direct current connections and must be treated as such. It connects to the earthed side of the battery. The three-plate connections have the other direct current line in the middle flanked by the two alternating current ones. These last two may connect either way round, as reversal at that point will not affect the rectifier operation at all.

The rectifier can be cleaned and its electrical function checked for the correct working of each diode. These must pass current one way but not the other and a meter or battery and bulb will act as a tester. Do not move the central clamping nut or the device will fail. The nut tension controls the efficiency of the unit and must be left alone. Care is therefore needed when fixing the device to the machine.

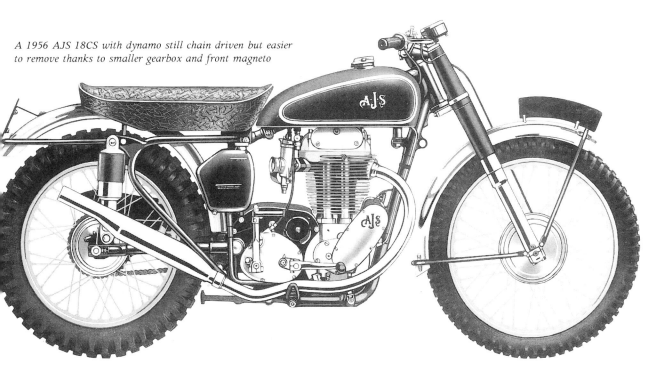

A 1956 AJS 18CS with dynamo still chain driven but easier to remove thanks to smaller gearbox and front magneto

Coil ignition and an alternator were used on this 1962 model 16

Alternator control

On the face of it, the stator coils connect to the rectifier which connects to the battery to complete the circuit. Unfortunately, there are complications. First, the output needs to be controlled to suit the load, and secondly, it would be nice to be able to start even with a flat battery. To cope with these problems introduces complications in the switches and wiring and the result can be confusion.

The control is done for 6-volt systems by stator coil switching. The basic control is that two coils are permanently connected and with the lights off the remaining four are short-circuited to reduce the output of the two in use. With the pilot light on, the four are open circuit so they don't affect the two and with the headlight on all six are connected. This means that the light switch has to be joined electrically to the charging circuit.

The light singles used a different system with two sets of three coils in the alternator. When running with no lights three coils were connected and the current was sent down a resistance wire to balance the load. With the pilot light on, the resistance wire was switched out of circuit, and with the headlamp on all six coils were connected.

For the other models problem two was overcome by switching four coils to supply the ignition circuit

and on the electric side it is just a question of joining wires, so anything is possible.

To add to the problem, Lucas also changed the wire colours on the early alternators as the originals tended to become indistinguishable. First they were light, mid and dark green. Then light green, green and yellow and dark green. Finally, green and white, green and yellow and green and black. If you don't have an original stator, rectifier and harness you could have variations.

Further complications arise in that where the machine has magneto ignition the above applies with two coils always in circuit. For models with coil ignition it was common to have four in use and the mid and dark green connections reverse. The lead from rectifier to light switch, usually light green, may be simply disconnected and taped up as this had a further training effect on the output. The connections were often reversed for winter riding, especially if a sidecar was fitted, and changed back for summer to avoid a boiled battery.

To sort out what you have and how to connect it you need to work out the alternator leads and circuit, the rectifier leads and the switch circuits. Then use the wiring diagram for the model and trace out what happens in each switch position. Not easy, I know, as the diagrams don't normally give the switch circuits, and without those it is hard. Hence the need to check the switch itself with a meter and write it all down.

BELOW *Typical Lucas cvc MCR2 which controlled many dynamos for many makes*

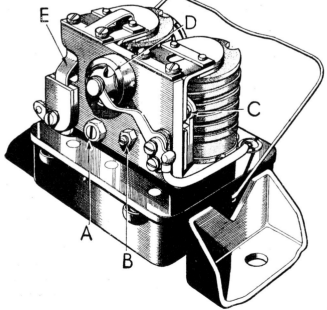

direct to leave two to assist the battery on an emergency basis on the singles and twins. On the light singles, emergency starting was achieved by using all six coils for ignition. On the twins, where a 12-volt system was in use, a zener diode was employed for control. The same part was fitted from 1964 onwards with a heat sink to dissipate the excess energy of the alternator.

If the connections are not as they should be or the switch contacts are dirty then all manner of charging problems will arise. The situation is further confused by variations that were available over the years and which may have been incorporated in a system. The mechanical components are generally interchangeable

Alternator voltage conversion

This is a popular way of getting more out of the system and can easily be carried out. It simplifies the wiring as all six alternator coils are permanently connected to the rectifier, which has the zener diode fitted between its supply terminal and earth. The actual details vary according to the machine circuit but can be sorted out using the wiring diagrams and the information already established for the switches.

When first introduced, the then available zeners could not cope with controlling the full output when there was no headlight load, so the switched connection was still needed. This had two coils which were on permanently for machines fitted with a magneto and four where coil ignition was used. Modern zeners can cope.

Battery, ignition coils, bulbs, possibly the rectifier and maybe the ignition condenser will need changing. The horn is not essential but any ancillaries need to be remembered.

Coil ignition

This was first used in 1958 on the road singles and light singles, and went on the standard twins in 1959.

Battery carrier mounting used for the cvc for a while on the rigid models

With this system the twins had a distributor for their coil ignition but this was not used on the 745 cc twins until 1967 when it had the backing of a capacitor system, fired by the points, which acted as an emergency circuit or the main one if no battery was fitted.

The road light singles kept to a simple coil ignition system with the points in the timing cover and their cam driven by the camshaft. The early CS models differed and used an energy transfer system but retained the points to fire it. They changed to coil ignition with a battery for 1961.

Distributor and points

The standard twins had this from 1959–66 and all twins were thus equipped from 1967 onwards. Essentially, you clean and inspect. Replace the points, oil the advance mechanism and make sure there are no cracks in the cap or the rotor arm. See if the bearings are in good order and that the spindle turns freely. Attend to anything in trouble and rebuild.

Do make sure the points wire connection is the correct side of its insulation washers and check it with the meter.

Inspect the small pivot points in the advance mechanism and repair or replace as necessary. Replace the advance springs if these are tired and check you have the correct type of advance unit installed.

No dynamo or battery needed here by Gordon Jackson while riding in the 1954 Hurst Cup Trial

Energy transfer and AC ignition

In these designs some of the alternator windings are connected directly to a special ignition coil. This allows the machine to run without battery on the lines of one fitted with a magneto, but the ignition timing can be critical. Points cam and advance unit are specially designed for the job and must be used for it to operate effectively. The distributor range is limited and essential to the workings. Otherwise, it is checked over as the others.

Ignition timing

This is often a source of great concern to owners and in one sense this is important. On the other hand, the actual figure used may be less so. What is often forgotten is that the engine may be 20 or more years old, worn in various ways and running on a different blend of fuel to that available to it when new.

So, while the original figure makes a good starting-point it is not sacrosanct. The old-fashioned technique of advancing the setting until the engine pinks on a rising road and then backing it off a little still works even if it is awkward to carry out on some models.

Check the timing you decide to use on full advance and on both cylinders on a twin. The retard figure is much less important so it may be ignored, although the particular will check it to be sure. It is not uncommon for a variation to arise between twin cylinders and this should be removed if possible as the engine will run much better. Beware of slack in the drive when checking and for slack in distributor bearings which can give a false reading. Recheck if in any doubt.

Electronic ignition

A worthwhile modification for late-type machines and available in various forms to replace magneto or coil ignition. It is also possible to adapt them to existing parts to retain the original drive system.

The installation instructions supplied with the kit should be followed carefully, especially regarding the timing. Electronic advance is normal, so the mechanical device must be discarded or locked up and the timing will have to be checked with a strobe. Therefore, a timing mark will be needed and this must be checked with a timing disc before the ignition is set up.

In addition to the electronic ignition kits, a further option is open in the form of capacitor ignition using the alternator as a power source, a 12-volt zener diode control, a storage capacitor and the original points and advance mechanism. Effectively, a variation of the earlier energy transfer system but much better in use and, in essence, the same as the one installed from 1967 onwards.

Sparking plug, cap and lead

The plug should be replaced by a modern equivalent, although many owners do like to keep the original if it is to hand. Some refit it for a concours but for normal use a new plug should be fitted. Check that the plug top is tight as it can cause a misfire if slack. Grades are listed in Appendix 7.

The cap should be the type that contains a suppressor and the leads must be in good condition. Make sure the ends are clean and make a good connection or an odd misfire may appear.

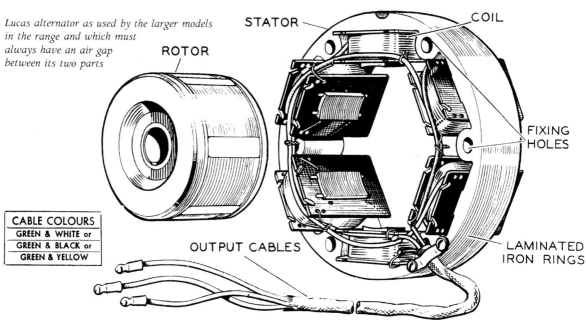

Lucas alternator as used by the larger models in the range and which must always have an air gap between its two parts

ROTOR

STATOR

COIL

FIXING HOLES

LAMINATED IRON RINGS

OUTPUT CABLES

CABLE COLOURS
GREEN & WHITE or
GREEN & BLACK or
GREEN & YELLOW

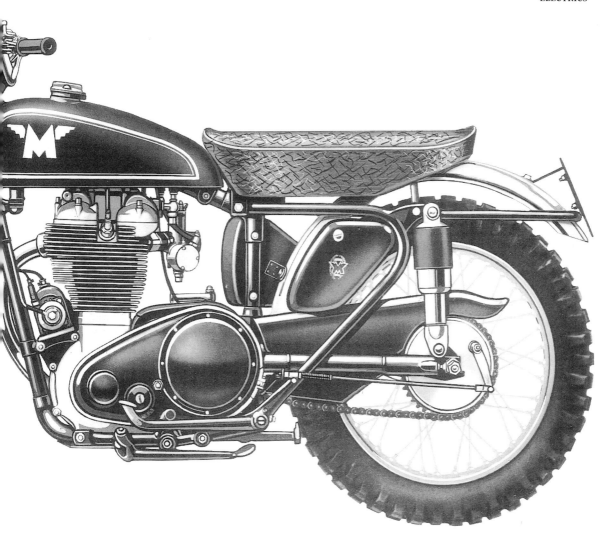

A 1956 G80CS with front mounted magneto which was chain driven from the exhaust camshaft

Lighting

Renovation of the lights is mainly by replacement as most of the parts are fragile and are either complete and working or in pieces. The bulb containers may need repair work carried out and finishing, which should be done in the same way as any other items.

For any machine being used on the road the current legal requirements need to be considered as some of the earlier fittings do not comply with them. In particular, rear lamps have increased in size which was essential for modern traffic conditions.

AMC used a variety of lighting systems over the years but, essentially, most changes were brought about by alterations to the electrical system or by styling.

Headlamp and switch types

The post-war AMC models were first built in a traditional manner with a separate headlamp shell which had a small panel set in it. This carried the ammeter with the light switch behind it. For 1948 the headlamp glass was changed to a domed shape and the next year a new shell, exclusive to AMC, was adopted and also went on the new twins. From 1950 a quickly detachable shell with plug and socket for the wiring was listed for the competition models. This concept was updated with better light units as they came along but otherwise stayed in use.

The next change came for 1952 when the underslung pilot lamp made its unwelcome appearance. It went two years later when AMC added two pilot lamps, one on each side of the headlamp, in its place. For 1955 a deeper headlamp shell, which also carried the speedometer, was fitted while the twin pilots remained. With this shell, the ammeter was located to the right and the light switch to the left.

The twin pilot lamps went for 1958 and for that year

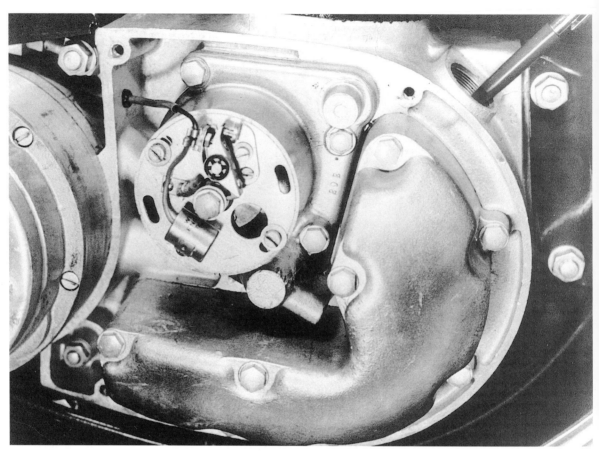

Points of the 250 engine surrounded by the built-in oil tank

the road singles with coil ignition had an ignition key
and switch added into the light switch. Otherwise, the
shell, ammeter and speedometer stayed as they were
with the existing parts, minus the twin pilots,
continuing on the twins. The exception to this was the
CS twin, which copied the competition models, when
these were fitted with lights, in having a qd lamp and
fittings in the 1950 style. The same arrangement was
also used by the CSR twins.

The light singles made their debut in 1958 and used
the same layout with a 6 in. Wipac lamp. Thus the
shell carried speedometer, ammeter and separate
lights and ignition switches. There was no change for
1959, other than the addition of the ignition switch
with the light switch for the standard twins, but for
1960 the headlamp shell of the touring singles and
twins was made more compact. It continued to carry
an ammeter and speedometer but also housed separate
switches for the lights and the ignition. The sports
twins continued with a single lighting switch in the
1958 shell and the competition ones with their qd
design.

For 1962 the models with coil ignition changed to a
switch with key in place of an unsecured knob and

during the year a cowl with fascia was offered as an option for the CSR twins. This carried the ammeter in the centre with the light switch behind it, rev-counter to the left and speedometer to the right but was no longer listed the next year.

The arrangements continued as they were for the AMC singles and twins but not the machines fitted with the Norton twin engine. For these there was a simple shell only carrying an ammeter while the light switch went on the fork top between the speedometer and rev-counter.

Stop and tail light

The singles only had a tail light at first and fitted the round Lucas MT211 to all models up to 1948 and the competition ones to 1950. For 1949, the road machines, including the new twins, changed to a rectangular lamp with a metal body with two apertures to the rear.

This was changed for a rectangular red plastic type 525 with stop and tail facility for 1953 on all road models and again for 1955 to the 564 with built-in rear

reflector. This then remained in use for all road singles and standard twins. The CS and CSR twins fitted the oval 529 red plastic lamp for 1959–62, after which they used the 564 alone for 1963. For 1964 it was joined for export models by the 679 which was used by itself for export 745 cc twins of 1964 and with the 564 for the home market from 1965 to the end.

On the competition singles the round 480 type was specified for 1951 and the oval red plastic 529 for 1954. In 1957 this had the stop facility added and this light was used up to 1962 with the 564 specified for 1963. For 1964 the CS singles had the 564 for home and 679 for export but from 1966 only the 679 was listed.

The light singles had a Wipac rear light with the option of the stop facility. This arrangement applied to all the road models with a change of lamp for 1962. In typical Wipac fashion the stop light came from two bulbs added to the lamp in addition to the normal tail bulb.

All bulbs should be as per the list.

The 1958 16MCS which continued with the magneto and dynamo and the option of full lighting

ABOVE *Later Matchless single with alternator and points was this 1962 G3*

BELOW *Central sparking plug and cap as used on the 1966 G85CS*

Horn

For most riders trouble with the horn comes in two forms. First, it does not work, which turns out to be a fault in the horn button or wiring, and second, is locating it on a basket job.

The first problem should be bypassed by checking with direct wiring between horn and battery. The second is dealt with below. If current is reaching the horn and nothing is happening then it may need adjustment. This may be by a screw in the back or a nut under a cover or there may be no adjustment at all. Where provided it should be moved not more than one or two notches at a time. On a scale of 24 notches equals one full turn of the screw. Six notches from just not sounding should be about right but the current flow should also be monitored and anything over 5 amps indicates a need for specialist attention.

Don't move the centre screw as this controls the basic points setting and needs special equipment to set. Given this and care, the horn may be stripped and the case renovated in the same way as any other part.

All models fitted the Lucas HF1234 up to 1955 and this remained in use on the competition models to 1961 for the 348 cc version and 1959 for the 497 cc one. The road models fitted the HF1441 for 1956–61 and this also served the 497 cc CS machines for 1960–1 when they were equipped with road electrics.

The light singles used the HF1849 up to 1961 but for 1962 all models changed to the 8H. This stayed in use on the singles, light singles and CS singles to 1966 while the twins from 1964 onwards and CS singles from 1967 onwards changed to the 6H.

Horn position

At first the two marques differed, with the AJS mounting the horn behind the cylinder and Matchless mounting it in front, using suitable brackets. By 1947 the AJS horn had moved to the left saddle lug and this was also used by the competition models unless a bulb horn was fitted.

With the introduction of the spring frame the AJS horn moved back behind the cylinder while the twins both hung their horn under the front of the petrol tank. For 1952 the horn on the Matchless road singles adopted the same position as on the AJS, thanks to the move of its magneto.

For 1954 the twin's horn was rubber-mounted from a frame downtube lug and for 1956 all road models had the horn moved under the dualseat and within the new enclosing side panels. For most of them that was where it was to stay. The early CSR twins had the horn back under the front of the tank but the light singles tucked it away under the seat as on the rest of the range. The CSR twins followed suit for 1960.

The light single CSR had the horn bolted to the top left front engine mounting for 1965 and the 745 cc CSR

Early competition Matchless in the 1946–7 period when they differed little from the road models

models copied this for the same year. This position was adopted by all road models for 1966, possibly due to some very adverse criticism of the earlier horn. This had been described as inaudible above 30 mph in traffic!

Battery

The problem on some models is appearance because while the battery lived outside enclosing panels, its looks were an important aspect of the left side of the machine. It is possible to obtain facsimiles of the early black-bodied 6-volt battery which is one solution. Another is to adapt an old battery by cutting out the interior and fitting a modern one inside it.

For the rest, keep it clean, check the specific gravity and smear protective jelly on the terminals to keep corrosion at bay. Keep the battery working so if it has been removed from the machine run it down with a 3-watt bulb and then recharge it. This will prevent it

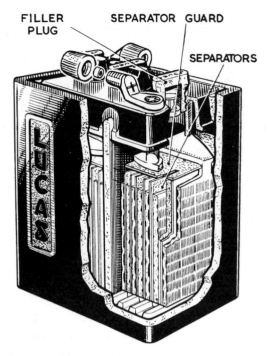

FILLER PLUG · SEPARATOR GUARD · SEPARATORS

ABOVE *Typical battery of the 1950s as used by AMC and many others*

BELOW *A 1966 G15CSR with its swept-back pipes*

from collapsing when asked to do some real work.

Up to 1963 all models had a 6-volt system, but from 1964 the twins changed to 12 volts which was done by fitting twin 6-volt batteries.

Ammeter

There is not much one can do to repair one of these, so either you have one working or it just acts as a dummy to keep the original appearance. In this case, one terminal can be used as a junction point but if the insulation of the case is in any doubt it is best to keep the wiring away from it altogether. The Lucas CZ27 was fitted up to 1948, the CZU for 1949–63 and the 2AR from 1964 onwards.

Wiring

The prime sources of electrical troubles, with poor connections, poor earths and intermittent leaks to earth being the major problems. Switches can also cause many headaches if the contacts are not clean and making good connections.

If you intend to use the existing harness it must be checked over carefully for any signs of damage or chafing. These must be repaired. All wires must be checked for continuity and a wiring diagram is most useful for this. Most of these given in manuals are really circuits and very hard to use in practice so it is well worth drawing your own. While doing this you can lay it out as on the machine and add the switch internal connections so it becomes easy to see where the current is supposed to flow.

You will find that one section deals with charging the battery and connects generator and control. The other deals with the consumption side and all flows from one point. The item using the current may be directly connected, as is the horn, via the ignition switch to the coil or via the light switch. Total isolation of the battery from the system did not come until later. The horn current is not taken through the ammeter so the lead to this comes before the instrument, and the same applies to some stop lamps.

If you have to rewire, first sort out the wiring diagram and then decide on the wire type and gauge you will use. Early models had black rubber-covered wire, possibly with a coloured or numbered sleeve at the end. This form of insulation perishes so it is no longer used and wires were colour-coded from 1952 onwards to ensure correct connections. The gauge depends on the current carried and it is as well to err on the fat side to keep voltage drop to a minimum.

A new harness is best built up on the machine, as this will ensure it fits well. Tape it into place while doing this and then remove as one unit and bind the wires into one bundle to keep the weather at bay. Either tape or heat-shrink tubing can be used for this as long as the finished harness will accept the

The Matchless G3LCS for 1958, when it took real strength to scramble machines of this type

necessary movement in the headstock area. Elsewhere it must be held firmly so it cannot fray away and is not trapped or pinched at any point.

Joints and connections need careful attention. Joins in the wires are best made with modern connectors, each wire being crimped or soldered to its terminal. When doing this, avoid nicking the wire when stripping the insulation, although this is not easy, and don't use an excess of solder. In avionics, inspection count the strands to make sure none are missing, inspect each for a mark and expect to see each one just outlined by its solder shroud. Get half-way to that standard and you won't have any problems.

Crimp connectors normally call for special tools but a serviceable job can be made using pliers of one sort or another plus common sense. Make sure the wire is firmly held and not slightly loose. If the wires are soldered in place don't let the solder run back into the wire or its rigidity will cause it to fracture under vibration. On the same lines when dealing with older types of switches with terminal posts just roll the wire into a ball under the fixing screw. If you do use solder play safe by clamping the wire securely a short distance from the terminal. Electrical strapping will look neater than tape on the final assembly.

Switches

These must be checked for their correct operation using a meter. The older type can be taken apart for cleaning, but watch for rollers with springs behind them that can fly out and roll all over the floor. Recheck the operation after assembly. Draw the connections on your wiring diagram so you can see how the components connect up in each switch position.

In addition to the more complex lights and ignition switches also check out the dipswitch, horn button, stoplight switch and cut-out for correct operation in the same way. As you connect them into the circuit check each, in turn, to ensure correct operation without any errant connections.

Earthing

All the older machines rely on the cycle parts to do this job, which is why they often have problems. Having carefully restored the protective paintwork of frame, forks, mudguards and panels, it is rather a shame to damage this finish to complete the earth return.

The answer is to run an earth wire from each item back to the battery or to a suitable junction point. The wires must be of a suitable gauge to carry the current from all items to which they are connected and are best earthed, both to the frame and the engine, at one point. Don't forget that the ignition system must have a complete circuit for both high- and low-tension loops.

Fuse

These were not fitted to early machines but are a good insurance for all. At worst a single 35-amp fuse in the main battery line can save the day in the event of a short circuit, while for more sophistication a modern fuse box with several fuses and spares can be wired into the circuits. Separate protection for the lights and ignition makes sense but this can be extended to a fuse for each circuit.

ABOVE *Start of the 1951 Pioneer Run with a G9 alongside Jock West on a 1904 245 cc Matchless*

RIGHT *Fun and games on a 1948 AJS single at a Greenwich MCC gymkhana*

8 The finish

This is the process that produces the final appearance, whether that is polished, plated or painted and the result always depends on preparation. The final top coat is the easy stage, it is the work carried out to bring the coat's surface to the required standard that takes time and effort.

The production finishes used by AMC were to either polish castings or leave them as cast, to plate certain major items and the details with either chromium or cadmium, and to paint the steel parts that made up the bulk of the cycle side and also certain cast-iron items using the stove-enamelling process.

Petrol tanks and wheel rims were both chrome-plated and painted on the earlier models while the plastic and rubber items were as moulded. Transfers were added as a final touch at certain points.

Cleaning the parts

Right at the start you will have removed the outer dirt from the machine, but now each part needs attention. The process used depends on the part, its job, its material and the required finish. For internal items the cleaning process is probably all that is needed but the visible items take more.

Cleaning can be done mechanically or chemically depending on the surface smoothness desired and the shape and area in question. Some of the chemicals are not readily available in the small quantities needed by the amateur and all must be treated with caution and only used when protective clothing is worn. Read the instructions carefully including the warning notes and what to do if you splash yourself.

Detergents

A household washing powder straight from the kitchen is most useful for cleaning castings. They are best done in a heated saucepan and before immersion all steel items must be removed. Don't leave the parts in for longer than is necessary as many of these products are acidic in nature and will attack the castings. After the cleaning process wash all the detergent away with hot water and then dry the casting.

Often this is all that is necessary to restore an engine or gearbox casting that is simply dirty with ingrained oil but do make sure all the detergent is removed.

Mechanical

At its simplest, this involves scraping the finish, usually paint, away with a knife or some similar tool. This is slow, tiring and tedious but will get you down to the bare metal in time. It can also damage the surface if you are not careful enough to prevent the knife digging in.

More usually it means some form of blasting process where small particles are blown at the item to be cleaned so they knock the finish off. The speed, severity, substrate damage and visual finish depend on the abrasive material used.

For removing rust, paint and corrosion, aluminous-oxide grit-blasting is suitable for motorcycle parts. Iron grit or shot are not and would badly damage castings and blow holes in sheet metal, so avoid them. A less common and more delicate process is vapour-blasting, which carries the abrasive medium in water, but the most popular method for smaller items is bead-blasting.

This uses glass beads so it does not take material away. It is also used on castings that have been grit-blasted as that process tends to open the metal pores. The beads close them up again, flattens the surface out and gives it a polish that can range from matt to gloss.

All parts should be thoroughly cleaned and oil, grease and loose rust removed before they are taken for the blasting process. Threads, cylinder bores, tight tolerance holes, headstock bearings, oilways and tapped holes will all need protecting, not so much from damage as to make sure nothing is trapped which could cause damage later. It is only too easy to block an essential oilway with beads and a wrecked engine will result in minutes.

Blanking off can be done using nuts, bolts, pieces of tube, several layers of masking tape or even Blu-tack. This last is excellent in recesses as it just absorbs the beads which come away with it afterwards. Items such as headstocks in frames can be sealed using a length of

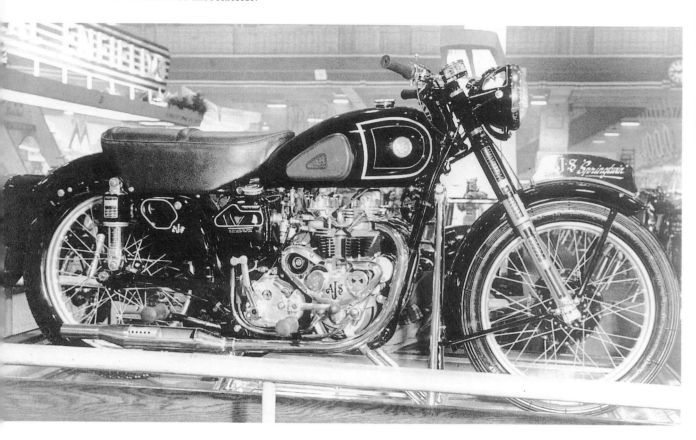

Superb cutaway 1952 model 20 AJS Springtwin on show

studding, two metal discs and rubber discs cut from an old inner tube. Don't forget a screw for the grease-nipple hole or your work will have been wasted.

The alternative to blasting is to remove paint, rust and, inevitably, some metal using emery. The manual method involves cloth strips which can be useful on frame tubes but for most items mechanization is essential. This takes the form of an electric drill and an emery flap wheel and is used more to remove deep scratches from the metal and to blend the damaged area into the rest. As with the blasters you should let the tool do the work without forcing it for the best results. Don't use a sanding disc as it will take off too much and most likely score the surface.

The extension of this type of work is to finer and finer grades of abrasive so that you finish up with a polished surface. This was normally applied to the timing cover, gearbox end cover and outer primary chaincase but is often extended by owners to many more of the light-alloy castings. This will reduce the metal's heat dissipation and may not be as original but many owners like to have more polish than normal and that is their right and decision for their machine.

Polishing can be done by hand, with mops or by a combination of the two. Industrial polishers use large mops driven at speed by a good-sized electric motor as they take a lot of power. They can also round off edges

and draw out drilled holes in a very short time so if you do have access to such equipment, practice on something that is scrap before beginning on your AMC parts.

Small mops can be used in an electric drill and must be kept charged with mop soap. Again, proceed with care, especially where there are sharp edges you wish to keep. Before mopping the easy areas you should deal with the awkward crevices. It is very tempting to do it the other way round but is not advisable.

The manual way of polishing involves wet-and-dry emery-cloth in paraffin. You need medium and then two grades of fine and it is a tedious and dirty job. The recesses can be done with an emery stick and this may be driven by a drill. The major areas can be done using a Loyblox, which is a block of rubber impregnated with emery grit that can be used wet or dry.

The final touch is a polish with Solvol Autosol or Belgom Alu applied with a soft cloth.

Chemical

There are chemical cleaners available for light-alloy parts and, as with the detergent mentioned above, they must be thoroughly washed away after use. Most are acidic in nature so care is necessary when using them and the instructions must be followed.

More usually, chemical cleaning means a paint-stripper and this is another messy operation but one that is quick and effective. Wear protective clothing and avoid contact by wearing gloves and eyeshields. It is a nasty substance.

Spread plenty of newspaper, put out the parts for stripping and paint the liquid on. After a while the paint will start to bubble up and often comes away in sheets. A scraper may be needed to help it along and all the old paint must come away. Then get rid of the old paint and paper remembering that it is now an industrial hazard. Burning is a good method if possible but will smell and must be done out of doors.

The parts will need to be cleaned with water if the stripper was so based, or thinners and wire wool. You *must* make sure that all the old paint and stripper is removed or the new coat will lift within days of application.

At this point you may find that under the paint there were patches of filler from some long distant repair. These will all have to come away so you can get down to bare metal and check on the exact damage. Don't be tempted to leave it as, having been disturbed by what you have done so far, it will be close to falling out anyway.

Douglas Bader receives a 1960 G3C for the Outward Bound School from Jock West at the Earls Court Show

Rust

You now have the steel parts in an ideal state for them to rust. However they have been cleaned, they will immediately begin to oxidize and any handling only makes matters worse due to the acids of the skin. So proceed to the next stage quickly.

If there is a delay and surface rust forms then it will have to be removed again before the finishing process is continued. There are a number of products available to do this and most have a phosphoric acid base. Many will also act as a primer for painting, but if the part has to be plated, wax or oil would be a better protection as they can be removed by degreasing.

Parts that are due to be painted should be given one coat of etch primer as soon as possible after the blasting or stripping process. This will keep the rust at bay while you draw breath.

Restoring the surface

If the part is to be plated then a metallic surface is essential and defects cannot be resin-filled as they can for painted items. Thus, it may be necessary to weld or braze, depending on the material, in order to obtain the required surface in the right substance.

This technique will work for castings and the heavier steel parts but sheet steel components in

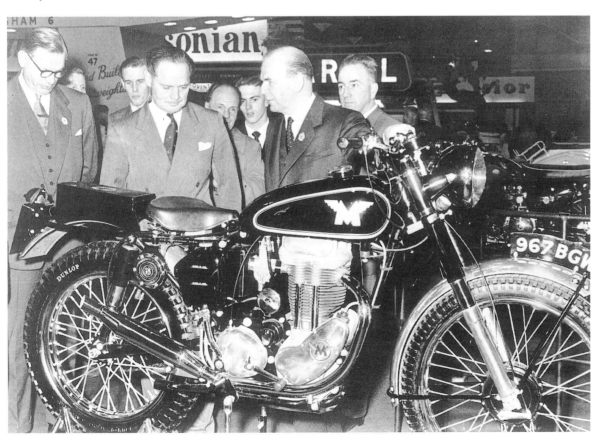

Very nice G11 from 1959 with some special fittings which did nothing to detract from its good looks

general, and the petrol tank in particular, need sheet metal skills. If you have these you will have the hammers and dollies to do the work but if you don't then you had best farm out all but the simplest tasks.

Even professional restorers often send petrol tanks to a specialist, as a repair usually entails cutting the bottom out to give access for the panel beating and then welding it back in again. A skilled job and not one to be attempted unless you really know what you are doing.

During preparation it is well worth rounding off the sharp corners of items such as engine plates and frame lugs as this will reduce any tendency to chipping. This usually starts from a sharp edge so their removal will improve the appearance in the long term.

Filling

Steel or iron parts which have been left for years are likely to have a pitted surface and it is not practical to fill these with braze or clean the surface down to remove them. The former would take forever and the latter would weaken the part far too much.

One answer is a resin filler, which may come as a brushed-on liquid or a two-part resin and hardener kit. Several coats will be needed to give body to the surface and ensure that all traces of pitting have gone. Once this is done the part will need to be left for several days to harden fully.

An alternative is lead filling as used for cars. The area to be treated has to be tinned first and this is done using a flux containing powered lead. This is brushed on and warmed with a blowlamp. Do not use a welding torch as the heat will be too high and too local.

Then continue with the lead, which comes as an alloy of lead and tin in sticks. The blowlamp will allow the lead to be kept movable without it running and a hardwood spatula will let you push it about. Wear a mask, try not to put too much on, remember you can always add more if needed, and finally dress down with a file and flattening paper.

The surface then has to be rubbed down and this is done using 320-grade wet-and-dry emery, used wet. It is a tedious job as the aim is a smooth, even surface that blends in with the rest of the part without bumps or hollows. This is not easy to get completely right first time but hollows can always be given another coat of filler so you have another chance.

Pinholes in the surface are dealt with using stopper in a similar way.

Once you are quite certain that the complete surface is perfect you can move on, but don't delude yourself. Any mark or imperfection will shine through no matter how many coats of paint you put on.

Painting

The traditional method of applying paint is by brush with a number of coats and the surface rubbed down between each. This was far too slow for mass-produced machines so the job was speeded up using spray or dip techniques and stove-enamelling paint. This gave a hard finish with a deep gloss that was hard wearing.

In contrast, a brush technique either took a great deal of time to apply or did not have a good finish and was easily damaged. Fortunately not any longer, although time and care is needed if a really good finish is wanted. What is now easy to obtain is good coverage, a deep gloss and a hard surface that won't chip easily and even if it does it can be touched in without much trouble.

Most restorers, therefore, use a synthetic enamel and the most common make is Tekaloid which is favoured by many professional men. Others simply shop at a high street store and produce very good results using either the enamel as it comes or as a two-part product. The second item acts as a hardener so the drying time is reduced and it is also possible to low-temperature bake the finish.

A short drying time is characteristic of cellulose which is normally used for spraying. It has to be mixed with thinners, is volatile and flammable, and must be handled with care as it can be medically dangerous.

A fast drying time is desirable as it helps to combat the home restorer's greatest enemies when painting, which are dust and midges. For this reason some do use a cellulose but in the end the finish depends far

The 1951 AJS 18S with the chrome-plated and lined tanks as used at that time

more on the preparation, clean atmosphere and operator care than the paint type.

To get this there are certain guide lines to follow. Paint after rain has washed dust from the atmosphere. Choose a warm, still day and damp down the working area. Wear clothes that do not harbour dust so avoid wool. Work in an area free from draughts and don't open the door once you have begun. But don't forget you do need air to breathe with. Don't breathe on the work and hang it from wire, not string, with the least important face pointing upwards. Use a tack rag on the surface immediately before you start and leave the working area as soon as you have finished painting.

The paint is applied with a brush and the name Hamilton is the one that comes up most often. A 1 in. wide brush will cover most items but a $\frac{1}{2}$ in. may be needed for details and a 2 in. for mudguards or the rear panels. Break the brushes in on something unimportant and wash out dirt with clean paraffin in several stages until it really is clean. Tap the handle against a piece of wood to shake the surplus out, do not finger the bristles or wipe them with a rag. After use, clean in paraffin, wash in warm soapy water, then clear water and leave to dry.

When painting pour some paint into a clean cup and load the brush from that. Do not put the brush in the paint tin. Apply with long, flowing strokes with the brush running down the part under its own weight to avoid brush marks. A light touch will give a lovely finish.

Two or three coats are usual and between each the surface has to be rubbed down using 500-grade wet-and-dry, used wet. This gives a smooth surface and allows you to see where the next coat has to go, not always easy on a dark, glossy surface.

There are two areas where the above will not work so well. One is where there is heat so brake drums and cylinder barrels are better stove-enamelled, which

means masking off and filling using materials which will cope with the baking temperature. The other is the petrol tank where the problem is resistance to petrol and staining. Fine if you never spill anything when refuelling and the cap seal does its job, but otherwise consider going to an expert.

Some restorers give the tank a coat of polyurethane lacquer but this is not advised as it will react with any spilt petrol and act as a paint stripper.

Paint colour

Black is black for most of us but colours seem to come in so many shades and suffer from fading, which leads to matching problems.

Also remember that all paints are not the same and while you can spray synthetic on to cellulose it won't work the other way round. Using a sealer or isolator may work but don't expect too much. Better to get back to the basic surface.

You should keep to one type of paint for all stages and colours, including any lining you do.

Paint colours are given in Appendix 4 and in more detail than in *AJS & Matchless—the postwar models* (Osprey Collector's Library) so should therefore take precedence over that volume with regard to the information given. Matching is another matter and an area of original paint that has been shielded from the light will act as the best guide. The inside of the toolbox or the underside of a clip are possible places but, of course, if your machine has been fully repainted at some time then this matching is lost.

LEFT *Plenty of onlookers but few customers for this 1959 G2CS which had too many pounds in both price and weight*

It may be possible to judge what you are after from a brochure or a contemporary magazine advertisement but otherwise you will have to find a machine to study. Museums, shows and meetings are all possible sources. Or you may be able, or lucky, to find a part in its wrapper in the right colour. Worth buying whether you need it or not just for the match.

Once you know what colour you need you then have to get the paint shop to mix it for you. Start from the British Standard Colour Chart as this should get you near what you want, but expect to have to experiment a little. Persevere on odd parts until you are satisfied you have it correct or to the shade you want it to be.

Spraying

This takes more cash to get the equipment and tends to be expensive in paint as much goes past the work on to the walls. The technique has been much described but as with the brush, practice, preparation and no dust are the keys to success.

Investigate paint types as some give off a lethal vapour and are not for the amateur at all. Learn how to operate the spray gun, the effects of your techniques and changes to them. Practise first.

Observe all safety precautions, which are more stringent for spraying due to the fire risk and the fumes. Keep a fire extinguisher of the correct type to hand. Make sure ventilation is good, don't have naked flames, gas heaters or open radiant fires and check on your electrics in case anything can spark. Wear a mask when working.

ABOVE *Nice two-tone finish used by AMC for many models and here seen on a 1961 model 31*

Coatings

An alternative to painting is plastic coating or powder coating. These will not give the gloss required by the perfectionist but the coats are tough. There are limitations on colour choice, filler cannot be used as it won't stand the process temperature and plastic coating can strip off if rust gets under the surface at any point.

So, again, preparation is important and will reflect in the final appearance. Dip-coating can be done at home on items such as stands, as the main requirements are means to heat the part up to around 300°C and a container for the powder into which the part is dipped. An old, clean oil can is a good start.

The Matchless G2 of 1962 with distinctive tank styling but otherwise much as always

Plating

Plating, like painting, depends on preparation for a good result. This means cleaning the surface and polishing it without damaging it. So once more the files, emery and elbow grease are needed but with some of the small parts the biggest problem is holding them.

You can pay the plater to do this but it is a labour-intensive job so costly and the more you can do yourself the better. Some parts you cannot replate as no one will touch them or allow them in their chroming bath. The two common ones are silencers and wheel rims as they would contaminate the bath solution.

After preparation, the trick is to find a good plater who is interested in your motorcycle work and it is a good idea to seek recommendations. Whether or not you are aiming for a concours job, expect to pay for good workmanship, which is always less expensive in the long run than a cheap job.

The major plated parts are finished with chromium but other plating processes are needed as well. Nuts and bolts that are not chromed are normally either cadmium- or zinc-plated. Bright nickel may be found on the spoke nipples.

Aluminium castings may be plated, although this does nothing for heat dispersion, or they can be anodized. This improves their corrosion resistance and the film formed on the surface can be dyed in a range of colours with matt black helping the heat and looking very smart. Note that the process acts as an insulator so don't forget that your electrics need a path for the current.

Lining and transfers

Signwriters do this freehand and one solution used by many restorers is to farm the job out. Alternatives are plastic tapes which are simply laid on and either left at that or varnished. Or masking using pvc tape to give the outline required. An alternative for the straighter parts is car lining tape which has a centre strip which is removed to leave two outers spaced parallel to each other. Tricky but not as much as trying to do it freehand. Don't forget that the lining paint must be the same type as the one it is being applied to or you will have trouble. Remove the tape before the paint is fully dry so it can flow smooth. Gold lining will then need a clear coat to protect it and yacht varnish is often favoured.

Transfers are the final touch to a machine and should be applied with care according to their directions. Make sure they go in the correct place and, when dry, protect with a thin coat of clear varnish.

Stainless steel

An alternative for many steel parts that are normally chrome-plated is stainless steel. Many owners refuse to use parts made of it but in the right application and the correct grade it can say goodbye to a corrosion problem for ever.

There are a good number of stainless steels, some magnetic and able to be hardened, some not fully corrosion-resistant and so on, as with other metals. With the correct specification all will be well, as long as the part is correctly machined.

Airport duty for the police using a rigid 1954 Matchless single

9 Frame and stands

With these items you have something solid to work on so most minor repairs are easy to do. Bent brackets can be heated and returned to their correct position and cracks around them welded. Holes may need welding and redrilling if elongated or tapping out if their threads are damaged.

All this is easy to do but the real work on the frame is to check its alignment. This can be done with string and straight edges but does take a good eye to spot areas where there is a problem. A straightforward bend due to a crash is easy to see but the twist that five years of sidecar work may induce is more subtle.

Getting the frame straight again is a specialized job and should be farmed out. Before this is done check it over for cracks which will need welding, for the fit of the head races in the headstock and the rear fork pivot, as attention to these areas will involve heat which could cause distortion. Best to get all the minor work out of the way so that once the frame is straight it can be painted.

The stands need similar attention and are often distorted due to misuse. Expect to find damaged pivot holes needing attention and check that the spring attachment is in good order and will hold the spring as the stand moves. Inspect the stand feet as these do wear and may need to be built up again to ensure the machine stands correctly when parked.

Rigid frame

This was only used up to 1955 and only for the singles. It came as two main parts, front and rear, which combined with the engine, gearbox and engine plates to form a rigid structure.

The first changes came for 1948 when a sidecar lug was added to the downtube just beneath the headstock on the front half. On the rear part the cross-tube that had taken the saddle spring stud became a simple cross brace and two short, vertical, threaded tubes appeared to support the saddle springs. At the same time frame parts for the competition models were

A 1953 competition AJS being used for trick riding

listed for the first time and these gave different wheelbase and head angle figures.

The two road halves were amended for 1949 so that the front could also be used with the pivoted-fork rear and the new twins. The front then remained as it was until 1954 when there were detail changes with more for 1955. The rear half was altered for 1950 and 1951 but then not again until 1954.

The competition front half changed for 1950 when the all-alloy engine was introduced and in 1954 when an all-welded design removed 4 pounds of weight. The rear half altered for 1949, 1950, 1951 and 1954 as the machines became more specialized and trials-orientated.

Pivoted-fork frame

This was introduced for 1949 and from 1956 onwards all models had this type of frame. AMC used a built-up construction for their frames and the first pivoted-fork type had a front, rear loop, two rails and a bridge.

The front comprised the headstock with top, down and seat tubes and at first was common to the rigid models. The loop was made from the two bent tubes which ran back to the top rear unit lugs and then down and forwards, these two being joined into one by a single cross-tube. The rails ran along either side below the crankcase and gearbox to extend from the bottom of the downtube to the pillion footrest and silencer supports. The bridge was a massive light-alloy casting which united the frame members together and to the gearbox plates.

The bridge was common to all the sprung singles, twins and competition springers up till 1955 but all the other sections had a number of changes. For the front, the first change was to accommodate an air filter in the 1951 twins. The next was for 1953 adding a lug on the downtube for a new head steady on the twins. For 1954 it was joined by a cross lug to rubber-mount the horn and for 1955 the seat tube was altered to tidy up the oil tank and battery carrier mountings while providing space for the air filter hose.

The sprung singles had a similar cycle with changes for 1953, 1954 and 1955, the last as for the twins. The

Last year before a new frame for a 1955 G80S with jampots and those nasty pilot lights

competition singles changed their tank mountings for 1954 and to accommodate a dualseat for 1955.

The rear loops had a similar cycle, although the singles and twins shared common parts. The first change was for 1952 with another for 1954 when the cvc was moved to brackets welded to the top loop tube under the seat nose. For 1955 the pillion and silencer supports became fabricated from sheet, welded to the lower ends of the loop tubes and given tapped holes for sidecar lugs. The CS models also changed their rear loop for these three years in the same way, but always fitted a different part.

The rails were common to all models and were amended for 1954 and shortened for 1955 when they no longer had to support the pillion rests or silencers.

The frames all changed for 1956 when the seat tube became vertical with a malleable iron lug brazed to its lower end to take the rear fork pivot. There were four in all with one each for the road singles, twins, competition and CS machines.

For 1957 all models changed to the AMC gearbox and this resulted in new front frames for the twins and competition trials singles plus the 497 cc road singles. The smaller road single kept to its 1956 frame as did the CS singles. The twins kept their frame to 1959 while the road singles all used the 1957 497 cc frame for 1958–9. The trials model changed its frame for 1959 when the sub-frame was reduced in size and the

rear fork design altered and the CS singles had a frame change for 1958 to allow the twin engine to be fitted. The result then had a steady lug added to become the twin CS and CSR frame for 1958–9.

During this 1956–9 period the rear loop continued to be bolted into place as did the rails. The singles and twins used the same loop for 1956 but altered this for 1957–9 when Girling rear units were fitted with the exception of the 1957 348 cc single. This had its own part for that one year alone. There was a different loop for the CS singles which changed for 1957 and again for 1958 when it also went on the CS and CSR twins.

The trials 348 cc model had a change of loop for 1957 when the rails became part of the loop and this design was modified for 1958. For 1959 the frame reverted to separate rails, which were new parts, while the loop became a small triangular sub-frame. The main frame had its rear pivot bearing modified for 1960 while the sub-frame was altered during 1964, but otherwise these two major sections and the rails ran on as they were to the model end in 1964.

The rest of the range received a new frame with duplex downtubes for 1960. The front part was common to singles, twins and CS singles and served the first two to 1963 and the last to 1965. For 1962 only, there were optional frames listed in blue for AJS and red for Matchless, as most models were offered in these colours for that one year.

The frame front changed for 1964 to accept Norton forks and this part continued for the AMC road models. Machines fitted with the Norton twin engine had their own frames with one for standard and another for the CSR version for 1965 but just the standard one after then.

For the G85CS of 1966 there was a welded, duplex frame, very similar to that of the Rickman Metisse, which saw that model out and was a single part. The other frames from 1960 on continued to have a separate loop bolted to the front frame and for 1960 there was one for the road singles and standard twins with another for the CS singles and sports twins.

The CS singles kept to the same loop up to 1965 while the road models were offered a coloured option for 1962. The sports twins had a loop change for 1962 as well, while the others had theirs for 1963. A common loop was used for 1964 and served all models from then on except the CSR twins of 1965–7.

The light singles had a built-up frame comprising front with single tubes, sub-frame and two channels which ran beneath the engine unit. The front was amended for 1960 and alternative types were used for the CS, which simply had a heavier gauge downtube, and the 348 cc models. The standard frame was offered in colour for 1962 and also for the CSR the same year.

The road models had a common sub-frame for all years with the 1962 colour option but the CS original was modified for 1961. The engine cradle channels were one for the CS and another for the rest of the range but there were four types of the other channel. There was one for the standard, S and CSR models, one for the 348 cc model and two for the CS with the second going in for 1961.

Rear fork

The design of this and its bearings changed little over the years and in fact the bearing assembly of a sintered bronze bush in a steel housing was used for all models from 1949 to 1969.

This ought to help but in fact repair is a problem as the bushes in the rear-fork pivot on a 1 in. diameter steel tube pressed originally into the alloy bridge behind the gearbox. This, at least, could unbolt from the rest of the frame but from 1956 onwards the tube was pressed into the main front frame. Lubrication was by oil, carried within the tube which was sealed with end caps secured by a spoke and nipple plus gaskets, a system which can also be seen on the Norton Commando in later years.

The original fork went on the singles, twins and CS singles and was altered for 1954 with a revised chainguard mounting lug and again for 1955 when the full width qd hub appeared. For 1956 only, another fork was listed for the competition models but otherwise the 1955 fork stayed in use to 1961 with one exception.

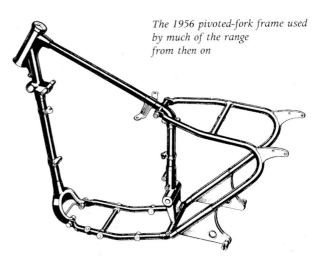

The 1956 pivoted-fork frame used by much of the range from then on

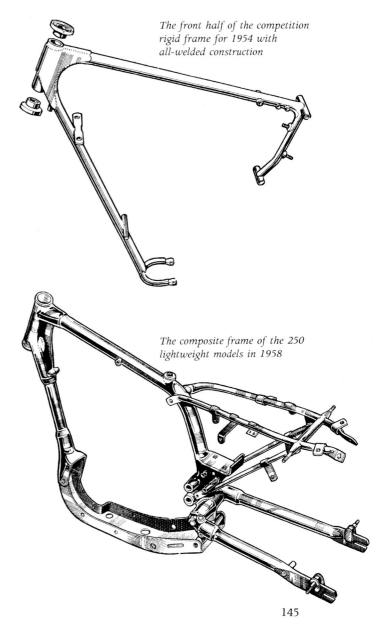

The front half of the competition rigid frame for 1954 with all-welded construction

The composite frame of the 250 lightweight models in 1958

145

This was for the trials model which for 1959 changed to a two-part fork. This had the pivot pin brazed to the right leg with the left pushed on to the end of the pin and retained by a cotter. The right arm was modified for 1960, after which this arrangement continued to the end of the model.

Meanwhile, the rest of the range had a revised fork plus colour options for 1962 and this fork remained in use for the CS singles to 1965 and the CSR twins for 1963. The standard twins and road singles had a further revision for 1963 to suit the change to standard Girling units and all models had the fork altered to suit the Norton hub for 1964. This fork then served the whole range right through to 1969 except the G85CS. This differed from the others in that it had to fit between the frame plates rather than around a lug.

The light singles had a rear fork built up in the same way as that of the 1959 trials model with the left arm pinned to the pivot pin with a cotter. One assembly served the CS models and another served all the others.

Head races

Expect to renew these on a restoration, unless they are in perfect condition and even then change the ball bearings. The cups were a pair for all models to 1953 and the road machines from then to 1963. The competition trials models from 1954 had their own dissimilar top and bottom cups. The lower cone was common to all up to 1963 while the upper was altered for 1948.

All these models had 56 balls of $\frac{3}{16}$ in. diameter,

equally split between the two bearings, and the trials model kept its two-odd cups for 1964 while the CS singles ran on with the original type. Other than these, the road models switched to Norton forks for 1964 with different cups and cones held apart by 36 balls of $\frac{1}{4}$ in. diameter.

The standard light singles had their own pair of races, dissimilar cones and 34 balls of $\frac{1}{4}$ in. diameter. The CS, 348 cc and CSR models used their own top and bottom cups with the cones from the larger models along with 56 balls of $\frac{3}{16}$ in. diameter.

Front stand

This was only fitted up till 1955 and doubled as the rear stay for the front mudguard, to which it was fixed with a single nut. It went on both rigid and sprung road models and two types were used. The first fitted inside the fork legs and was replaced for 1948 by the second type, which went outside the legs and was used from then till 1955. It was not used by the competition models at all.

Rear stand

Just one rear stand and spring was listed from 1945 to 1955 and this was only used by the rigid road and competition singles.

The rigid 1955 G3LC with revised frame and small cylindrical toolbox under the saddle

The 1960 standard model 31 AJS with the new duplex frame and finished in the optional two-tones for the tank

Centre stand

These first appeared with the spring frames in 1949, with one for the singles and another for the twins. Both had longer legs for 1951 when the singles type also went on the CS models. These had an alternative listed for 1956, which also went on the springer trials model of that year, but returned to the 1951 type for 1957–9.

That 1951 stand also stayed on the road singles till 1955 and went on to the CS and CSR twins for 1958–9. On the standard twins, their 1951 stand was replaced for 1958 and the new part stayed in use till 1961. The trials model kept its 1957 stand right through to 1964 but the road and CS singles, along with the sports twins, had a new common stand for 1960–1 to suit the new frame.

For 1962 the CS singles changed to the trials stand and kept that till 1965. The road models had new roll-on stands that made parking easier with one for the singles and standard twins, and another for the CSR twins. There were also coloured stands to go with the optional finish, for that year only.

The CSR stand continued for 1963 but the others changed to fit round the new silencer with one part common to the singles and standard twins. For 1964 there was a new stand common to all the road models

The 1960 duplex frame as used by both twins and singles from then on

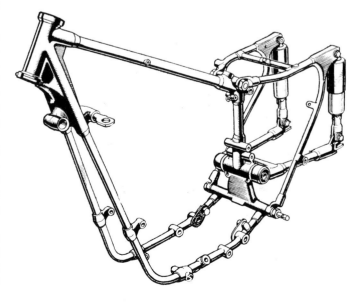

The 1961 AJS 16C with its light sub-frame and many features from the past

Spring-loaded prop-stand of the 1946 G3L and details of the chaincase and rear-brake pedal used in that era

and this went on the 745 cc standard twins as well. The CS version of this size used the competition stand at first and another for 1967 onwards while the CSR twin had its own from 1965.

All these models had a common return spring from 1949 to 1969. The light singles had another and their original stand was altered for 1960 to add roll-on feet. It was further modified for 1961 and served all models, except the CS which had its own part. The coloured option was listed for 1962 only and not for the CS.

Prop-stand

The AMC machines had this feature from 1945 and it was first modified for 1949 when the spring-frame was introduced. A year earlier another was listed solely for the competition models, but from 1950 a single prop-stand served all the singles.

This was to go on to all the road singles from then on, plus the CSR twins. The standard twins had their own stand from 1949 and this went on all models till 1966 and all the 745 cc twins till 1969. There were coloured versions for 1962 and the one other stand was the one fitted to the trials models for 1958–64.

Four springs were listed in all with changes for 1950, 1951 and 1954 with this last one continuing in use till 1969.

10 Suspension

All models had telescopic forks with hydraulic damping and most fitted the AMC Teledraulic fork first seen on the army G3L of 1941. The light singles used a light version of these at first but changed to the sturdier type for the CS, CSR and 348 cc models. From 1964 the larger singles and twins fitted the Norton fork as part of a rationalization programme.

The early post-war models had rigid frames but pivoted-fork rear suspension was offered for road models from 1949 and competition ones from 1951. After 1955 all models had this form of rear suspension. The rear units were of an AMC design for some years, with slim ones known as candlesticks fitted for 1949–50. These were changed to the latter units called jampots for 1951–6 and both types differed from other makes in having clevis ends for their attachment to frame and rear fork. From 1957 Girling units with clevis lower and standard top fittings were used until 1963 when standard Girlings took over.

Telescopic forks

Most of these are similar in nature, and restoration follows common lines. Strip the forks, following the procedure given in the manual, and examine the parts for wear. Check each leg for worn bushes or sliders which may call for repair or replacement.

Bent fork legs are common and rolling them on a flat surface will reveal this. Wear can be overcome by hard chroming and grinding to size if new parts are not to be found. This will also deal with any pitting of the surface, but where this is minor it can be filled with epoxy resin which is rubbed down when hard.

Expect to renew fork bushes and seals but most of the other internal parts operate in oil and seldom wear. Check the springs for tiredness and shortening. If this has happened try to find new springs of the correct rate. Packing can be and is done but will affect the rate and may restrict fork movement. It can also give rise to clashing sounds if things have worked out against you.

All threads need to be carefully checked and repaired as required. As they hold the forks together or the wheel in, they do have a bearing on your well-being. Check the lower legs especially for any signs of damage.

If the fork tubes have been bent then it is most likely that the crowns will also be bent or distorted. Sometimes this manifests itself in the head races becoming tight at one point but slack at another. The crowns must be true to the forks and the frame and their threads checked.

Assemble to the book, make sure the head races are correctly adjusted and that the fork legs are parallel so they can move freely without binding. Fill with the correct grade and quantity of oil and try to get the same amount in each leg.

Telescopic-fork types

After the war AMC continued to fit the wartime forks to all their models. These had a long damper rod in each leg screwed into the top nut and working in a tube secured to the base of the lower leg. The left one of these had a stud set in it for the brake anchor and the handlebar clamp was held by two bolts.

For 1947, triple-rate springs plus buffer springs were fitted but there were more changes for 1948. On the outside there was a light-alloy top crown with four fixings for the handlebar clamp and two lugs on the left lower leg. These were for two high-tensile bolts which anchored the backplate, while inside went longer springs and a new shuttle damper.

The same fork was used for the 1949 singles, but for the twins the brake backplate was anchored by a torque arm so there were no bolt lugs on the left lower leg. The singles copied this arrangement for 1950 when the lower crown became a steel stamping and special competition forks were introduced.

A further set appeared for 1951 to suit the competition springers and for all models there was a change back to the early damper design. In addition, the drain plugs were recessed into the legs to stop them being sheared off by high kerbs and the lower crown became a steel forging.

For 1952 the lower legs were polished, instead of being painted black as before, and the spring shrouds made longer. There was a new malleable iron top crown with a neater speedometer mounting and a new handlebar clamp secured by three cap screws. The next year the lower crown left lock stop was formed and drilled to accept a steering lock bar which was in turn held in place by a small padlock. In addition the top shrouds were no longer held in place by screws but allowed to turn between rubber mouldings to fit the headlamp shell and the fork tube clamp screws changed to the cap head type.

There were new fork legs for 1954 which were smoother and easier to clean. The legs changed again for 1955 when the mudguard front stays were deleted for the road models so there was no longer any reason for the front lugs on the legs. The stanchions were increased in diameter from $1\frac{1}{8}$ to $1\frac{1}{4}$ in. and there were new crowns. The lower was forged while the upper was in malleable iron and shaped to suit a new headlamp shell. There were new tapered shrouds between the crowns, and the brackets welded to them had horizontal upper edges to match the new headlamp shell.

For 1956 the fork legs had cleaner caps which were cast with the legs and then machined off. There were

ears on the top crown sides to guide the control cables and the top nuts were modified. They went from a deep dome and hexagon to a lesser dome with cap screw recess, plus a rubber plug to keep water out of that recess. There was also an adaptor beneath the nut for the damper rod.

The next alteration was for 1958 when the sports twins used the older style top crown with the speedometer mounted on it rather than in the headlamp shell. They also used the fork legs with twin-stay lugs. For 1959 the trials model went back to the smaller diameter stanchion in a better steel to reduce weight and for 1960 the road models had more trail.

The next major change came for 1964 when all the road models went over to Norton Roadholder forks to leave just the competition ones with the AMC type. This arrangement continued from then on with the forks from the trials model being used by the G85CS to keep its weight down.

The light singles had their own simpler version of the forks with pressed-steel crowns but retained the hydraulic damping. The steering column was separate

Matchless G12CSR of 1961 with telescopic front forks and Girling rear units with clevis lower ends

When only rigid machines were to be had some riders fitted options such as this Clark rear linkage on a 1947 16M

from the lower crown and the fork shrouds were in one length from the top crown to the lower legs. These legs had cross-tubes at their ends for sleeve nuts on the front-wheel spindle.

This fork was used by the standard and S models but the CS fitted the Teledraulic fork with two stay lugs on each leg. The 348 cc model had the same fork but with one stay lug and the smaller diameter stanchions, this also went on the CSR model.

Steering damper

This was listed as an option from 1949 on and in all cases the condition of screw threads, discs and detail parts needs to be checked and renovated as required.

The original type was revised for 1951 with a new upper plate and damper knob with the latter labelled to suit the marque. The damper was altered again for 1955 with a new fork crown top nut and finally for 1964 to suit the Norton forks. From 1959, the 1951 version went on the competition models and was also available in turn on the light singles in CS, 348 cc and CSR forms.

151

*Early spring frame with candlestick rear units on a 1950
G80S*

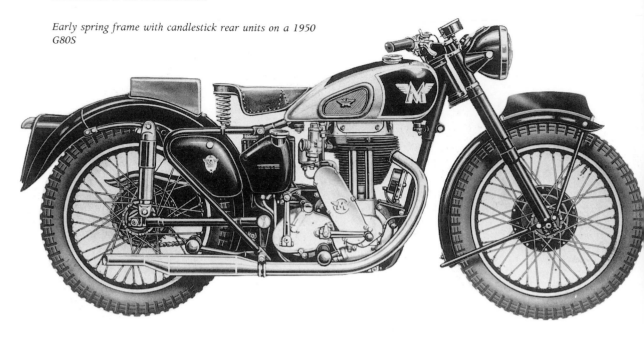

*Exploded drawing of jampot unit which can be repaired
with care*

The candlestick rear unit drawn to show its construction

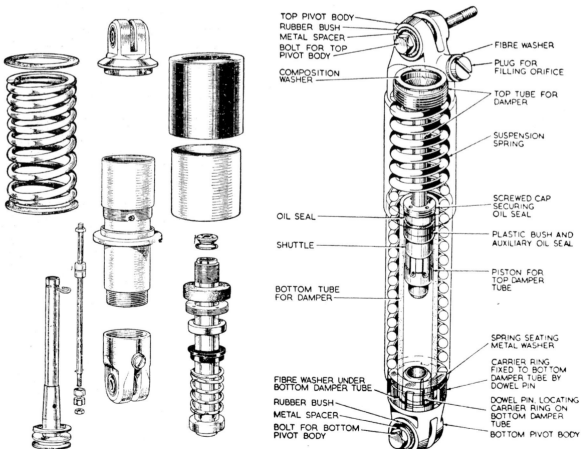

TOP PIVOT BODY
RUBBER BUSH
METAL SPACER
BOLT FOR TOP
PIVOT BODY

COMPOSITION
WASHER

FIBRE WASHER

PLUG FOR
FILLING ORIFICE

TOP TUBE FOR
DAMPER

SUSPENSION
SPRING

OIL SEAL

SHUTTLE

SCREWED CAP
SECURING
OIL SEAL

PLASTIC BUSH AND
AUXILIARY OIL SEAL

PISTON FOR
TOP DAMPER
TUBE

BOTTOM TUBE
FOR DAMPER

SPRING SEATING
METAL WASHER

CARRIER RING
FIXED TO BOTTOM
DAMPER TUBE BY
DOWEL PIN

FIBRE WASHER UNDER
BOTTOM DAMPER TUBE

RUBBER BUSH
METAL SPACER
BOLT FOR BOTTOM
PIVOT BODY

DOWEL PIN. LOCATING
CARRIER RING ON
BOTTOM DAMPER
TUBE

BOTTOM PIVOT BODY

A 1951 AJS model 20 twin with jampots, saddle and plated tank

RIGHT *The top crown as adopted for 1952*

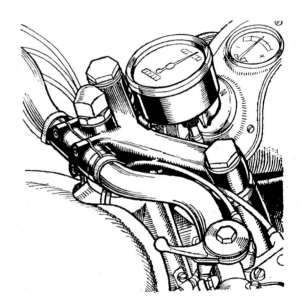

Rear suspension units

For some years AMC chose to go their own way with these which differ from most in that they can be dismantled and renovated. This aspect is helped by the owners club which produces parts and holds the tools needed.

The early candlesticks differ from the jampots in their construction and are critical as to oil content. This should not exceed 50 cc of SAE20 oil, as an excess can burst the oil seal. It is possible to drain and refill these units but the procedure in the manual must be followed carefully and completely.

The jampots had a larger damper which took 85 cc of oil so were less critical and less prone to ruin their seals. Even so, the contents should be measured with care and filling instructions obeyed. The jampot springs were shorter and fatter than the candlestick so no longer sat between the top and bottom pivots.

Instead, a ring was screwed on to the lower leg to support the bottom of the spring and for 1955 the design was changed to a ring and circlip seated in the lower leg. The year before, the lower spring cover had a detail change so in all there were three versions of the jampot with solo or sidecar springs. The last jampots were fitted up to the end of 1956.

For 1957, AMC changed to Girling units with the lower end altered to a clevis fork to suit their unique arrangements. At the top went the normal Girling bush. In all there were four units listed with one each

for the road models in solo or sidecar form, one for the trials machines and one for the scramblers.

All the solo units changed for 1958 and the road model type continued on the singles and standard twins to 1962. The CS singles used the same unit as the CS and CSR twins over this period while the trials model had one change for 1958 and then another for 1959, which ran on to 1964 and the end of that machine. For 1961–2 one special unit was listed for the twins and another for the CS singles when these models were exported to the USA.

For 1963 all models, other than the trials, changed to standard Girling fixings to the pivoted forks. The AMC machines had one unit listed for the singles and

The 1963 model 16 AJS with standard Girling units at the rear

standard twins while another served the CS and CSR twins. The first was also used by the standard twins with the Norton engine for 1965–9 but both the CSR twin of that period and the CS of 1967–9 had their own units. On the CSR twin the lower spring covers were left off to expose the spring and this also applied to the G85CS model.

The light singles had their own Girling units with one for the 248 cc road models, one for the CS version and one for the 348 cc machines.

The Girling units offer limited scope to the restorer because while the outer covers and springs can be removed the actual damper unit is sealed. The rubber mounting bushes can be renewed but repair of the unit required that it is dismantled, which for most people is not possible.

Given machining equipment it is feasible to strip, repair and rebuild units but it is a specialized business. If replacement units cannot be found then an alternative will have to be fitted. These are available and from the suppliers' lists it should be possible to find one with similar closed and open lengths, and fixings and spring. In many cases these new units have improved (and sometimes adjustable) damping, and can be stripped for repair when this is needed.

In all cases check that the eyes at the ends of the unit and the frame attachments are in good order and will carry the loads they are called upon to support. Note that where the springs are partly exposed this can have an adverse effect on the life of the dampers. It is well worth fitting covers or gaiters to keep road dirt off the damper rods and away from the unit seals.

11 Painted parts and plated details

This chapter covers the mass of major parts and minor fittings which are mostly steel pressings and nearly all painted. A few are forged or diecast and some plated with chrome or cadmium.

The steel pressings need to be checked over for repair. This may entail a simple bending job to straighten a bracket or a complex panel-beating job for such items as mudguards. Often the parts will need to be welded either to mend cracks or to rejoin things that have come apart. Excess holes will need to be filled, and the external signs of all this work removed before the finish is applied.

The problems in this area arise not so much with the repairs which are usually straightforward, but in collecting all the parts and ensuring that what you have gathered up is correct for your model. In all too many cases, changes did not affect fit or if they did the parts could be modified to suit. Thus, machines built up from parts can often have cycle details from many models and worst of all can be the basket jobs.

The latter need very careful checking over from the first. It is easy to see that you have a pair of mudguards, although less so to be sure they are the correct pair, but much more difficult to be sure you have a full set of engine plates or torque stays. The following sections are thus not concerned with the repair of the parts, which follows stock lines, but with their correct identification.

Knowledge of part numbers and changes will all help to ensure that the cycle spares bought from a dealer or at an autojumble will be correct for your project.

Engine and gearbox plates

The singles began with several different arrangements to suit the two marques and the two engine sizes. Thus the AJS models had a pair of front engine plates while the Matchless ones had a channel section as this did not have to carry the magneto. At the rear, one pair of plates served both makes of 497 cc single but the 348 cc models differed with two of one part serving the AJS but the Matchless having a left and right one.

This arrangement continued till 348 cc engine 8000 of 1948, after which the 497 cc rear plates were used by all models so one part only had to be listed. This changed for 1949 when a cover was added over the rear plates for the AJS single only. That year the twins first appeared with left- and right-angle plates at the front and a pair of plates at the rear.

The singles continued with this arrangement of front plate until 1952 when the Matchless adopted the AJS part. This served all singles to 1957 and the competition ones to 1965 with something else for the G85CS. From 1958 the road singles had a new part with two off fitted from then till 1966. The rear plates of the road models stayed as they were until 1952 when there was a new part fitted to both rigid and sprung models. This changed to suit the new sprung frame of 1956 and again for 1958, after which it stayed as it was.

A special rear plate for the competition singles first appeared for 1950 and was joined by one for the CS versions in 1951. Both were altered for 1952 and again for the new frame in 1956. They were once more revised for 1957 with the trials one later changing for 1959 and the CS for 1960.

The original AJS rear plate cover went on the Matchless singles in 1952 and was changed to a snap-on type for 1956. The next year it was kept for the road and trials models with another for the CS ones, but for 1958 there was one for each machine type. The road model then continued till 1966 but the trials one changed for 1959 and then this ran on to 1964. The CS stayed with its 1957 cover until 1960 when it adopted the 1959 trials cover.

The twins kept their front-angle plates up to 1959 but for the 1960 duplex frame changed to a channel section which stayed in use to 1966. The rear plate, which was used in both locations, was changed for 1952 and became handed for 1956. This pair served all models till 1958 and the standard and de luxe models from then on. They were joined by a second set which went on the sports models for 1958–62. From 1963 the CSR version used the standard plates. New front and rear plates, both handed, were needed to carry the Norton engine of the 745 cc twins and the rears were changed for 1966.

Matchless twin prepared for the 1951 Clubman's TT when lights and silencers were not compulsory

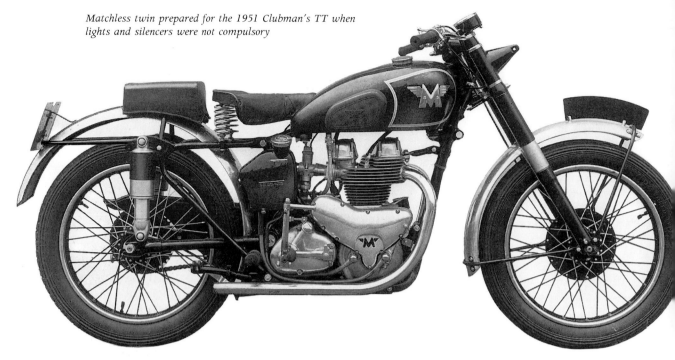

A rear plate cover was fitted from 1957 and the original served the de luxe, CS and CSR models from 1960. That year another was introduced for the standard model and both were then listed up to 1966. Another served the 745 cc twins.

The light singles only had rear plates to join the gearbox and engine to the frame and one handed pair served all models and years. A cover went over them with one each for the 248 cc, 348 cc and CS models.

Engine steady

This joins the top of the engine to the frame and in all cases the parts must fit properly and without strain if they are to do their job.

At first, only the 497 cc engines had a steady and it was not until 1953 that one was fitted to the 348 cc singles. The original was altered for 1949 and this part, plus a clip, served all till 1959. A second clip appeared in 1954 for the competition C models only and continued on them till 1964. With it, only from 1960, went the 1949 steady, while another without clip went on the road and CS singles from 1960 onwards.

The twins began with a pair of handed tubular stays, a clip and plate, which joined the front of the engine to the frame. For 1953 this was simplified to a single triangular plate with a large centre hole and for 1958 this hole altered to two small slots. There was a new part for the 1960 frame and others for the Norton engines with one for 1965 and another for 1966 onwards.

The light singles had one stay for the 248 cc road and 348 cc models, with another for the CS version. These served all years.

Exhaust-pipe and silencer brackets

In the main these are simple strips of steel, bent once or twice, with a hole at each end and then chrome-plated. There are a good number listed, as often they differed between the 348 and 497 cc singles and again between road and competition machines.

All need to fit correctly and to hold the exhaust system without straining it. In addition to the brackets, AMC also used supports which were lengths of bar, threaded internally. These screwed to an engine plate stud and had the pipe bolted to them in turn. They appear on both singles and twins.

Magneto shield and platform

These are only to be found on the singles and the shield was only fitted when the magneto was in the forward position and not at all after 1955. It thus first appeared on AJS models only with one version serving the road machines to 1951 and another the competition ones for 1950–1.

There were two new parts for 1952 but while the competition one continued for the next year the road one was reduced in size. This smaller shield was then only fitted to the 348 cc road models for 1954–5. The rest of the range had another part for 1954 only but this was not listed for the AJS competition models, only the Matchless ones.

The mounting platforms also varied at first with one for AJS and two for Matchless, one for each engine size. Matchless fitted one part to all models for 1949–51 but from 1952 the original AJS part was used by all singles which retained a magneto. This continued till 1963, with a change of 1964, the last year of the trials model although the CS ran on till 1969.

Undershield

This was fitted to the competition and CS models and was first listed for the former for 1949. It was revised for 1950, and this part went on the CS machines the next year and continued to serve both model types up till 1958.

That year the 1950 part also went on the CS twin and remained there for 1959 while continuing on the CS single for those two years as well. From 1960 a new part was used by the twins, for that year only, and the singles to 1965. For the G85CS there was a front-engine shield and low-level crankcase protectors. The trials model had a new shield for 1959 and continued with this through to 1964.

Fork shrouds

These cover the fork tubes between the two crowns, and in most cases have a bracket welded to them to support the headlamp. Only on the light singles do they extend down the fork to the lower leg, and in this case their fit needs to be checked when they and the headlamp are bolted up. They must run clear of the leg because if they scrape they will damage themselves and then continue to wear away both parts.

The shrouds began as simple tubes, for the headlamp shell was supported by stays up till 1948. For 1949 the shrouds grew shell lugs and were handed left and right, while the original part continued on the competition models without lights till 1952. Up to that date the shrouds had been retained by screws but for 1953 they were made free to turn about the fork tubes. A rubber washer went under each to give a fit and this change allowed for easier packing for export.

The addition of twin pilot lights for 1954 meant a change to the shroud lugs and for 1955 they were altered to a tapered form. This was due to an increase in the stanchion-tube diameter, which in turn affected both the spring and its cover. The shroud taper was to match the new cover and these parts stayed in use till 1959 when they were joined by a chrome-plated pair.

During this period the competition models fitted either a plain tubular shroud or the standard part if a headlamp was fitted. From 1959, the standard 1953 parts were used in the latter case while the tubes remained in use otherwise, except for the G85CS.

The 1959 standard shrouds remained in use for the CS singles fitted with lights for 1960–5 with the plated type standard for 1962. For the road models there were new shrouds for 1960 to suit the new, smaller headlamp with either a painted or chrome-plated finish but only the first remained for 1963. For 1964 and the Norton forks there were new shrouds which were altered for 1965 onwards.

On the light singles the shroud was a simple tube at first and extended below the lower crown to the fork leg. Handed shrouds with lugs to carry the headlamp shell were introduced for the standard model for 1960 and continued from then on. Previously, the headlamp shell was carried from the fork-top pressing. The CS light singles used the 1953 standard shrouds or the type without lugs while the 348 cc and CSR models had their own parts.

Matchless G3 of 1962 with massive tank badges and little else altered

Fork cover tubes

These went below the lower crown and extended down to the lower fork leg. As with the light-single shrouds, they must run true and not scrape or the parts will be damaged and worn very quickly.

The original covers were fixed by the same screws that retained the shrouds so there were three fixing holes in the top flange. For 1953 they lost the holes as they were held in place by the fork springs and they were also lengthened a little. They were increased in diameter for 1955, along with the stanchions and springs, and in this form continued to 1963.

From 1959 to 1962 a chrome-plated version was also listed and from that year the competition models fitted the 1953 covers to suit the lighter forks used. There was a special cover for the CS singles from 1962 onwards and another for the 745 cc models from 1964 on.

The light singles fitted the 1959 competition cover to the CS, 348 cc and CSR models while the standard ones kept to the long-fork shrouds.

Headlamp shell

These are all similar in shape but there were quite a few variations over the years. The shell is none too easy to repair but often ones from other models can be used if necessary. Threads, general shape and condition need to be checked and the finish was usually paint but could be chrome-plating.

The first shell was simple with flat glass and a small panel carrying the light switch and an ammeter. For 1948 the glass was fluted and for 1949 it was domed and a pre-focus light unit was fitted. From the next year the competition model was listed with a version of the older type while for 1951 the road model lamp was altered in detail only.

The competition models continued as they were up to 1958, but for 1952 the road ones were fitted with the underslung pilot lamp. This went for 1954 when twin pilot lights, one on each side of the shell, were adopted, while for 1955 the shell was deepened to carry the speedometer, with the ammeter to the right and light switch to the left, ahead of it.

The road models next changed for 1958 when the twin pilot lights were dropped and the singles changed to coil ignition, with the switch for this combined with the lighting one. The CS twin fitted the same shell as the road single but pierced to take the older light switch.

For 1959 it was altered to take the combined switch for the standard models with the same shell also being used by the de luxe twins. The competition, CS single and sports CS and CSR twins all changed to a shell with a sealed beam light unit and this remained in use from

The 1961 G12CS as prepared for the American market with high bars

158

AJS model 16 or 18 for 1963 with large tank badges but otherwise as the Matchless

then on for the trials model and to 1961 for the sports twins.

The rest of the range changed to a shallower shell for 1960 with one for both singles and twins and another for the CS singles when fitted with lights. This last changed twice more for 1962 and 1967 with the 1962 shell also fitting on the 650 CSR model for that year alone. The standard road model had another shell for 1964 which saw them out while the CSR twins had changes for 1963 and 1964. The 745 cc models continued in the same vein with one shell for the standard machine, which was modified for 1967 to add a warning light, and another for the CSR with a chrome-plated finish.

The light singles began with a Wipac headlamp mounted from the top fork pressing but for 1960 it was held by the fork shrouds, as on the rest of the range. The new part was also fitted to the 348 cc models, changed for 1961 and later went on the CSR machines. A different lamp was listed for the CS versions and was also altered for 1961.

Mudguards, their stays and front stand

All these parts are associated together and as there were a good few changes over the years some care is needed to ensure that all the correct parts are to hand. If they are not then the mudguards may be fabricated from others or from stock parts. The stays and supports can also be made from strip or tube as required. When flattening the ends of a tube for the mounting hole add a piece of flat stock inside the tube.

This will give it more body and stop the walls from cracking.

Above all else do make sure the mudguards are properly secured and cannot revolve round the wheel. Check that they sit correctly with a good line to the tyres and that all the stays and supports line up and bolt down without strain. Only when you are fully satisfied with the mechanical aspects should you move on and complete the finishing.

Front mudguard

This began in a conventional form with a bridge that bolted to the fork legs. It was supported by a pair of strip stays at the front and a stand with a single nut fixing at the rear. The mudguard and stays were altered in detail for 1947 while the stand was revised for 1948 when it fitted outside the fork lugs instead of inside and then continued in that form to 1955 and the end of the rigid models, having also been fitted to the sprung road singles.

The competition models had a light-alloy mudguard supported by a bridge riveted to it and a pair of loop stays. These went to the two mudguard ends and each had two cross-plates welded to it, each of these with two bolt holes. The parts were altered in detail for 1949 and the mudguard remained in use to 1957 and the loops to the end of the line. While the alloy blade saved weight, much of this went back on with lock-spreading plates which were also prone to corrosion.

The road machines were altered for 1950 with ribbed blades supported by a single tubular loop at the front while retaining the stand at the rear. For 1954 the mudguard was given flared ends with rolled edges and for 1955 it had a new shape and lost its front stay. This new form with the bridge valanced to the guard continued on the 1956 model with a minor revision. This reflected the appearance of a rear loop stay held to the mudguard by two fixings in place of the stand.

For 1958 the competition models were given a wider guard and this was used by the C, CS singles, CS twins and CSR machines for varying periods. It served the CS singles and twins till 1960, after which these had another form. The same change happened to the C models but not until 1964 while the CSR kept to the 1958 guard to the end of 1963, except for 1962 when the alternative was listed.

The standard road models had a deeper section mudguard for 1959 with a new rear loop stay. The valance was thus able to carry the registration number so the plate was no longer listed for these machines but the mudguards were listed with or without a suitable panel if in colour. The guard was shortened for 1961, although the stay remained the same, and formed to a D section for 1963 which did mean a new loop stay. This then remained in use on the Norton forks adopted for 1964, but with a new blade which had a separate bridge.

The CSR twin had a new, chrome-plated blade and stays for 1964 to suit the Norton forks and these had their own bridge, while others were used for the 745 cc CSR models. The 745 cc CS machines had chrome-plated parts and the standard model mudguards also had this finish from 1967 onwards.

The light singles began with a deeply valanced mudguard with integral bridge. This bolted to the fork legs via a clip and was supported by a rear loop stay. For 1960 the bridge became a separate part and the revised blade was also fitted to the 348 cc model which had its own bridge and stays to suit the Teledraulic forks fitted.

The S model had the same blade with a chrome-plated finish and this also went on the CSR up to 1965. This used the bridge and stays from the 348 cc machine and had a polished light-alloy blade for 1966, which was its final year. The CS also had an alloy mudguard and used one of the stays from the heavy singles range to support each end of it.

Rear mudguard

There was a good number of these and for nearly every year there was one for each marque as well as each model, the difference being the transfer fixed to the tail. There was little duplication of use of either the blades or the fixing stays or brackets, other than with the sprung singles and twins. These shared parts for the touring models as did some of the sports ones.

The rigid models began with a mudguard supported by a double stay, shaped into a vee, on each side. A separate lifting handle was also fitted and the rear number plate was held by four bolts. During 1947 this

was changed for a single bolt plate while for all the year the two stays and the lifting handle were formed into a single arch.

The parts were amended for 1949 and again for 1950 when the mudguards were ribbed. At the same time the rather awkward arch was revised into a rear loop-cum-lifting handle and two simpler stays, one for each

Sporting Matchless G15CSR twin for 1965 with rearsets but normal bars

side. The joint area between the two halves of the blade was revised and shrouded for 1951 and there were new parts for 1952. The stays and loop then continued as they were but the mudguard gained a flared end for 1954 and a further modification for 1955, the last year of the rigid frame.

The sprung road models began with a ribbed, well valanced mudguard held by a bracket at its front end and a top support on each side with these bolting to the subframe near the rear-unit mountings. The supports were amended for 1951 and again for 1953 when the mudguard tail was made detachable. There was a further change to the guard for 1955 when a rear

reflector was fitted but not to the other parts.

A new mudguard appeared for the new frame of 1956 with a new bracket but the old supports, which changed for 1957. The guard was made deeper for 1959 and changed to a D section for 1963 onwards, and for both changes there were new supports and bracket. The final arrangement continued on the touring twins till 1969.

The competition models and sports twins had light-alloy blades for most years and the first was supported by two loops. All the parts were altered for 1949 and again for 1950, after which they continued as they were till 1955. For the pivoted fork frame of the 1951

161

*The 1953 Matchless G80S with little chrome but a very
good paint finish*

competition models there had been another alloy
blade with a front end bracket and a support loop.
This bolted to the sub-frame to run back and round
the mudguard tail. The blade was shortened for 1955
and then for 1956 all the competition models had a
new pivoted-fork frame. The blades for C and CS
versions differed but the rear loops were the same for
1956. For 1957 the C models had another blade and
loop while the CS ones just amended the loop.

Both blades were made wider for 1958 and the C
model for trials had a bridge support added but used
the 1957 rear loop. It was revised into its final blade
form for 1959 but the rear loop continued to alter with
new ones for 1959, 1960 and 1964.

The CS parts also went on the twins in CS and CSR
form for 1958 and again the blade was wider and
supported by a bridge and the 1957 rear loop. The

parts all changed for 1960 and the new frame when a
bridge was added to the supports. The rear loop was
changed for 1963 and these parts then served the CS
singles to the end.

The CSR twins with AMC engines had a new
chrome-plated blade for 1964 which was held by twin
front brackets and twin rear support tubes. These
parts continued on the 745 cc tourer from 1965
onwards while the similar size CSR model kept to an
alloy blade. This was new, as was its bracket, and it
had one rear loop for 1965–7 and another from 1968.
The 745 cc CS twin kept to a chrome-plated guard but
with the CSR bracket and 1968 rear loop.

The light singles were much simpler with a deep
pressing, acting as the rear guard without any need for
stays or supports except on the CS models. These had
alloy blades held by a front bracket and rear loop stay.

ABOVE *An early G9 fitted out with Plessey radio gear for police use in 1951*

BELOW *First year for the competition singles was 1946 when this 16MC appeared*

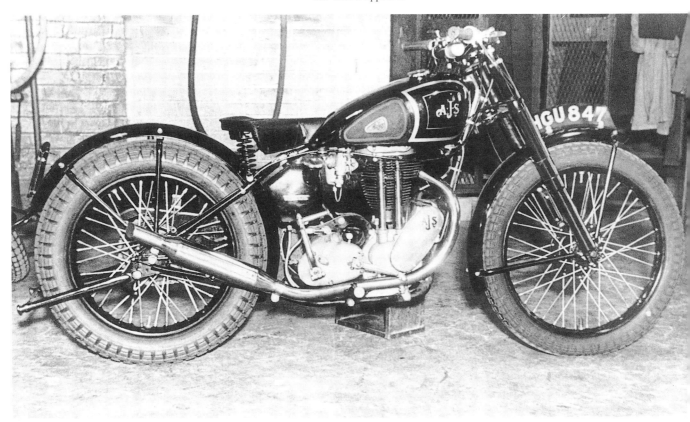

ABOVE *The 1963 G80CS was by then being outclassed by the lighter two-strokes but was still a nice motorcycle if you had the strength*

For the other models there was a mudguard each for the standard and 348 cc ones, a chrome-plated one for both the S and CSR models up to 1965, and a final alloy one for the 1966 CSR machines.

Front number plate

This is no longer a legal requirement in the UK but many owners like to keep it and either display the registration number or the model type and year. The original plate was amended for 1947 when a rubber bead was added between it and the front mudguard, and this arrangement was used by all the standard models up to 1958. The mounting brackets were exclusive to AMC, rather than being common to other marques of the period. After 1958 the side of the mudguard was used to carry the plate.

The competition models, including the CS light singles, had a different plate with a cut-out to clear the front stay loop and this part served all the singles and the sports twins to 1963. For 1964 these fitted the standard 1947 part while the 745 cc CSR twins were listed with this part, or another, new alternative.

Rear number plate

This is still required and is governed by local regulations which must be followed. In the early days the numbers were painted directly on to the plate but later came transfers, pressed-aluminium, plastic self-adhesive numbers and finally, the modern yellow reflective plate.

BELOW *Early twin was this 1950 AJS model 20 which differed from the Matchless in respect of seats and silencers as well as badges*

BOTTOM *One of the first of the 18CS models, in this case being tried by Harry Louis before shipment to California*

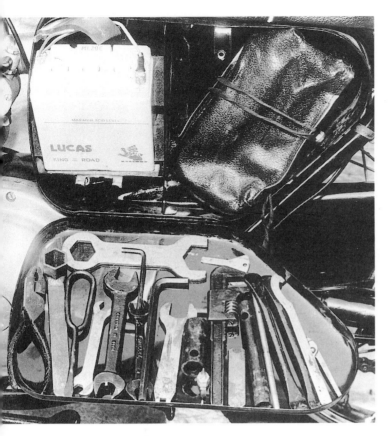

ABOVE *Toolbox and laid out tools for a 1960 model 31*

BELOW *The cylindrical toolbox used on the competition models from 1950 for some years*

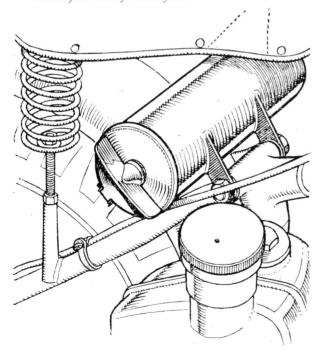

The original plate carried a round Lucas tail lamp and was boxed in to the rear mudguard. It was held by four bolts but during 1947 this changed to a single bolt. The plate was next altered for the rectangular rear lamp of 1949 and then for the ribbed mudguards of 1950 when an alternative was listed for the sprung road models.

It was amended for the rigid models for 1952 and for rigid and sprung machines for 1953 when an all-plastic rear lamp was fitted. These last plates were 8 in. wide and for 1954 only were joined by others of $9\frac{1}{2}$ in. width, which must have been for export use as they were not seen in the UK. Otherwise, the rigid one ran to 1955 and the sprung one to 1958. The latter was altered for 1959 to suit the deeper mudguard and again for 1963, for the D-section type adopted then. This last plate was not boxed in to the guard and was also fitted to the CSR twins from 1963 and the 745 cc CSR twins from 1965 onwards. The standard 745 cc twins had another plate, as did the earlier CSR twins up till 1962.

The competition machines had their own plate from the start and for 1950 it became a simple flat sheet supported by a strip bracket. The plate became 8 in. wide for 1952 and was amended for 1955. For 1954

The street scrambler G12CS from 1960 built for off-road use as well as on the tarmac

only, it was joined by one $9\frac{1}{2}$ in. wide, but otherwise continued in use to 1962 with a change of bracket for 1959. There was a new plate and bracket for 1963 and the plate changed again for 1964.

The light singles had their own plate to take the Wipac rear light and the original also went on the 348 cc models up to 1961. From 1962 another was used, while the CS machines had their own plate and used the 1959 competition model bracket from the heavy singles. From 1962 the CS model fitted the plate used by the CSR twin of that year.

Side and cover panels

Panelling first appeared in 1956 in two forms and came because the oil tank and toolbox had been altered in shape to suit the new frame of that year. One panel went across the frame, between the tank and toolbox, and was pierced for an air-cleaner hose. The second panel was only fitted to the twins and was held to the oil-tank side by two screws, but with an air gap to insulate it from the tank heat.

The centre panel was listed at first in two forms to suit the singles and twins. These were joined by two

more for 1958, with one for the CS singles and the other for the sports twins. All changed for 1960 when the frame was altered with one part for the road singles and another for all the twins, both touring and sports. All but the CSR changed for 1963, when a new tank and toolbox shape was introduced. For this, a two-part panel was used with one set for the singles and one for the standard twins. The CSR fell in line with this for 1964 and the machines continued in this manner till 1966. The panels were not used by the 745 cc twins.

The oil-tank cover began as a plain part but for 1957 was given a small pattern of ribs. This took the standard twins up to 1959, after which the cover was changed to suit the 1960 oil tank. It was modified for 1962 and then given a new shape for 1963 when the tank was altered.

The standard cover was joined by one for the sports twins for 1958 and this was amended in 1959 and 1962. It was altered to the final tank shape for 1964 and continued like that to the end of the AMC twins. The 745 cc twins in standard and CSR form both fitted the cover from the 1963 standard 646 cc twin.

On the light singles there was only a panel on the

left as the one on the right was, in effect, the toolbox. The left-panel shape was common to all models, except the CS, and all years with suitable changes to its colour and transfers.

Battery carrier

This can be one of the most heavily corroded parts on the machine due to the action of the battery acid when it fumes. Damage can be severe but all traces of the cause must be fully removed before the part is repaired and finished. It is then worth taking precautions to avoid the problem re-occurring.

The range began in the typical English style with the battery carrier on the left of the machine under the saddle. For 1948, the strap was chrome-plated and for 1949 the cvc was mounted from the carrier to sit just aft of it. The sprung singles and twins had their own carrier which went on the CS models for 1951 while the competition machines had their own part. An alternative was listed for the 1951 twins only.

The cvc became flexibly mounted for 1952 so there were three new carriers with one each for the rigid and competition models and one for all the sprung machines. The next change was for 1954 when the cvc was moved under the seat nose, so the carrier lost its support for this item. Finally, for 1955 the carrier mounting to the frame was simplified and one part served all models except the rigid competition ones which kept the 1954 item.

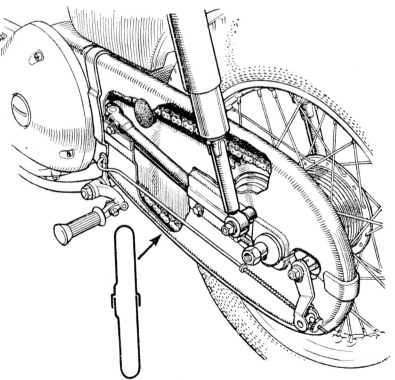

Rear chaincase provided for the light singles in 1958 as an option and commonly fitted to keep the chain happy

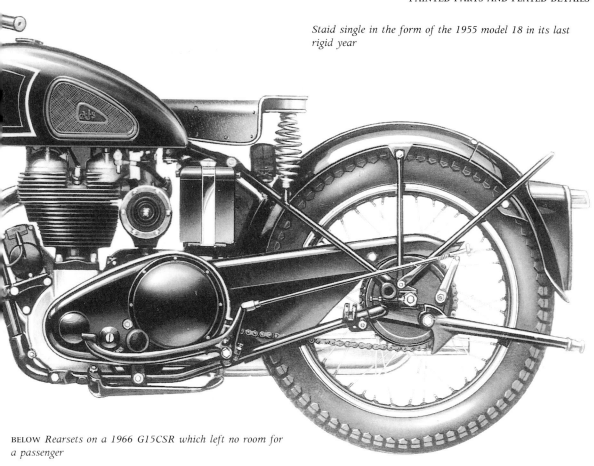

Staid single in the form of the 1955 model 18 in its last rigid year

BELOW *Rearsets on a 1966 G15CSR which left no room for a passenger*

The lightweight single in the form of the 348 cc Matchless G5 of 1960

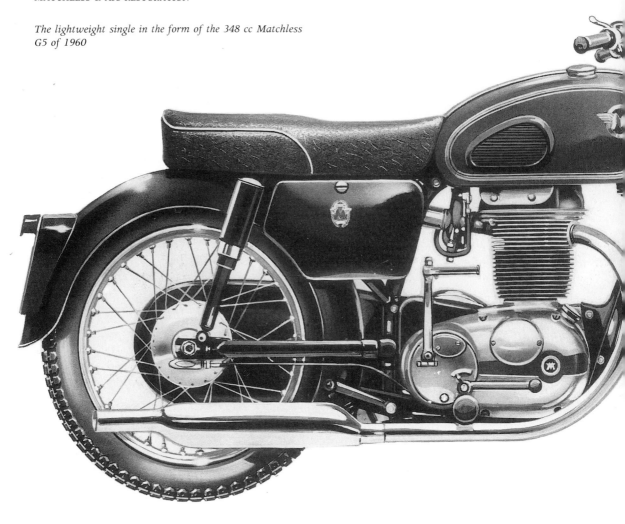

The form of the carrier changed for 1956 for the road models as it went inside the toolbox, although it still bolted to the frame of the machine on the left side. It continued in this way from then on until 1960 when the battery was reduced in size a little and the carrier became part of the toolbox with the battery held in it by a rubber strap. In 1963, the toolbox shape altered and the carrier was once more listed as an assembly with parts.

For the competition models an older form of carrier continued as one served for 1956–63. It also went on the CS single from 1956 and the CS and CSR twins for 1958. For 1960 the CS and CSR models had the carrier built in as for the other models, and for 1962 the CSR alone had a carrier. It was not altered to suit the new toolbox shape until 1964 but then went on to serve the 745 cc models in standard and CSR form.

The light singles had their own battery carrier hidden by the toolbox on the right of the machine. This served all models and years older than the CS, which had its own part which was altered for 1961.

Toolbox

This began in a traditional form fitted on the right of the machine above the upper chainstay. One box served all the rigid models to 1949 and for 1950 the road ones had a modified box set between the chainstays. At the same time the competition models changed to a tubular box set across the frame under the saddle.

The sprung singles and twins introduced for 1949 had twin toolboxes with one on each side in the bend of the sub-frame. The right side one alone was used on the CS singles from 1951 onwards. All the boxes changed for 1956 when the road models adopted a longer type which enclosed the battery and cvc as well as the tools. This was amended with ribs on the lid for 1957, to match the oil tank, and further altered to suit the new frame of 1960.

The competition models of 1956 had a single box on the left of the machine which was similar to the early sprung model boxes. It was modified for 1957 and on

the trials machines replaced by a tubular box for 1959. This sat just above the gearbox and remained in use till 1964.

The CS machines used the competition box for 1956–9 and then changed to the C-type tubular box for 1960–2. After that, another type was listed for the machine when used on the road, trail or in enduros. The 1956 toolbox also went on the CS and CSR twins up to 1959 but after that the longer type, as used for the standard models, was fitted.

The standard models had a new toolbox shape for 1963 which they kept from then on and this was used on the CSR twins from 1964. The 745 cc models had a similar toolbox but without the need to fit to a centre panel.

The light singles toolbox was the right-side panel which had the space for the tools formed on its inside. It had colour and transfer variations but the same shape remained common to all models and years other than the CS. This had a tubular box mounted low down behind the cylinder.

Chainguards

These are parts that are usually covered in grease, damaged by chains and bent or distorted by owners struggling to fit the rear wheel. So the first job is to clean what you have, which may take several sessions before you get all the grime off. Then repair and finish as any other steel item, making sure it fits as it should.

If there is any doubt, you need to fit gearbox and rear wheel back into the frame assembly to check that the chain will run clear of the guard regardless of suspension movement. If it touches anywhere it will wear the finish away in no time and always rattle.

Chainguard and chaincase types

The chainguard of the first post-war models had a deep inner wall to run behind the bottom chain run and also carried the type pump between two welded-on pins. It was amended for 1947, when its end was flared, and again for 1949 and 1951. It took its final form for the rigid road models for 1954.

The competition machines had another guard and for the rigid versions this was amended for 1950, 1951, 1954 and 1955. The sprung machines of all types had a chainguard with different shape and fixings which did not carry the tyre pump, and the original was altered for 1954 and 1955. It then continued on the road models for one more year and was then amended for 1958 when one was listed for the singles and one for the touring twins. A single revised chainguard was used for all the road models for 1963 and continued on the 745 cc models, although it was chrome-plated for the CSR versions of these.

The competition models had a common new part for 1956 and this then went on the CS singles from then on and the sports twins for 1958. These last changed to the touring twin guard for 1959, while the trials competition machines had a new guard for the same year and both then kept these items to the end.

The light singles had their own guard with one for the road models, which was chrome-plated for the S and CSR versions. The CS machines had their own guard which was amended for 1962.

A chaincase was available as an option for the light singles from their start in 1958. One assembly served both the standard and 348 cc models which were the only ones for which this was available. The option was not listed for the rest of the range until 1963 when it appeared in two forms to suit singles and twins. It continued on the first of these to 1966 and for the twins to 1967.

Footrests

These are nice, sturdy items that can usually be repaired. For once you have something to get hold of, and the correct shape can be restored by heating the

As the plate says it is a 16MS and is fitted with both the rear rack and panniers for 1956

bent area and knocking it back into place. Clamp it in the vice to do this. If it is worn away it may be necessary to build the material up again and then reshape it with a file.

The first post-war footrests were not a pair as one ran out from its mounting and the other stepped back. For 1947, two of the latter type were used, and for 1949 only, the mounting bar was made integral with the left rest and matched with a new right. The problems of removing a bent part forced a change for 1950 with a simple stepped-back footrest that went on both sides of the machine and served rigid and sprung models with single or twin engines. It was amended for 1953 because the chaincase was altered and this part was then used by all the road singles and touring twins to 1966. It also went on the CSR twins from 1961 onwards, the 745 cc standard twins and the 745 cc CSR twins for 1968–9.

The competition machines began with a pair of one-part for the 348 cc models and a second-part for the 497 cc ones. From machine 8000 of 1948 the latter became common to all. A new part was listed for both sides of the machine for 1950 and continued on the left for 1952 when the right one was altered. Both changed to one new part for 1953 and this went on both sides of the model from then till 1964.

The CS singles had their own rest which went on both sides for 1951, but only the left one for 1953–6. The right was altered for 1953 and again for 1956 when the frame was changed. There was one new part for 1957–9 and this also went on the CS twins in 1958. For both singles and twins there was a new left rest for 1960, but the singles went back to the 1957 rest for 1963 before changing to another form for the G85CS of 1966.

The CSR twins had their own rests for 1958 and

changed the left one for 1960. As mentioned above, they went over to the standard model part for 1961 and continued with this except for 1965–7. For these years folding rests were listed and another folding type was shown for the G15CS twin built from 1967.

On the light singles one footrest served both sides of all the road models while another pair was listed to the CS machines.

Footrest rubbers

These are best replaced, as new ones help to put the finishing touch on a restored machine. There was little change to the part over the years with one part serving all models, including the light singles, up to 1963. Another took over for 1964 and then ran on till the end.

Pillion rests

These may need to be straightened as well as cleaned, and particular attention should be paid to the pivots and threads. The pivot should be just tight enough to keep the rest in position without making it too hard to move.

The rests were always optional equipment and the first type was used up to 1955. For that year another part appeared for the sprung-frame models and was then listed alone up to 1962. It was joined by another for the sports twins of 1958, but both were superseded by a new part for 1963. Another was used by the 745 cc twins and a further part by the light singles.

The original footrest rubber also went on the pillion rest up to 1962, except on the light singles. These had their own part which went on all models from 1963 onwards.

Brake pedal

This is another part which is often damaged but is not too hard to restore. The pivot may well need attention which could involve machining and then fitting a bush, should it be worn. If bent, it will need to be heated before it can be straightened and worn surfaces can be built up and then filed to shape.

The original pedal was amended for 1950 and was used for both rigid and sprung singles with another for the twins. The sprung model types were both changed to a less curved form for 1955 but the rigid one stayed as it was for that final year. New parts went on both singles and twins for 1956 but from 1959 the singles fitted the same part as the twins. Both changed to another part with a stop-light screw boss for 1963 and this served all the singles and touring twins from then on.

The competition models had a pedal each for the C and CS singles at first and for the first of these there was a change for 1956. However, for 1959 it reverted to the original part and kept to this right through to 1964. The CS model changed for 1955 and then adopted the part used by the 1956 C machine and kept that from then on. Another pedal served the G85CS.

The 1956 C-machine pedal also went on the sports twins for 1958–63, after which they fitted the standard part. This was used by the 745 cc CSR twins for 1968 onwards but for 1965–7 these models fitted a different item.

On the light singles there was just one pedal listed and this was fitted by all models and years.

Rear brake rod

These need to be straight, and both the fork hole and adjuster thread must be in good condition. Any damage found needs to be repaired.

The original rod was altered for 1949 and again for 1950 when the original was used again for the competition models. The road machines had a change for 1955 and another for 1956 and the new frame. This rod was used by them till 1962, was altered for 1963 and returned for 1964 to the end.

The competition models had a rod for the CS models but they and the C type changed for 1956, and again for 1959. The C machines used the standard 1950 rod for that year and then returned to the original part for 1960 onwards. The CS machines went to the 1956 standard part and used that for singles and twins, including the CSR versions, from then on.

The light singles had one rod for the road models and another for the CS models. The latter was the original 1945 type.

Optional equipment

This included a rear carrier, panniers, locking bar, crash bars, legshields and a cowling at one time or another. As options, none are essential for a restoration but the fitment of one from the correct period can set off a machine very well.

A rear carrier was listed immediately after the war by using the army one and this continued for 1947 with its pannier lugs removed. It was amended for 1949, and then again for 1950 and 1951. A second part was added for the sprung singles and twins, while there were a special pair for the Swiss market in 1950 only.

The carrier was revised in form for 1956 and the new frame. It was positioned on the machine in an inclined manner and for 1958 it was joined by another part, which had its platform horizontal to the ground. Both were revised for 1959 but for 1960 there was just one new, inclined platform carrier to go with the new frame. It was listed up till 1962. The light singles had their own carrier listed for all the years.

Panniers were listed for 1945–6 and then dropped until 1951. They were available up to 1962 while the

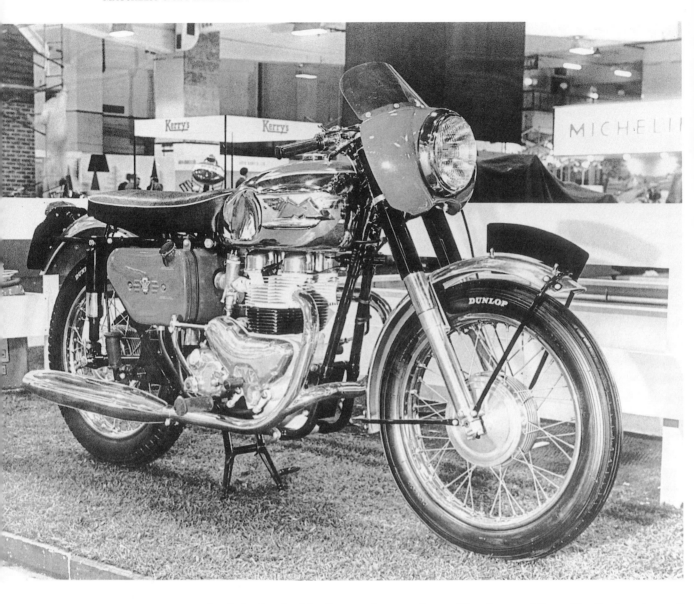

A 1962 G12CSR fitted with the short-lived headlamp cowl based on the ones used for road racing around that period

light singles had their own set from 1960.

The locking bar was introduced for 1953 and fitted over a lug on the lower steering crown once the bars were on full right lock. A small padlock was then used to retain the bar and fitted to a hole in the lug. The locking bar was listed up till 1962 and another appeared for the light singles in 1961.

Crash bars were listed for the heavy singles and twins from 1957 onwards and were joined by rear crash bars from 1963. Both, in various forms, then continued on to the end. Legshields for these models did not come until 1967 so up to then owners fitted proprietary parts. Bars for the light singles appeared in 1960.

The headlamp cowl was announced in May 1962 and was a fibreglass moulding with a fascia and a small screen. It was listed only for the CSR twins in red or blue to match the marque colour and was similar in shape to the front number-plate cowl fitted to the firm's racing singles.

Unlike them, it carried a rubber-mounted Lucas light unit and matching speedometer and rev-counter, plus ammeter and light switch. It was only offered for a brief period and did not appear in the 1963 parts list.

Oddments

These need to be seen to just as much as any other item. The parts list will show what is needed and all must be collected, checked, mended and finished just as any larger part. Their fit can be important as they may align other pieces, so care with these details can pay dividends.

12 Wheels and brakes

This is an area where a good few operations have to follow one another in a definite sequence, so an early start is advisable to avoid a hold-up later on when it may not be convenient. Once the machine is without wheels it becomes very hard to move about unless reduced to parts. It might be worth considering slave wheels if this is a problem for you.

Restoration begins by removing the wheels, taking the tyres off and separating the brake backplate from the wheel assembly. Each can then be dealt with in turn.

Spoking pattern and rim offset

The wheel assembly comprises the hub assembly, spokes, spoke nipples and rim. Before doing anything else, get your notepad out and measure the rim offset and draw the spoke pattern. This first is a vital piece of data and the second will give you real problems if you have to work it out from scratch. This can be done but it is not easy.

The rim offset is taken by placing a straight edge across the mouth of the brake drum and measuring from that to the edge of the rim. Just to make sure, also measure from a firm point at the other end of the hub and note the rim width. Take several measurements to see if there is any variation.

If the rim is buckled or has been removed from the hub, it is back to basics. You will have to work out where the rim should be in relation to the frame and you have two points of reference to help. First is that the wheels are normally central to the frame and forks. Second is the sprocket offset, which you can measure on the gearbox and wheel.

Alternatively, find another machine and check that.

You may have to measure another wheel if you start with the bare hub and don't know the spoking pattern, but with a complete machine you can make notes. Consider each side and start by checking the rim to see which way round it is. No problem with a full-width hub, but when it is offset the spoke lengths and angles differ from side to side.

Now note where the valve hole is and check that the spokes on either side run away from it to give the best access. If they don't the wheel has been built incorrectly at some time and you can expect to find most of the spokes bent near the thread. Note how the spoke to one side of the valve hole runs, whether its head points out from the wheel or into its centre, and any feature of the hub which will enable you to locate that spoke in the same hole.

Relating the rim, spoke lay and hub for that first spoke will give the key to the wheel build. From it the others will fall into a pattern. Working round the rim, the spokes will alternate from one side of the hub to the other. Every third spoke will be laid the opposite way to the first and its head will face in the reverse direction, unless straight spokes are fitted. Every fifth will echo the first in angle and lay.

To finish the notes for side one, you need to work out the spoke cross pattern. On one side a spoke may cross one running the other way two, three or four times. Note the position of the first spoke and the one that crosses it nearest to the hub. Trace it to the rim and note its position in relation to the outer end of the first spoke.

Now note how side two relates to side one. Don't forget you reverse things if you turn the wheel over. One spoke on side two will give you the start to the pattern, but check it out anyway as an extra precaution on your notes for side one.

Wheel dismantling

If you want to repaint the hub you will have to take the wheel apart and rebuild it later. Hence the notes above. The rim is removed by undoing all the spoke nipples which may be easy or could call for penetrating oil and a little heat. Note that there can be four types of spoke in each wheel with differences in length and head angle, so these points need checking. Keep the spokes in batches and note which goes where on your spoke diagram or you will have to sort that out as well. Note that for some wheels certain spokes cannot come away until others have been removed. This sequence must be known as the rebuild has to be done in the reverse order.

Norton hubs and wheels were used by AMC in their later years as shown here by a 1967 G15CSR, which also has engine and forks from the same source and a common gearbox

You now have a rim, batches of 20, 36 or 40 nipples and bundles of 20 or 40 spokes for the heavy singles and twins. Some of the light singles have batches of 9, 18, 27 or 36 spokes with 20 or 40 for the CS machines. Plus the hub assembly with attendant brake drum and the rear sprocket.

Hub, drum and rear sprocket

After the war AMC continued with their unusual design of wheel bearings with taper rollers, of which the actual spindle was the inner race. This design remained in use for the front hub into the 1960s but was replaced in 1949 at the rear. In other respects the hubs were normal, beginning as off-set and then changing to full width.

Regardless of type, the bearing retainers need to be removed, some having left-hand threads, and all the parts dismantled, cleaned and inspected. Before the spindle is removed the hub and brake drum should be checked for run-out but if there is any, it should not be corrected until the new bearings are in place.

In some cases the hub and drum were built up and the individual parts should be inspected. For others, the rear drum was in one with the sprocket and for this the whole part will need renewal if the drum is

scored or belled or the sprocket worn or hooked. The new part should be checked for true running when on its new bearings.

Where parts are not available it may be possible to skim the brake drum which will also deal with oval or belled drums. The sprocket teeth can be built up and recut by a specialist. The hub itself should be carefully inspected for damage or cracks. Repair may be awkward and must not be attempted unless you are confident that the result will withstand the load placed upon it.

The parts will need careful masking before finishing and the threads must be left clean or the locating rings may bind. Check this before the final assembly.

Front-hub types

AMC began with an offset, one-piece hub which contained a $6\frac{1}{2}$ in. diameter brake drum. For 1948 this was changed to 7 in. with $\frac{7}{8}$ in. wide shoes, and for 1950 the drum was made separate from the hub, of which three were listed.

A full-width hub with straight spokes was introduced for 1954 and the next year was replaced by a similar but narrower hub of barrel form. Both these kept to the 7 in. brake size and the second was used by the trials model to 1958, the CSR twin to 1963 and the other road models and the CS singles to 1962.

The trials model went to a $5\frac{1}{2}$ in. drum for 1959 to save weight and stayed with that from then on. The majority of the road models and the CS singles had a new hub with only five fins but wider $1\frac{1}{8}$ in. shoes for 1963, while the CSR twins kept the 1955 hub. All models, except the CS singles, changed to a Norton full-width hub with an 8 in. brake, $1\frac{1}{4}$ in. wide, for 1964 and this went on all road models from then on. The G85CS used the 1963 full-width hub with the fins machined away from 1966.

The light singles had their own full-width hub with 6 in. brake, 1 in. wide, and this served the standard, S and 348 cc models. The CS used the offset 1953 hub with 7 in. brake and the CSR had a full-width hub with 6 in. brake and $1\frac{3}{8}$ in. drum width, although the shoes were only $1\frac{1}{8}$ in. wide.

Rear-hub types

The hub itself was a spool at first, so all the spokes were the same, with the drum and sprocket in one and bolted to the spool. The drum was $6\frac{1}{2}$ in. diameter at first but increased to 7 in. and $\frac{7}{8}$ in. width for 1948. For 1950 either five or six bolts were used to join the drum and hub but from 1951 the five-bolt type was listed alone. This suited the wider hub introduced for 1950 when there were three listed, but this dropped to two for the following year.

The next change came for 1955 when a full-width

The simple drum brake fitted to all models for 1945–7

hub, to match the front, was adopted and, while still with a separate, one-piece, drum and sprocket, this too was a new part. This continued till 1963 for the road models and 1965 for the CS singles, but the trials machines changed to an offset hub with $5\frac{1}{2}$ in. diameter drum for 1959 onwards.

The road models went to the full-width Norton hub for 1964 with 7 in. drum and $1\frac{1}{4}$ in. wide shoes while the G85CS fitted the conical racing hub as used by the 7R and G50 with its $8\frac{1}{4}$ in. drum. The light singles had a full-width hub with 6 in. drum and 1 in. wide shoes for all road models. The sprocket bolted in place and the CS machines used the 1959 trials hub of $5\frac{1}{2}$ in. drum diameter but with both drum and sprocket separate parts.

Wheel bearings

The range began with the special taper rollers of which the spindle was part. At the front this was used for all models up till 1962, for the CSR twins the next year and the trials model for 1963–4. At the rear, the inclusion of the spindle as part of the bearing ceased after 1949 but the use of taper rollers continued for much longer.

The rear bearings became a pair of standard taper rollers and these were used by all models to 1962, for the CSR twin for 1963, the trials model for 1963–4 and the CS single for 1963–5. In every case, the bearings must be carefully adjusted as if too tight they will be ruined very quickly. The requirement is for 0.002 in. end float which should just allow perceptible rock at the wheel rim.

Do not allow the drag of the oil seal to disguise the

end float and be especially careful if you have the quickly detachable rear wheel which became an option for 1955. The spindle must be an easy sliding fit through both bearings, or one may be overloaded when the spindle nut is tightened.

The bearings were changed to ball races starting in 1963 and these were used front and rear by all road models from 1964 and the singles and standard twins for 1963. This also applied to the front of the CS single from 1963 onwards, but not the rear.

On the light singles all the road hubs turned on ball races but the CS was on rollers as it used hubs from the standard range.

All the races need to be a good fit in the hub and on the spindle. Except where it is part of the race the spindle is easy to replace if damaged, but for the hub it may be necessary to use Loctite to ensure the race does not move. Races must be fitted square and the drift or press used must bear directly on the race being inserted and not load the balls or rollers and their tracks.

Sometimes, with a ball race, the wheel spindle is tight once assembled. What can happen is that as you push the outer home the inner is held back by the spindle so it finishes out of line from its nominal position. To correct you use a hammer as a precision tool and just lightly tap in the required direction.

Brakes

All were single leading-shoe, but regardless of type they require the same attention. Strip, clean and examine for wear, damage, distortion or cracks. Repair as required. Check the fit of the backplate to the wheel spindle, the condition of the cams, the cam levers and the return springs. If the springs are tired, replace them.

You are likely to fit new brake shoes or to reline the ones you have. With the former, check that the brake drum is the standard diameter and has not been skimmed at some time. If it has not, still beware of pattern shoes as some have minimal lining material and will seem to be worn out even when new.

From 1948 AMC changed to this larger brake and used this two-bolt anchor for a short time

The taper-roller hub bearings used by AMC for many years and which, in some cases, used the spindle as the inner race

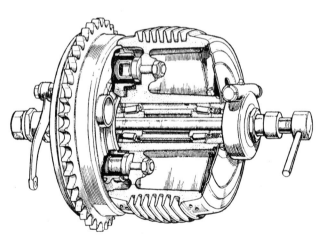

Section of the full-width AMC rear hub which shows the taper-roller bearings and drive pins from sprocket to hub

If you reline the shoes yourself you will need clamps to hold the liners in place, drill and counterbore to form the holes, and riveting tools. Work out from the centre and chamfer when finished.

Should you go to an expert he will, or should, want the wheel and backplate. He will check and skim the drum first if this is needed and then reline the brakes with oversize liners which can be turned down to fit. This was normal practice on racing machines when they all used drum brakes.

Front-brake types

The parts were to suit the brake size so most only altered for the 7 in. brake of 1948, the increased width of 1963 and the larger Norton brake of 1964. The cam lever varied to suit the backplate changes and it was this last that had the most alteration.

The first backplate was to suit the $6\frac{1}{2}$ in. brake and located to a stud in the fork leg. For 1948 the size increased to 7 in. and the backplate was held in place by two bolts in lugs on the leg. The plate itself was next altered to a torque-arm location for 1949 on the twins and 1950 on the singles, with a separate shoe pin appearing for 1952.

For 1953 the backplate was amended so that the cam lever pointed forward while remaining low down on the plate. It was further amended to suit the full-width hub of 1954 and the barrel-shaped hub of 1955. The backplate was revised for 1956 so the cam lever was at the top of the plate, just behind the fork leg, although it continued to point forward.

The backplate remained in this form to 1962 for all models and 1963 for the CSR twin, when the rest of the range had a new plate to suit the hub with five fins. For 1964 all the road models went to the Norton backplate while the CS single continued with the 1963 part and the trials model with a $5\frac{1}{2}$ in. backplate with anchor bolt that it had used since 1959.

The light singles had their own sets of parts, except for the CS which used the 1953 brake, but there was variation in the backplate and hub cover to suit the standard, 348 cc and CSR applications, sizes and front fork types.

For any model fitted with the Norton front brake, the two leading-shoe option becomes available and featured a backplate with an airscoop and three air outlets, a rod link between the two cam levers and a separate cam and pivot for each shoe.

The Norton backplate and cams were modified for 1972 when a support plate was added inside to brace the cams and pivots to one another. Reports suggest that the Norton brakes varied a good deal in performance but that they could be improved. The first step was to bush the centre of the backplate so it was a good fit on the spindle. Next was to cut the air scoop off and to weld or blank off the hole as this stopped water getting into the brake. The air scoop would direct water in, even if its intake was blanked off, hence the need to remove it entirely.

Further possibilities were to fit a brake stiffening kit which helped to stop parts moving under load or to fit AM4 green linings. These had to be fitted by an expert, machined to suit the drum diameter and well backed off on their leading edge to avoid grabbing. It was suggested that the two combined could be too much for road use. The stiffening kit plus a 30 mm longer cam lever arm to the cable can also make the brake more effective.

Rear-brake types

There were few changes for the rear brake once its size had increased to 7 in. for 1948. The backplate was altered for 1951 and 1956, the latter when the adjuster moved to the front end of the brake rod.

The trials model altered to a $5\frac{1}{2}$ in. brake for 1959, while the road machine fitted the Norton one with $1\frac{1}{4}$ in. wide shoes from 1964. The CS singles kept to the 1955 hub and 7 in. brake to 1965 but the G85CS used the $8\frac{1}{4}$ in. drum of the old conical racing hub from 1966.

The light singles all had a 6 in. brake with 1 in. wide shoes for road use while the CS model fitted the $5\frac{1}{2}$ in. brake from the 1959 trials machine.

Spokes and nipples

These need to be straight and with good threads. It is false economy to replace only some if more than one or two are past redemption; better to respoke completely. Carefully check the length, gauge and head angle you require before shopping and inspect what you buy to make sure you get what you want.

If the spokes are being replaced, a new set of nipples are worth getting as well. Remember that their diameter is to suit the spoke gauge and that the rim holes must suit.

It is possible to buy stainless-steel spokes, although opinions vary as to how this material can cope with the bending of the head angle and the stress pattern to which spokes are subjected. If made to really close tolerances they should be no trouble, but avoid anything cheap or poorly finished.

Wheel rims

All AMC models had steel rims of the WM section form. Diameters used were 17, 18, 19 and 21 in. and width numbers 1, 2 and 3. All the heavy singles and twins had 40 spoke holes, while the road light singles had 36. Security bolts were listed for the competition models on front and rear wheels, while light-alloy rims were listed as an option for the CSR twins in 1967–8.

If the rim is damaged or rusty it will have to be replaced as you are unlikely to find anyone who can repair the former or is willing to strip and replate to correct the latter. Thus you will need a new rim and the first point to consider is the tyre size you will finally fit. In many cases it will be worth going to a WM3 section rather than keeping to the listed WM2 if you wish to fit a fatter tyre. If you do this, remember it will affect the offset dimension, which will need changing by half the alteration in rim width.

Next is the dimpling and the holes. For a really strong wheel the spokes must lay at the correct angle in both directions and to achieve this the rim must be

Full-width rear hub as used by the larger AMC road models for many years and here seen on a 1960 model 31

pierced to suit. You also need holes for the tyre valve and any security bolts. Inspect the join in the rim as unless it is smooth you will never get the wheel to really run true.

The rims used are set out in Appendix 11, along with the tyres fitted to each model and some modern equivalents.

The rim finish was either painted, painted and lined, chrome-plated or the same with a painted, lined centre. Unless you are very sure that you can produce the painting and lining really well, send it to an expert. It is an area where any flaw will be only too obvious, so the cost will be worth it.

Wheel rebuilding

This is an area that many people fight shy of, but with care and patience good results can be obtained. Your notes will make the job much easier and should be consulted for the order of assembly and the precise location of each item. The rim must be the right way round.

Simply fit the first spoke and start its nipple so it cannot shift and scratch the rim. Then continue this process until you have all in place. It should be obvious if you have made a mistake as either spokes won't connect at all or they will be at the wrong angle. As long as spoke one is correct, the rest will fall into place.

You now have to true the wheel and could consider sending the assembly to an expert for this final important stage. Or you can do it yourself. Set the

ABOVE *A 1952 AJS model 18S which had offset hubs among its features*

BELOW *One type of AMC brake shown with collar which had slots to compensate for lining wear*

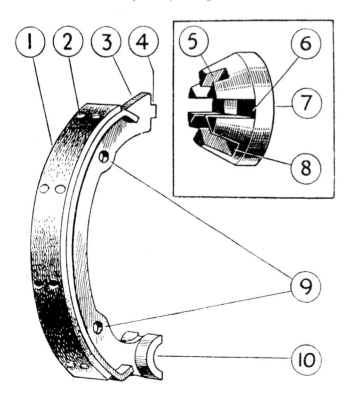

wheel vertical with the spindle held so you can spin the rim. Place a marker clear of the rim and spin it to check it runs true. Adjust spokes to suit, but work to get the radial position correct first and then go on to deal with the sideways error. If you start with a good rim and work carefully you should not have much trouble. Make sure every spoke is nicely tensioned without being overstrained.

Tyres, tubes and rim tapes

Your first problem could be finding something to fit. Much easier with some models than others. You now have the choice of 'old-fashioned' sizes (or some of them), more up-to-date low profile tyres or the latest metric offerings which are low profiles with their inches translated into millimetres.

Regardless of which you decide on, do fit a rim tape in good condition after you have checked the spoke nipples for protruding spoke ends. A new inner tube really is mandatory, don't even think of patches. The tyre itself must suit the rim section and the front and rear must be compatible. The faster the machine, the more important the tyres and their type, but they must never be ignored.

ABOVE *Rear end of a 1962 AJS single so it is either a model 16 or 18 but the cycle parts were common*

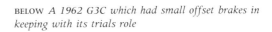

BELOW *A 1962 G3C which had small offset brakes in keeping with its trials role*

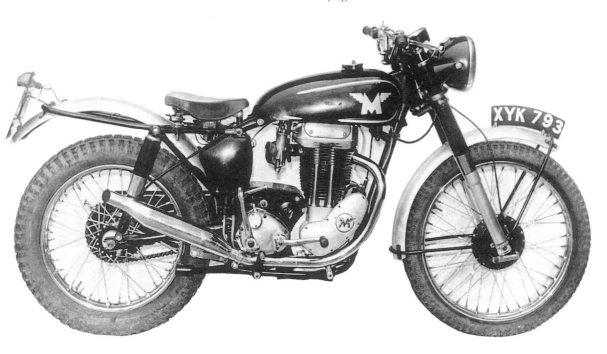

Norton brakes on a 1964 Matchless G3 which also had Norton forks

If you fit modern tyres you must make certain that there is ample clearance for the fatter section in all positions of the rear suspension. Fit them with care and use your slim, smooth, polished tyre levers. Don't forget the security bolt. Do forget the tyre pressure table in the old manuals which has no relevance to modern tyres. Establish the wheel loading and check tyre data tables for the correct pressure. Check the rolling diameter, or revolutions per mile, for the old tyre against the modern replacement, in case it affects the speedometer reading to any real extent.

13 Cables, controls and instruments

There are few things that look worse on a restored motorcycle than cables drooping in loops, obviously far too long, or ones with the adjuster screwed right out and hanging on the last thread. There is nothing more dangerous than cables that are tight and which could be pulled by the forks as they move.

The control cables should be the proper length, be routed correctly and neatly clipped out of harm's way and in correct adjustment. They should also be of the correct gauge for the job or the throttle will feel heavy and the front brake full of sponge.

Every cable is an assembly of inner, outer, outer ends and wire nipples at a minimum and normally all have at least one adjuster in their length. To these parts end stops can be added and fittings to attach the cable to its lever and the machine. In just about all cases the outer length determines the sweep of the final job while the inner must be chosen to suit the wear on the parts and the length of adjustment available.

Each end fitting needs to be checked over and repaired or replaced where needed. This operation should include any plating required. Nipples may be re-used but must be fully cleaned first so it is best to remove all the old solder using heat, so you can assess the condition of the part properly. If beyond repair they should be replaced. If the exact size is not available, it may be machined from another, larger, nipple. Do make sure it is a good fit on the cable—free to slide into place but no more.

Soldering

This is the technique used to attach the nipple to the wire and the secret of success is clean parts. Solder will not adhere to surfaces that are dirty, tarnished or greasy, but is no problem on a clean surface.

The tools you need are soldering iron, solder and flux. The first may be electric, heated over a gas flame or heated by butane. The slim type used for electrical work will not have enough heat for cables and something of 60–70 watts is necessary. If you use a gas flame, first clean up the iron tip with a file and let the flame play on the iron an inch back from the tip to keep it clean. When hot it can be dipped in flux to remove any oxidation and then given a thin coat of solder.

The solder required comes in a stick. Do not use flux-cored electrician's solder as it is not up to the job, being designed for electric wires, not steel cables. Use plumber's solder instead. The flux can be a paste in a tin or a liquid. My own preference is for the first as it is convenient to be able to open it and dip the iron or cable in. A match is handy for putting flux on to the area where it is needed.

To cut an inner cable to length you use sharp, heavy-duty cutters or a cold chisel and block or a hacksaw. Before cutting, you must tin the cable to stop it unwinding and the process is the same as any soldering. First clean the wire really well, secondly, tin the iron and thirdly use the iron to tin the wire, adding solder if needed. Keep it to a minimum and try to avoid blobs.

You can now cut the wire and solder a nipple on the end. To do this successfully you have to splay the wire ends out to sit in the countersink in the nipple and this operation can be done as follows. Clamp the wire vertically in the vice with the nipple sitting on top of the vice jaw. Before holding the wire firmly, slide it down to about level with the top surface of the nipple. Tighten the vice but don't crush the cable, then tap the wire top with the ball end of a light hammer to splay the strands.

Now hold the wire lightly in the vice with a clothes peg between the nipple and the vice jaws. Leave the vice slack enough for you to pull down on the wire. Tin the iron and apply solder to the nipple to build up as required. While it cools keep a light pull on the wire and watch. The surface appearance will change as soon as it hardens. Leave for a short while and give it a good tug. Better it flies off in the workshop than on the road. File to shape, making sure it fits its lever and can turn if necessary.

Cable making

There are two ends to a cable, so there are two soldering jobs to do. As there are at least three, and

ABOVE *Nice straight bars on a 1965 G15CSR fitted with instruments side by side with light switch between them and ammeter in the shell*

BELOW *First post-war controls were even more congested on the bars with magneto advance and valve lifter, as seen on this 1946 AJS single*

sometimes up to six, cables to do, it takes some time to make a full set from scratch.

Start with the outer and determine its run and thus its length. Fit its ferrules, having checked that they in turn will fit their housings at both ends. Solder on one nipple to the inner and assemble to the outer, complete with all fittings. Some owners like to lubricate the cable at this point but this practice means that the end has to be cleaned again. My own preference is to assemble, clean, solder and then oil.

In either case, the important aspect is to get the inner wire length correct. To do this, connect the already soldered end and offer up the other. No need to clip anything to the frame or even have the parts on the machine at this stage, as long as the operation at the ends is correct. Set the adjusters to suit the controls. Thus, screw in the front brake adjuster if the brakes have been relined as movement will all be in one direction. The clutch is better in mid-travel as this will allow for wear or swelling plates if you have the latter problem. The throttle, air and magneto should be set to allow the controls to work to their inbuilt stops without the adjusters hanging out of their housings.

Now solder the second nipple in place and clean it up. The cable can now be lubricated and the only way to be sure the oil has gone all the way through is to pour it in one end until it comes out of the other. Funnels formed round the end are a common suggestion but my own method is to use a pressure device which goes round the end and is pumped up with a bicycle pump. Rather messy but very effective and there are others available.

Controls

The handlebar these fit to varied to a degree and in later years was extended to include western, continental and sports styles. The original type was altered for 1951 when a tapped hole appeared next to the twistgrip for a horn button. It was amended for 1954 and the next year joined by another bend for the CS models. The latter went on the trials machine for 1956 when the rest of the range no longer needed the horn button hole as this control was combined with the dipswitch.

The western bars appeared in the lists in 1958 and the Continental ones the next year when there was a new bend for all the competition models. The CSR twins had a new bend for 1962 and there was a suitable downswept one for the sports edition of the 348 cc singles that year. The bars for the road singles and standard twins were altered for 1963 and again for 1964 and the Norton forks when the same part also went on the CSR twins. A trio of bends served the 745 cc twins in standard, CS and CSR forms with the last available in low or lower styles to suit the rest of the machine's control layout.

The light singles had their own bend for the standard models and another for the S and CSR versions. The CS used the 1959 competition bend and the 348 cc machines were fitted with the 1955 bend from the heavy CS single.

The controls also varied over the years and a careful study of the parts list needs to be made to ensure the correct item. Some machines had two controls mounted together and these need extra attention. Each control needs to be stripped, cleaned, inspected, renovated as required and assembled. Care will be rewarded by smooth operation and pleasant feel. Twistgrip and left-bar grips should be replaced if required and the right part will enhance the final result.

The handlebars themselves may well have been changed or bent. If the former is the case, the criterion is whether they are comfortable for you, the new owner, or whether you want to change them back to the original kind. If they are bent, much the same applies but beware of straightened bars as they have been known to snap due to the metal being stretched.

Instruments

The ammeter has been mentioned which leaves the speedometer and rev-counter. Repair entails instrument mechanic skills and tools for the parts are smaller and lighter than the general run of motorcycle items. A magnifier and tweezers to hold things are well worth having. Treat the scale face with care but repaint the needle if necessary.

Two types of mechanism were used in the speedometers and rev-counters fitted by AMC and the chronometric type were superseded by the magnetic in 1964. The former was generally held to be the more reliable in the long term but is a complex mechanical device that just became too expensive for a mass-produced product. It has a camshaft, balance wheel, gears, levers and springs. To get at these, you first have to unscrew the bezel ring without marking it, which will then allow the works to be removed.

If you are an instrument fitter you should be able to strip, repair and rebuild a chronometric speedometer. If you are an instrument mechanic it could be as well to stop at the mileage recorder, which is easier to work with, although it still needs delicate care.

The later magnetic type is easier to work on, but only once you get inside it for the bezel is rolled on. This means care and maybe a special tool to unroll it off plus another to replace it. Once inside, it is much less complex but just as delicate as any other.

From the point of repair the rev-counter is simply a speedometer mechanism minus the distance recorder. The case is basically the same and only the dial differs, having its own calibration.

Along with the instrument head, its mounting and its drive must be considered. The first must be in good order and the second comprises the cable and the drive box. The cable needs to be inspected and replaced if either inner or outer are damaged while the drive box must operate smoothly. For all models and years the speedometer was driven from the rear wheel but the rev-counter drive came from a camshaft end. One was listed from 1960, but only for the twins, and later there was one for the Norton engines.

Speedometer types

The first point on any speedometer is the direction of rotation of the needle, which must match the cable. Next is the maximum scale reading, then whether in miles or kilometres and, most important, the revolutions-per-mile figure.

This is normally written on the scale just under the part number and for many models a figure around 1600–1700 can be expected if it is calibrated in miles, reducing to circa 1000 for the metric measurement. This is also the cable speed in rpm at 60 mph by definition, as at that speed one mile takes one minute to travel so if the cable turns, say, 1620 times in the distance, it had done the same in the time.

The final points in speedometer selection are the presence of total and possibly trip distance recorders, the method of returning the trip to zero and the mounting of the instrument.

BELOW *The handlebar layout for 1948 when there were four fixings for the bars*

ABOVE *Twins had many common parts with the singles so this 1952 model 20 was much as the sprung AJS singles*

BELOW *Bar layout for the 1965 G12 which kept controls to a minimum and set the speedometer in the headlamp shell*

The speedometer itself was listed in mph and kph forms for most years and the type was changed for 1955 when it went into the headlamp shell of the road models. Both these were of the 120 mph or 180 kph maximum scale reading, while the light singles managed with 80 or 100 mph heads. All changed to the magnetic type in 1964.

When hunting for a replacement speedometer, most of the requirements are easy to determine and to check, except for the important revs-per-mile needed to match the machine. For rear-wheel-driven machines the factors are the tyre revs-per-mile and the ratio between wheel and cable. The latter is controlled by the speedometer gearbox and the ratio is usually around 2:1. If either change so does the speed of the instrument cable, so adjustment is needed to allow for a change of tyre size or another gearbox.

The optimum cable speed can be found by calculation using the data available for the model in question, but only applies if the machine is to standard specification in respect of the features that affect it. If all is well, this is the figure to seek on the replacement speedometer, or something close to it.

On occasion, the calculation has to be used in reverse. If a good speedometer is to hand, but with the wrong cable speed, it may be possible to achieve the correct readings by using an alternative wheel gearbox. Calculators make it easy to do the sums once the data has been collected.

Rev-counter types

Both chronometric and magnetic types were used on the twins, all driven from the camshaft. The fitment first appeared as an option for 1960 when the drive gearbox was bolted to the engine and driven from the left end of the exhaust camshaft. On the Norton engines it came from the timing side and the cover

ABOVE *This 1967 model 33 is fitted with twin instruments and raised bars*

specified with this arrangement was the pre-1958 type with the early pressure-release valve. A blanking plate was also listed to cover the hole left if the gearbox was removed later.

Instrument-bracket type

At first the speedometer was mounted on a small bracket bolted to the top of the forks and it stayed there for all the competition models where these had an instrument. From 1955 the road models had the speedometer mounted in the headlamp shell and held by a bracket, and this arrangement continued to 1966 for the AMC-powered models. Those with a Norton twin engine had the speedometer mounted on a bracket above the forks and this extended to include the rev-counter when required. The light switch then went between the two instruments.

The original bracket was used by the road models to 1951 and for the competition ones to 1954. The replacement for the road machines continued on the competition ones in 1955 but was altered for 1957. It later went on the CS twins when these were fitted with road equipment, as well as the CS singles and trials models, but these last reverted to the original bracket from 1959. The CS models had a new part for 1961 and this stayed in use for them from then on.

When the rev-counter option was introduced for the CSR twins in 1960 it came with a bracket to support both instruments. The kit also included a new headlamp shell of the older style with just ammeter and light switch mounted on it. This kit was listed till 1962.

Another bracket was listed for the twins with Norton engines and was finished with chrome-plating for the CSR models and black for the others.

This model 33 is a 1965 model but is fitted with the petrol tank from the previous year

14 Petrol tank

This has already been mentioned in Chapter 8 and the tank truly is the crowning glory of any motorcycle, so its finish is important if you want the machine to look nice, but not to the extent that it does not match the rest of the machine. If the general paintwork is reasonable but a touch shabby, a super tank job will stand out and show up against it. Maybe better to leave the tank to blend in with the rest, or you may find yourself renovating all the paint you meant to leave alone for a season or two.

Any tank must be checked out for damage which could be dangerous. This means looking for splits and cracks, checking brackets, examining tap bosses and badge screw threads, and looking closely at the tank bolt holes in the base. If bolts of too great a length have been used or washers left out at any time, the base of the threaded hole may have been lifted so a small crack exists. All these faults need to be corrected.

The fit of the tank cap should also be checked early on in case attention is needed in this area. Where there is no real damage but the tank interior is rusty this needs to be removed as far as possible. If left, either the rust will block the carburettor or the rust area will develop a leak, or both. To remove the worst of the rust, drop a handful of small nuts and bolts or sharp stones into the tank and give it a good shake. Then wash out well. After this, a swill with a rust inhibitor fluid is well worth the trouble and, when the finish is complete, the inside should be treated with Petseal. This two-part liquid forms a coat on the inside of the tank and seals any small pinholes or doubtful area, so is well worth using in any tank which is suspect. However, do look on it as an extra insurance and don't expect it to hold a cobweb of steel together with petrol in it.

The tank's appearance is dependent on its external shape and if dented it will require attention. This is specialist work as has already been mentioned and usually entails cutting the tank open for access and rewelding it afterwards. Before deciding what work is needed, first remove all the loose items from the tank such as taps, cap, badges and panels. Then examine it to establish if it has any filled patches. If it has and you want a good job, they must be cleared away.

Work on the tank, even if minor, usually means a welding torch and there are many horror stories on the subject. The problem is removing all the petrol and the fumes before the torch is lit up. Methods used are to wash it out with water or to allow a car exhaust to flow into it, or both of these. After this, many experienced workers will stand well back, light the torch and point it into the tank. The theory, and it works, is that if there is any vapour left you burn it there and then while expecting a bang.

You may not be disappointed, in which case you will remember to wash the tank out better next time. What you avoid with this method is a bang when welding close up to the tank.

Tank finish

This can simply be paint, with the style coming from the badges and trim, or paint plus lining, or two colours of paint plus separating line, or, worst of all to cope with, chrome plate plus painted panels and lining.

This last was used from 1949 to 1956 and is very specialized. The sequence of jobs is plate, paint and line and a good job will be expensive. It will also be worth the money.

As with any finish, preparation is all and for other than plated tanks follows the same lines as any other steel item. The exception is the avoidance of polyurethane lacquer which would react with spilt petrol to lift the paint. Otherwise, the final result will simply reflect the care with which the metal surface has been prepared and the skill with which the paint is applied, rubbed down and polished up. As with mudguards a brush finish can be fine as long as you can keep the dust off it. Care will be repaid by a smooth, glossy surface. An internal coat of Petseal may be a good idea, depending on what you discovered during your early examination. Protect the tank finish while applying, as a dent at this stage could be annoying.

Nice lines of the 1954 G9 are set off by the tank, seat and megaphone silencer

Tank types

This is a complex section as the tanks often varied a little between the marques as well as between singles, twins and competition models. In addition, there were often options which began simply but became complex for the 1959–62 period.

The post-war models began with a 3-gallon tank, which went on both makes and all machines with just a change of paint, lining and marque transfer. This tank remained in use on the AJS machines up to 1948 but the Matchless ones were modified for 1947. This change was to provide four tapped holes to take the flying wing badge used instead of a transfer, but the selection of 3BA screws to hold it in place was less than helpful.

The first option appeared in 1948 when a chrome-plated finish with painted, lined panels became available but only for export. This practice continued up till 1956 but the home-market tanks stayed with their paint and lining alone. All were new for 1949, thanks to a new bayonet-type filler cap, and the plated Matchless tank went on the new twin as well as the export singles. The AJS twin had its own 4-gallon tank.

Up to this point the competition models had used the standard model tanks but for 1950 they were given smaller ones which managed without kneegrips. These tanks were altered for the next year when the AJS one was fitted with an oval tank badge and the Matchless changed its transfer for a plated flying M. They were also joined by two more tanks for the CS singles and for 1952 all four had new badges, but the tanks stayed as they were, and also for 1953.

The 1949 road tanks were amended for AJS in 1951 to suit the oval tank badge and again for 1952 along with Matchless that year for the new badges which were a metal 'AJS' and a round Matchless with wings. The twin tanks copied this with AJS continuing to fit a 4-gallon tank while Matchless used the smaller one from the singles. All models were amended for 1953.

There were changes for 1954 with the twins and 497 cc road singles fitting a $3\frac{3}{4}$-gallon tank and a round plastic badge was incorporated on the AJS tanks. the 348 cc singles stayed with their 1953 tank that year but fitted the larger one from 1955. While the Matchless models continued with their round, winged badge (now also in plastic), the AJS one came in two forms. One was in silver with chrome-plated screws for use on the plated tanks, while the other was gilt with bronze screws and went on the painted tanks.

The twin tank continued to be chrome-plated but this remained an option for the singles till 1956. For that year the 593 cc twins had tanks with plated sides, while those for the 498 cc models kept to their earlier style. For 1957 the twins changed to painted tanks with separate, chrome-plated, side panels and the tank in black was common to both marques of the 498 cc machine. The 593 cc versions differed due to their colour and this arrangement continued for 1958. Meanwhile, the standard singles continued as they were up to 1959 but from 1957 with an option of the painted tank with separate side panels finished in chrome plate. They also had a panel in a contrasting colour for 1958 only.

The competition model tanks changed for 1954 when they were all equipped with a hinged, wing-nut

The 1958 model 14 AJS with its apparent unit construction engine

filler cap and, as standard, were of 2¼-gallon capacity and in light alloy. They had no kneegrips and the marque name was by transfer with tanks for C and CS models in each make. All continued for 1955 but for the next year one 2-gallon tank became common for both C and CS models of each marque. These again had no kneegrips, were in light alloy and continued as they were for 1957 when there was an option for the CS models. This was the standard size tank finished in black to take the chrome-plated side panels to suit road or enduro use. There was another light-alloy standard tank for 1958–9, still of 2-gallon capacity and in black, without kneegrips, plus another for 1958 in steel of the same size, as well as a larger road tank in colour. The year 1958 also saw the first CS twin appear and as standard this had the 2-gallon steel tank fitted, although the larger road style option was available. The CSR of the same year came with this fitted as standard, complete with its colour finish and chrome-plated side panels.

More variety in colour came for 1959 and the tank sizes increased for the twins, although the standard road singles remained with their 1954 tanks. These were also available in single or two-tone colour, as were the larger tanks fitted to the twins. The competition singles stayed with their 1958 alloy tank as standard but had options of the same size tank in colour, or a larger one, still in alloy, in the standard black. The CS twins also kept their 1958 tanks as standard with coloured options in two sizes.

Most of the tanks were changed for 1960 to suit the new frame with a considerable list of options. In part, this came from the listing of standard and de luxe twins with different finishes, plus that of the CSR, with most options for each model. The plated side panels also remained and where these were used the tank, even when in the same colour, had another part number as the lining differed. With two marques and different tanks for singles and twins it must have been a production nightmare.

The trials models alone kept to their earlier tank with the 1958 one continuing in use although joined by an array of options in black or colour, steel or alloy and three capacities to add to the confusion. The CS singles made do with a mere three options for each marque and these were also options for the CS twins.

Matters simplified for 1961, when the tank badges were made larger, with the standard tank common to both singles and twins. Another with plated side panels was an option and standard for the de luxe twin, while the CSR kept to its coloured tank as standard. Various coloured and two-tone finishes continued to be offered, albeit with the colours reversed on the tanks. The competition models stayed as they were.

There were new badges and tank mountings for 1962 when the chrome-plated side panels and two-tone finishes were dropped. Options were much reduced with just the standard CSR tank, also used by the sports 348 cc single, offered for the rest of the road range. There were specific tanks listed for the USA with one for the CSR and one for the other road machines. The CS single continued with its 1960 tank, which it was to keep for one more year, while the trials model had a new and final tank plus a colour option. One two-tone option hung over from 1961, no doubt to clear stocks.

For 1963 the road tanks had recesses formed in them with the kneegrips stuck in place. One tank was for the CSR model and another for the rest of the road

Famous flying M used by Matchless for many years and here seen on a 1949 G3LC

range and these continued on till 1966 with a badge change for AJS in 1965 and for Matchless during that year. The CS single tank was altered for 1964 and again to suit the G85CS of 1966. There was another tank for the models with the Norton twin engine which was joined by an alternative for the CS twin of 1967. This last went on the CSR for 1968.

The light singles had their own tanks with painted finish. The standard tank was altered for 1960 when it also went on the 348 cc models and was joined by two options, in black or coloured with plated sides. The options continued till 1962 and the coloured and plated one was fitted as standard to the S models.

These, and the standard and 348 cc machines, had a new style for 1962 with the tank in colour with a broad white band running along each side. An alternative in the same style was listed for the standard model for the USA but the CSR had its own style. This plated more of the tank side to produce a different effect and was used by that model alone. The CS models had their own tanks which were in colour and served all years.

ABOVE *Zig-zag tank lines and a diamond-shaped badge were both features of this 1966 model 31*

Filler cap

This began as a type with large finger grips on the outer part. When turned it unclamped three fingers from inside the tank neck which thus allowed the cap to be removed. It was amended for 1948.

The cap type changed for 1949 when a quarter-turn, bayonet one was introduced and remained in use for nearly all the range, including the light singles, from then on. Exceptions were the competition models from 1954–65 which had a hinged wing-nut cap, whose internal mechanism was much as that of the 1945 one. It went on the C singles and CS twins and singles but not the CSR twins. These last had another cap type for 1968 while the G85CS of 1966 had a snap action racing filler cap.

Tank badges

Handle these with care as they are often fragile. Check that they are not cracked or damaged, and fit as they should. Make sure the fixing screws, which were 3BA for most years, fit and don't bottom in their holes.

The first post-war models just had tank transfers and this practice continued on AJS machines till 1950. Matchless changed to a chrome-plated, flying M badge for 1947 and used this up till 1951. It went on the competition ones as well, except in 1950 when they had a transfer.

For 1951 all AJS models had an oval badge but both marques changed for 1952. AJS changed to a badge with its letters on a bar while Matchless fitted a round metal badge with flying wings. Both stayed in use for 1953 except for AJS export models, which had the 1951 oval badge.

There were new plastic badges for 1954 but only for the road models as the competition ones switched to transfers and stayed with them from then on. The only exception to this was when, in later years, one of the bigger tank options was fitted.

The Matchless badge remained in use as it was up till 1960 but the AJS one was increased in diameter by $\frac{1}{4}$ in. for 1956. In addition, it was listed in two finishes to suit painted or plated tanks. The first was in gilt and held by bronze screws while the second was in silver with chrome screws. The badge diameter for both marques was increased in size for 1961 with the two AJS finishes continuing.

There were completely new badges for 1962, both of which ran back from their usual position to the kneegrip. Both were large and flamboyant and because the kneegrips were rather far back the badges often dug into the rider's knees. They were soon known as 'knee-knockers' and were not to all tastes. The AJS one was replaced by a diamond shape for 1965 and kept this from then on. The Matchless changed to a smaller badge with the flying M motif during 1965 and stayed with that to the end.

The light singles used the stock badges when launched in 1958 and changed with them to the larger size for 1961. For that year alone the S model AJS fitted the plated tank badge rather than the painted tank one but reverted to the same part as the rest for 1962. There were no further changes and the CS models used the same badges as the other models, year by year.

Tank side panels and trim

The chrome-plated side panels were introduced as standard for the twins in 1957 and were an option for the singles. The same pair of panels was used for all years and applications, and in time went on the de luxe and CSR twins while becoming an option for the standard ones.

The panels had a coloured bead round their edge and for AJS models this was a light blue in colour. For Matchless, the bead was red for a black tank and black for a red tank up till 1959. After then only the red bead was listed up till 1961, after which the panels were no longer fitted.

Sporting style used by a 1966 model 14CSR to attract the buyers

In addition to the plated panels, painted ones were offered for the singles and for 1958 only. These were in gold with the light blue bead for AJS and off-white with the red bead for Matchless.

The introduction of the two-tone tanks for 1959 brought with them a pair of embellishers which went on the sides between the colours. At the same time a plated bead was fitted on the top of the tank on its centre line and these parts were all amended for 1960 when the tanks were altered. The embellishers were only used up to 1961 as that was the last year for the two-tone finish but a revised centre bead remained on for 1962. The light singles also had a tank top bead for 1960–1 on the road models while a plastic bead was used round the edge of the large tank badges fitted to the road AJS models of 1962–4.

Kneegrips

These were a feature of machines from the 1920s gradually becoming more common as speeds rose and the need for something to clamp on to became more pressing. As tanks fattened in the 1930s they also served to protect the finish.

The kneegrips were handed and carried the marque logo up till 1961. The original AJS parts had the name within a line similar in shape to the part outline while the Matchless ones had the flying M symbol. For 1957 these were revised so the AJS was within a roundel, as was the Matchless, although the M retained its wings.

This changed for 1962 when the larger badges were fitted and the kneegrips became common to both marques. The parts used dated from 1958 for they had first been fitted to the light singles and were to continue for all the road models of that range right through to 1966. Unlike the older items they were stuck to the tank and not mounted on a plate and held by screws. They were revised for 1963 when fitted into a recess on the tank sides and remained in use from then on. They were also used by the CS light singles.

Taps

AMC fitted push-pull taps with cork seals without too many changes over the years. Adaptors for the taps appeared in 1954 for the light-alloy competition tanks and remained in use from then on for those models.

In all cases the tap needs to come apart and have the sealing arrangements checked over and repaired as

Massive tank badge as adopted by Matchless for a year or two and here on a 1963 G80

The AJS tank badge as in 1961 and here on a tank finished in two-tone colours

required. Then check that the filter is undamaged and that the taps work freely. Make sure they don't leak and do pass a full flow of petrol before they are used on the machine. Leaks at that stage are a bind and can produce a fire.

The post-war models began with two in-line taps, each with filter and push-knob control bar. For 1954 the competition models had their taps screwed into one short and one long adaptor which remained in use till 1959. After then they fitted two short adaptors up till 1965 and in the CS twins from 1967.

The tap type changed for 1955 for the road and rigid competition models and for 1956 for the CS singles. The new tap had a horizontal push-pull knob with the outlet in line with this and attached to its lower end by a banjo bolt. This allowed the pipe run to be easily aligned and the same arrangement was used for the tap adopted for 1957. This went back to the 1945 cross-bar control and this type remained in use in various forms from then on.

Versions with reserve facilities were brought in for 1960 and fitted in one position while the earlier form continued in the other. Alternatives went in the competition and sports twin tanks but from 1963 the road models returned to one tap type, used in pairs, and this remained in use till 1969, other than on the 1967 CS twin.

The light singles used the existing range taps so they had two of one type at first and a pair for 1960, reverting to one for 1963 onwards. The CS models had their own pair which were as those on the 1960 road twins. Conversely, the road light singles pair were from the heavy CS and sports twins.

The 348 cc lightweight, as built by AJS in 1962 as the model 8

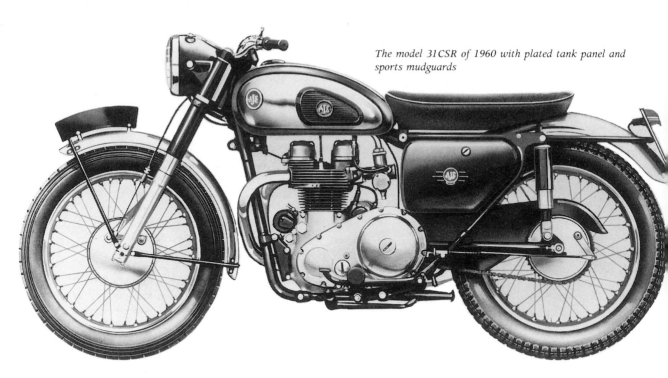

The model 31CSR of 1960 with plated tank panel and sports mudguards

15 Seating

AMC fitted a saddle and offered a pillion seat as an option for all models immediately after the war, with a gradual change over to the dualseat. This appeared as early as 1949 on the Matchless twin, but not the AJS one or the road singles until 1953. One went on the CS singles in 1954 but the rigid models and the trials competition machines kept to a saddle to the end of their production.

Saddle

A saddle is an assembly and should be treated as such. On top is the cover which is sewn to shape and then fitted with clips riveted around the edge. Under that went a felt underlay and this tends to wear and fray on the springs beneath. With felt and cover removed, what is left is the main frame and a series of suspension springs which run fore and aft.

The two main springs were attached at the rear of the assembly and a pivot bolt went at the front. This was supposed to pivot in a greased hole in the frame but is an area often neglected and the holes may well need repairing. A good fit will allow the saddle to rise and fall on its springs as it should, without side-sway which can be disconcerting.

The parts need to be refurbished and then reassembled. Once complete a new cover with under-felt can be fitted and retained with its clips. Fit the back first and work the material forward to the nose.

Saddle types

The 1945 saddle was mounted by a bolt through the nose and a stud running across the frame. Angle brackets on this were bolted to the springs but for 1948 the springs were fixed directly into small lugs on the frame chainstays. The competition saddle was similar to the standard part.

The saddle height adjustment was extended for 1949 by lengthening the nose bracket and providing three cross holes in it. This allowed the front as well as the back to be raised or lowered as required and the same seat with different springs went on the competition machines.

The rigid road models kept their saddle from then on but 1949 also saw a new part with short springs to suit the pivoted-fork frame. This was then used by the sprung singles and the AJS twin up till 1952. The sprung competition singles had a similar saddle which was listed for them till 1953.

The rigid competition models, used mainly for trails, had a new smaller seat for 1950 set back on an extended nose bracket. The seat changed to another form for 1954 and was replaced by another for the pivoted-fork frame adopted in 1956. This had a rather tall height so its bracket and springs were shortened for 1957 to reduce this. It continued in this form till 1963 but was replaced by a simple pad for 1964.

In addition to the saddles fitted as standard they were offered as an option on two occasions. One was in 1959 for all touring models and the other was in 1967–8 for the G15 Mk II.

Pillion pad

When separate from a saddle, passenger seats could be either sprung and built up like the saddle, or simply a rubber pad with a cover. AMC listed a pad but often owners would fit other makes to the rear mudguard. The firm also tried a tandem seat as an option for the road singles of 1953 with the pillion seat linked to the back of the saddle to form an embryo dualseat.

If a pad was fitted and water has got into the interior it is unlikely to be usable anymore so replacement will be necessary. Again, if the cover is damaged, a new one will be needed. Make sure you have sorted out the fixing to the mudguard before that item is finished.

When the pillion seat is of the spring type, repair is done in the same manner as for a saddle and again the fixing to the machine needs to be finalized before finishing and not after.

Only one pad was listed and was offered for all road models fitted with a saddle up to 1955.

Dualseat

These can be more of a problem as there were a good few variations used over the years and they can be

The final AJS trials model was this 1964 16C with its board seat

BELOW *The rigid model 18 AJS hung on to its saddle for a good number of years after this 1946 edition was built*

awkward to mend. They consist of a steel pan which can rust, a moulded interior which can rot, and a cover which may tear or split.

The interior moulding is the greatest problem as replacement may be the only answer and unless you can locate a suitable one you will not get the desired final seat shape. The pan can be refurbished, as for any other steel part, and the cover replaced by another which may be stitched from basic material.

Restoration is thus a specialist job and one you can expect to farm out in most cases, being impractical for most owners. There are always exceptions of course, depending on the size of the problem and the skills and resources of the person dealing with it.

Dualseat types

The first of these went on the Matchless twin alone for 1949 and for 1951 the cover material was changed to vynide. In 1953 the same seat went on the sprung singles and was joined by another for the AJS singles and twin. From then till 1959 the road model seats differed between the marques, but the CS singles had a common part.

There were new seats for 1954 and because of the different petrol tank sizes there were two for the 348 cc singles and two more for the 497 cc singles and the twins. The latter were used by all models for 1955 while the CS models had one seat for each year.

Due to the frame change there were new seats for 1956 with one for each marque and one for the CS single. This alone continued for 1957 when once more

BELOW *The lightweight models all had a dualseat from the start, as shown by this 1960 Matchless G2*

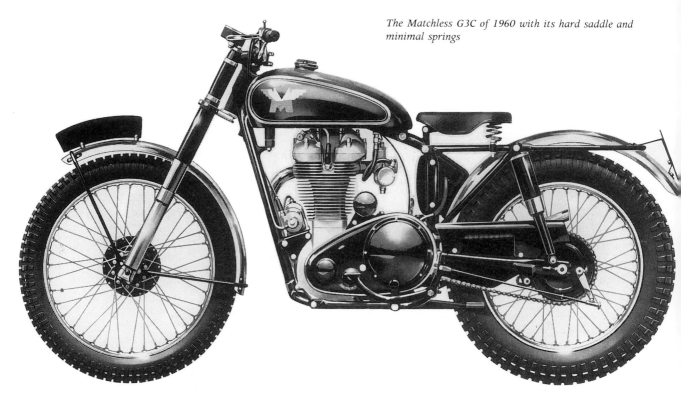

The Matchless G3C of 1960 with its hard saddle and minimal springs

the smaller singles had their own pair of seats, while the larger shared with the twins. As before, the latter went on the 348 cc models the next year, 1958, when there were new seats, with one for the CS singles and twins and another for the CSR models.

The CS seat continued for 1959 but the others changed with a pair for the singles, a pair for the twins and one seat for the CSR. From 1960 both marques fitted the same seats and there was one for the singles and standard twins and another for the CS and CSR machines. This last continued on the CS singles till 1965 and the CSR twins till 1963. The seats were joined by grey options for 1962 with one for the touring and the other for the sports models.

There was a new seat for the singles and standard twin in 1963 and this continued for them and the basic 745 cc twin to the end. It also went on the CSR twins for 1964–6 but the 745 cc versions had another seat which was altered for 1968. This last seat was also fitted to the G15CS from 1967.

The light singles began with a pair of seats plus another for the CS model which fitted all years of that machine. The standard models changed to a common seat for 1960 with a grey option for 1962 only.

AMC dualseats had cross-ribs up to 1959 and a suggestion of two levels from then on for the road models. The competition and sports seats were usually shorter and thinner without the wrap round of the touring forms. The light single seats were similar with cross-ribs at first and then a two-level line, except for the CS which had a thinner, shorter seat.

16 Assembly

This is often the most satisfying part of a restoration or rebuild, culminating in that heady moment when you swing on the kickstarter and the engine bursts into life.

It is also a time for avoiding haste as rushing matters can easily damage something you have spent time, money and effort on. Slow but sure progress is best with plenty of reference to your notes so you work in the right sequence. In the build-up to the final assembly you should have checked the fit of bolts to holes as you went along and all this work will now pay off in a straightforward fitment of the parts without snags.

The greatest problem is protecting the finish you have lavished so much care on, so cover, pad and mask where necessary and work slowly to avoid damage. Have a think about the order in which you intend to assemble the parts and arrange the items of each stage so they are together. It is good practice to do this as it is a further check that you have everything and that each item has been reworked as required. It will also ensure that you are not caught off balance with something partly together and being short of a vital bolt, with no free hand to locate it. If this does happen, go back and dismantle rather than chance damage occurring while your back is turned.

Start the assembly with the frame, fitting the rear fork, the head race cups and the main stand. You can now put the skeleton on your machine bench and prop the front end up. If you have any doubt at all on stability, clamp the stand down. Now fit the fork crowns and the forks themselves, adding the front wheel. If you fit the mudguard at this stage, it will certainly need protection, so is best omitted for the time being.

The rear guard may well have to be fitted early on and it may be necessary to add the wiring harness at this stage or at least fit the rear section, if this is threaded through frame and mudguard tubes and guides. If the machine is balanced on its centre stand, either fit the rear wheel or anchor the rear fork end to your bench.

Once you have a stable frame that is not going to rock about, fit the engine and gearbox while you have the maximum amount of room in which to move. Don't forget to check that you have not left anything out that must be fitted first. Sort out all engine fixings, plates and spacers in advance and place to hand. Spare rods on which to locate the unit may well be needed.

You are more likely to damage something while fitting the engine than at any other time, so first protect everything you can. Don't try to lift the weight into place unless you have at least two helpers to take the load while you slide the fixings in. With only two people, something is sure to be scratched.

Blocks underneath are one way to take the strain, but better is a means of lifting the engine from above. In view of the cost of a rebuild, it is well worth the price of a car engine hoist, which will be able to carry the load easily. Arrange the lifting sling so it is secure and holds the engine in the correct plane for its fixings to line up. If you have to tilt the engine to achieve this, you are more likely to have an accident and crushed fingers. Better to adjust the sling so the engine just drops into place.

Then fit all fixings and tighten. As with any assembly work, it is best to complete a sequence fully and not leave the final tightening for later in case you forget. However, it is not always possible, in which case leave the nut undone and give it a marker to remind you.

Continue the assembly as you wish and as the design dictates but leave the tank and seat as late as possible. Check wheel alignment once both are finally in place and adjust the chain tension correctly.

Don't try to start the engine until all is ready and keep the battery on the shelf until nearly finished. Before connecting it use your meter to check that the wiring is not shorting to earth somewhere and make sure you connect it the right way round. It should be fine, but better be sure than chance a spark at this stage. Then disconnect the battery again while you fill the oil tank and check the gearbox and primary-chain levels.

If the machine is still up on the bench, you will need help to get it down safely. Take care that you don't drop it at this stage, giving yourself plenty of room to work in. Once down, you can prepare to start up by opening the workshop doors to let the exhaust fumes out.

The petrol tank should have been left off while you get the machine down to ground level. Now fit it, connect it up and pour a small amount of fuel in. Half a gallon or two litres is fine to start with. Turn on and check for leaks. Connect battery and start the engine. Keep the engine speed low and check that oil is returning to the oil tank. Check the rocker feed and adjust if necessary and where the supply comes from

the return line hold your finger on the pipe in the tank to force some into the rocker box as soon as possible. Watch that the oil-pump pressure does not force the return line off its pipe or you could have a large puddle on the floor and a shortage of oil in the engine. Check that the generator is charging.

Next put the machine on its stand and run it up through the gears to make sure all is well in that area. Have a good look round the pipe connections to make sure there are no leaks and check the ignition timing with a strobe if this is called for.

Try the machine gently in your drive to check the operation of the clutch and brakes. If you have done

Once assembled the works had to give them a road test which is what is happening to this 1959 model 16C

Supreme tester was Hugh Viney here on a 1954 ISDT model 20 which differed in many minor ways from the standard model

your paperwork, are insured and still taxed after all this time, you can now get your helmet and go for a ride. If not, you will have to put it away for the moment.

For most owners in the UK that first ride of the restored machine is the prosaic one to the local dealer for its official test. Rather irksome after all your work but look on it as a top mechanic may regard scrutineering at a race meeting—a check that nothing has been overlooked. It may help to go to a dealer who knows something about older machines and who will

believe that taper-roller-bearing wheels should have a trace of side play and that a 7 in. sls drum brake will lack the bite of a double disc with hydraulic operation.

A chat when booking the appointment is well worth the effort and can smooth the way to your pass.

With the machine legal, enjoy a ride. After a few miles check the oil level and give the machine a look over to see if anything has worked loose. Get some more petrol before you run short and roll off some miles.

Then take the machine back to the workshop. Check items such as chains, brakes and cables which may have settled down a touch. Do your carburation check.

Enjoy your AJS or Matchless.

17 Paperwork

In this modern age, ownership and use of any road vehicle involves pieces of paper and some of these are documents issued by the authorities. This chapter concerns these in general and those specific to the United Kingdom. Details for other countries will vary and must be checked accordingly.

The first piece of paper was mentioned in the opening chapter and is the receipt for the machine or the bundle of receipts for parts if that was the way you obtained your model. It is very desirable that they contain the engine and frame numbers so you have proof of ownership of what you actually do have. Make sure they agree with what is stamped on the machine and beware of anything that looks altered.

The other documents you will need in the UK are registration form, test certificate and insurance certificate. The first is currently known as a V5, the second as VT20 and the last is obtained privately. With them you can then tax the machine for road use.

You should consider insurance long before you get to the road, as the parts and the machine as a whole need to be covered against fire or theft as soon as you get them. Try to obtain an agreed value for the machine and make sure you adjust this in line with the market. The insurance will need to be extended to cover road risks before you ride in public and it is worth shopping round for a company who specializes in older machines and caters for them. Otherwise your relatively sedate model G11 will be lumped in with modern 750 cc models of far higher performance and spares prices.

The V5 and VT20 are to an extent linked and also involve the number plate of your machine. Where a machine has been in use on a fairly continuous basis its original buff or green log book will have been replaced by a V5, which will record the correct engine and frame numbers along with the original registration number as displayed on the number plate.

As nothing is perfect there are even discrepancies when the documentation is all in order. For example,

Mrs Van Overloop of New Jersey with a Matchless single in American style

an AJS is bought from a dealer. It suffers an engine problem and the complete unit is changed, which is not recorded at the time. Eventually, the machine is withdrawn from use and, in time, sold off. The new owner rebuilds it and, on coming to register it, compares paper numbers with actual markings to find they don't tally—as they have not done for many years.

More difficult is a machine that has not been used for a period and has no V5. For the authorities to issue a form with a registration number appropriate to the machine's year, they need further proof and the onus is on the owner to provide it. Only in cases of rare or historic machines, well-known past owners or a similar reason is there much hope of retaining the original number, but it is always worth trying with an application.

As part of this exercise to keep the original number it helps to be able to link it to the machine and for this old MoT certificates or old licence discs are acceptable. Where these are not available, or to back them up, a letter from a recognized authority to confirm the date of the quoted engine and frame numbers, stating whether or not they were likely to have begun life together, should be obtained. Acceptable sources are the owners club, Vintage MCC, service-page writers of the specialist magazines (I am one of these) or the holders of the manufacturer's original records.

It is not normally possible to trace the original registration number from scratch and much of the official record no longer exists. The procedure needed would be to look at the firm's records to match engine and frame numbers. If this is in order the records will then give the name of the dealer to whom the machine was sent. He, in turn, would then need to be sought out and his records could give the registration number. In practice, few dealers from those days are still in business, and fewer still will have kept such records for the 20 or 30 years likely to be involved.

So you have to call on your Local Vehicle Licensing Office and take all your documents with you. There you fill up a form, as you would expect to do at any government office. This will trigger off a series of events which will culminate with the issue of a V5, if

Line-up of Matchless twins for the British South Africa Police in 1956

Collecting the papers is an essential part of buying and these relate to a 1958 model 14

all goes well.

The first thing likely to happen is a visit from the authorities or their agents to inspect your machine. This is done to check that the numbers all agree with those quoted on the form and that the machine is what you say it is and does exist.

This visit is not always carried out but if it is to take place the machine is best assembled to some degree. It is a good idea to register the machine long before the restoration is complete or before there is any need to tax it for the road. At the very least, it allows you to get the number plate finished.

After the visit and if all is in order, the vehicle documents can be issued. If the evidence is good the original registration number, or mark as they call it, may, in rare cases, be retained and entered on the main computer at Swansea. Normally this is not so but where there is evidence as to the age of the machine, the authorities will try to issue an appropriate number for the period. Should there be no way of linking the machine to any period, which may happen with a hybrid, a number with a letter Q prefix will be issued.

Following this, the machine will have to go for its official test as mentioned in the previous chapter. Book the test, make sure you have insured the machine for road use, pass the test (after all this I would be most disappointed if you did otherwise) and you can then tax the machine for the road.

Keep all the paperwork first, in case there are any queries at any time, and secondly, to go with the machine should you ever come to sell it.

Now you have to decide what to restore next year.

Engine and frame numbers

Up to 1963 AMC engines are easy to date as they carry a code system using the last two digits of the year followed by the model code and then a serial number. Thus, 49/18/12345 would be a 1949 model 18 AJS, while 57/G9/54321 would be a 1957 Matchless 498 cc twin model G9. After 1963 this nice, easy system was dropped and only a number was used. Details and dates are as follows:

| | | Model | Engine number | |
Date	AJS	Matchless	AJS	Matchless
9/64	16	G3	42791	42761
7/66			43066	43171
9/64	18	G80	134658	134939
7/66			135289	135336
8/64	16C	G3C	4827	4802
9/64	18CS	G80CS	4619	4958
8/65		G80CS		5179
7/66		G85CS		296
9/64	31	G12	10212	10254
7/66			10509	10784
9/64	31CSR	G12CSR	10211	10175
7/66			10659	10715
6/58	14	G2	501	501
9/59			4756	4756
9/60			7979	7979
9/59	14CS	G2CS	4756	4756
9/60			7979	7979
9/59	8	G5	500	500
9/60			2237	2237
5/62	14CSR	G2CSR	8750	8750
9/63			13275	13274
9/64			14107	13956
9/65			14833	14757
7/66			15506	15468

Norton engine numbers comprised two sections. The first of these was a number code, which was 20 for the 745 cc Atlas engine and after this came the serial number itself. The engine number was stamped on the left crankcase just below the cylinder barrel and some dates and numbers are given below:

Date	Number	Date	Number
2.64	108000	8.67	123666
9.64	111377	1.68	124372
1966	115871	2.68	126125
1967	119760	9.68	128646
5.67	120323	11.68	129145
5.67	121307	3.69	131180
5.67	121665	3.69	131257
8.67	123364	9.69	133668

Frame numbers

These are much more of a problem as they were used for more than one model and either marque in any one year. There are two distinct number forms with one for the road machines and another for the competition models. Also, it would seem that road frames were stamped up in batches and could then be drawn upon as production dictated. In the later years this fell off so frames could be in the stores for some time, which can throw this aspect out. It would seem that AMC simply began the post-war frames at zero or some low number and ran up from that regardless of the machine they went on. During 1952 they reached 99999 so they began again with a letter A prefix. This does not always occur, but after 1955 the frame design changed with all models having rear suspension. It altered to the duplex design for 1960, so the factory may have felt that appearance would be a guide in the dating as well as the number. Some sources suggest other prefix and suffix letters but the owners club records do not confirm this at all. Dates and numbers are listed below for guidance and should be used in conjunction with the rest of the data in this book, parts lists and model recognition features. Often the club can assist further and membership of this helpful organization is recommended. Engine numbers were stamped on the left crankcase just below the cylinder, while frame ones are to be found on the right side under the seat front area, often on a seat lug. These never start with a figure '0' and should not be confused with the lug casting number on the steering head as this will simply add to the number of machines already registered with the same 016117 part number. Casting numbers are raised but the registration ones are always stamped into the metal.

Heavyweight singles and twins: frame numbers

Date	Number	Date	Number
1946	500	9/54	A21057
1947	12760	9/55	37700
1948	23358	9/56	49350
1949	35000	9/57	59492
1950	47000	9/59	72300
9/50	59744	9/60	76550
9/51	74100	9/62	A83900
9/52	89501	9/63	85669

Late numbers by model

Date	16	G3	18	G80	31	G12	31CSR	G12CSR
9/64	87183	87120	86850	87144	86815	86828	86786	86712
7/66	88277	88307	87891	88257	87387	88405	88108	88339

Frame number notes

1 September 1959 number is for 20/G9 standard model; de luxe, CS and CSR number is 72228.

2 Start number for 30 is 38294 and for G11 is 38253.

3 August 1958 end number for 30 is 65925, for G11 is 65864, for 30CS and 30CSR is 65662 and for G11CS and G11CSR is 65967.

Competition frames

Date	16MC	G3LC	16MCS	G3LCS	18C	G80C	18CS	G80CS
1946	464C	463C			457C	467C		
1947	574C	680C			575C	576C		
1948	958C	981C			979C	978C		
1949	1746C	1542			1500C	1547C		
1950	2220	2200			2107C	2105C		
9/50	2642	2911C	2642	2806CS	2604	2604	2604	2604
9/51	2642C	3117	2642C	3104	2712C	2694C	2833CS	2754CS
9/52	3193C	3704	3106	3704	3704	3218C	3704	3221
9/53	3775C	4725	3861CS	4942	4609	3969C	4609	3967
9/54	4880C	5651	4956CS	5212	5012	4615	4747CS	4616
9/55	5660C	6243	5267CS	6391	5658C	5711	5093C	5251

Date	16MC,16C G3LC,G3C	16MCS,16CS G3LCS,G3CS	18CS	G80CS	G85CS
11/55		6396	6401	6395	
9/56	7350	7350	7350	7350	
9/57	7952	7952	7952	7952	
9/58	8490	8633	8572	8550	
9/59	8860	8671	8880	8880	
9/60	9500		9500	9550	
9/62			10550	10550	
7/63	10499				
8/64	10871(16C) 10841(G3C)				
9/64			10728	10936	
8/65				11082	
7/66					328
6/67					5348

Light singles frames

Date	14/G2	14CS/G2CS	14CSR/G2CSR	8/G5
6/58	1001			
9/59	5270	5270		6020
9/60	10183	10183		10183
5/62			12500	
9/63			16800	
9/64			17536	
9/65			18283	
7/66			19033(14CSR)	
7/66			18932(G2CSR)	

2 Model charts

AJS	Matchless	b × s	Years
16M	G3L	69 × 93	1945 46 47 48 49 50 51 52 53 54 55 56 57 58 59 60 61 62 63 64 65 66 67 68 69
16MS	G3LS	69 × 93	
16	G3	69 × 93	
16	G3	74 × 81	
16S	G3S	74 × 81	
16	G3	72 × 85.5	
16MC	G3LC	69 × 93	
16MCS	G3LCS	69 × 93	
16MCS	G3LCS	72 × 85.5	
16CS	G3CS	72 × 85.5	
16C	G3C	69 × 93	
16C	G3C	72 × 85.5	
18	G80	82.5 × 93	
18S	G80S	82.5 × 93	
18	G80	82.5 × 93	
18	G80	86 × 85.5	
18C	G80C	82.5 × 93	
18CS	G80CS	82.5 × 93	
18CS	G80CS	86 × 85.5	
	G85CS	86 × 85.5	
20	G9	66 × 72.8	
20dl	G9dl	66 × 72.8	
20std	G9std	66 × 72.8	
20CS	G9CS	66 × 72.8	
20CSR	G9CSR	66 × 72.8	
30	G11	72 × 72.8	
30CS	G11CS	72 × 72.8	
30CSR	G11CSR	72 × 72.8	
31	G12	72 × 79.3	
31dl	G12dl	72 × 79.3	
31CS	G12CS	72 × 79.3	
31CSR	G12CSR	72 × 79.3	
33	G15	73 × 89	
	G15Mk2	73 × 89	
33CSR		73 × 89	
	G15CSR	73 × 89	
	G15CS	73 × 89	
14	G2	70 × 65	
14CS	G2CS	70 × 65	
14S	G2S	70 × 65	
14CSR	G2CSR	70 × 65	
8	G5	72 × 85.5	

1945 46 47 48 49 50 51 52 53 54 55 56 57 58 59 60 61 62 63 64 65 66 67 68 69

3 Model alterations

These notes have been compiled from the main text and are to provide a quick guide for checking the year of a machine. The starting-point should always be the engine and frame numbers and the following is mainly concerned with external details that can be inspected when purchasing.

The notes run on and are generally applicable to later models of the same series. If in doubt, refer to the main text.

Singles

1945   All iron engine with coil-valve springs, valve lifter in crankcase, different bottom halves for 348 and 497 cc engines, separate gearbox, rigid frame, telescopic front forks, toolbox on right above upper chainstay, saddle, magneto in front of engine for AJS and behind it for Matchless, 348 cc exhaust pipe above footrest.

1947   Flared chainguard, 348 cc exhaust pipe as 497 cc one under footrest, lifting handle as part of the rear mudguard stay.

1948   7 in. brakes front and rear, two-bolt front brake anchor, four-bolt handlebar clamp, adjustable saddle springs, during year 497 cc bottom half used for 348 cc engines to make them common.

1949   Hairpin-valve springs, valve lifter in rocker box, seat height adjustable, rectangular rear lamp, rigid frame with sidecar lugs. Pivoted-fork models with candlestick rear units, saddle, twin toolboxes in rear frame corner.

1950   Ribbed mudguards, long carburettor body, offset silencer, front brake with torque arm, centre stand for pivoted-fork models, toolbox between chainstays for rigid-frame machines.

1951   Jampots for rear units, recessed fork drain plugs, horn button in right handlebar, light-alloy cylinder head.

1952   Matchless magneto in front of engine, B52 Burman gearbox, clutch access cap in chaincase, alloy front brake backplate, three-bolt handlebar clamp, underslung pilot lamp, positive earth electrics, colour-coded wiring.

1953   Front brake shoe lever pointed forward, fork shrouds free to turn, cap screw fork crown pinch bolts, plastic rear lamp, smaller magneto shield, steering lock bar, dualseat for all pivoted-fork models.

1954   Full-width light-alloy front hub, removable clutch dome cover on chaincase, twin pilot lamps, flared mudguards, auto-advance for 497 cc engine

so bulge for this in timing cover, oil tank filter position altered.

1955   Front hub narrower and with fins in barrel profile, full-width light-alloy rear hub, Monobloc carburettor, new silencer shape, larger fork diameter, modified jampots, frame with hole for air filter tube, pressed-steel lugs for pillion rests, deeper headlamp shell to carry speedometer, reshaped headlamp brackets, simpler oil tank and battery carrier mounting, front mudguard without front stay so also no lug on fork leg, rigid-frame models with barrel-shaped saddle springs, 348 cc engines with auto-advance and timing cover with bulge to clear.

1956   New frame with vertical seat tube and pivoted fork, long thin oil tank on right and matching toolbox on left, centre panel to join, cover over gearbox, shorter pushrod tubes and no cut-outs in cylinder head for them, front brake shoe lever positioned at top of backplate, rear brake adjuster at front end of brake rod, no front stand, rear brake backplate in steel with chrome cover riveted on, horn under seat, cables routed through fork crown, combined horn button and dip-switch.

1957   AMC gearbox, chaincase front dome smaller to suit removal of engine shock absorber, Girling rear units with clevis lower ends, ribbed oil tank and toolbox lid.

1958   No twin pilot lamps, alloy chaincase, alternator electrics, coil ignition, small timing cover with points housing.

1959   Deeper section mudguards without centre rib.

1960   Duplex frame, small headlamp shell, two-level seat.

1961   Shorter mudguards, larger tank badges.

1962   Ignition key added, roll-on centre stand, 348 cc engine with integral pushrod tunnels in cylinder, 348 cc sports version with inverted bars added to range.

1963   Front hub still full width but with five fins, standard Girling units, rounder shape for oil tank and toolbox, 18 in. wheels, narrower seat, D section mudguards, direct action stop-light switch, petrol tank with knee recesses, silencer without tail pipe.

1964   Norton front forks and front and rear full-width light-alloy hubs, short-stroke engines with integral pushrod tunnel, Norton oil pump.

1965–6 No changes.

Competition singles

1946   Based on road models with upswept exhaust, competition tyres, heavy gauge spokes, light-alloy mudguards, duplicated cables, optional lights, saddle.

1948   7 in. brakes front and rear, two-bolt front brake anchor, four-bolt handlebar clamp, adjustable saddle springs, during year 497 cc bottom half used for 348 cc engines to make them common.

1949   Hairpin-valve springs, valve lifter in rocker box, seat height adjustable, rectangular rear lamp, rigid frame with sidecar lugs.

1950   All-alloy engine, 'wader' magneto, smaller petrol tank, tubular toolbox under saddle, front-brake torque arm anchor, offset silencer.

1951   BA Burman gearbox, recessed fork drain plugs, frame with pivoted rear fork with jampots added.

1952   B52 Burman gearbox, clutch access cap in chaincase, alloy front brake backplate, three-bolt handlebar clamp, Matchless magneto in front of engine.

1953   Front-brake shoe lever pointed forward.

1954   Full-width light-alloy front hub, removable clutch dome cover on chaincase, all welded front frame half for rigid models, dualseat for CS machines.

1955   Front hub narrower and with fins in barrel profile, full-width light-alloy rear hub, Monobloc carburettor, new silencer shape, larger fork diameter, modified jampots, TT carburettor for CS models.

1956   Trials models with new pivoted-fork frame with shorter wheelbase, saddle, toolbox fitted on left only in rear frame corner; scrambles models with short-stroke all-alloy engine with integral push-rod tunnel in cylinder, Monobloc carburettor, road type frame, dualseat.

1957   AMC gearbox, chaincase front dome smaller to suit removal of engine shock absorber, Girling rear units with clevis lower ends, ribbed oil tank on CS models only.

1958   CS models with new seat, wider mudguards, oil tank set in further.

1959   Trials models with new frame with long inclined Girling units, new rear fork without bridge and with detachable arm held by cotter, small offset brakes front and rear.

1960   CS models with oil tank on left, GP carburettor, air filter on right, battery fitted under filter for road use.

1961–2   No changes.

1963   CS models with front hub still full width but with five fins, trials C models as 1960.

1964   Trials models with pad seat, shorter Girlings, CS engines with Norton oil pump.

1965   CS with no changes.

1966   G85CS with duplex welded frame, AMC front hub with fins machined away, 7R rear conical hub, AMC front forks, all-alloy engine, central oil tank, three-point footrest mounting.

1967–9   No changes.

Twins

1949   Engine with magneto and dynamo, separate gearbox, pivoted-fork frame with candlestick rear units, telescopic front forks, centre stand, saddle for AJS with adjustable springs and seat height but dualseat for Matchless, twin toolboxes in rear-frame corner, flared chainguard, 7 in. brakes front and rear, front-brake torque arm anchor, four-bolt handlebar clamp, rectangular rear lamp, silencers tubular for AJS but megaphone-shaped for Matchless, petrol tanks differ for two marques.

1950   Ribbed mudguards, offset silencer for AJS only.

1951   Jampots for rear units, recessed fork drain plugs, horn button in right handlebar, longer centre stand legs, vynide seat cover for Matchless, frame modified for air filter.

1952   B52 Burman gearbox, clutch access cap in chaincase, alloy front brake backplate, three-bolt handlebar clamp, underslung pilot lamp, positive earth electrics, colour-coded wiring, engine breather in crankshaft drive end.

1953   Front-brake shoe lever pointed forward, fork shrouds free to turn, cap screw fork crown pinch bolts, plastic rear lamp, steering lock bar, dualseat for AJS machines, two-bolt rocker covers.

1954   Full-width light-alloy front hub, removable clutch dome cover on chaincase, twin pilot lamps, flared mudguards, oil tank filter position modified.

1955   Front hub narrower and with fins in barrel profile, full-width light-alloy rear hub, Monobloc carburettor, new silencer shape for AJS only, larger fork diameter, modified jampots, frame with hole for air filter tube, pressed-steel lugs for pillion rests, deeper headlamp shell to carry speedometer, reshaped headlamp brackets, simpler oil tank and battery carrier mounting, front mudguard without front stay so also no lug on fork leg.

1956   New frame with vertical seat tube and pivoted fork, long thin oil tank on right and matching toolbox on left, cover over oil tank held by two screws, centre panel to join, cover over gearbox, front-brake shoe lever positioned at top of backplate, rear-brake adjuster at front end of brake rod, no front stand, rear-brake backplate in steel with chrome cover riveted on, horn under seat, cables routed through fork crown, combined horn button and dipswitch, introduction of 593 cc models.

1957   AMC gearbox, chaincase front dome smaller to suit removal of engine shock absorber, Girling rear units with clevis lower ends, ribbed oil tank cover and toolbox lid.

1958   No twin pilot lamps, alloy chaincase; CS model with sports engine, siamezed pipes, scrambles frame, small tank, speedometer on fork crown, fat tyres, competition mudguards; CSR model with sports engine, siamezed pipes, standard tank, competition dualseat.

1959   498 and 646 cc engines in standard, de luxe, CS and CSR forms; standard and de luxe in frame with vertical rear units, others with tuned engine

Three young ladies off on holiday in 1951, but the two on the left will be hard pressed to stay with the G9

with siamezed pipes in scrambles frame with inclined units; standard with alternator and distributor; rest as before with magneto and dynamo; deeper section mudguards without centre rib for standard and de luxe with light alloy for sports models; CS with small tank and CSR with large.

1960   Duplex frame, small headlamp shell, two-level seat, new head casting with extra fins.

1961   Shorter mudguards, larger tank badges.

1962   Ignition key added for coil ignition model, roll-on centre stand, road frame for CSR.

1963   Front hub still full width but with five fins, standard Girling units, direct action stop-light switch, petrol tank with knee recesses, silencer without tail pipe, narrower seat for both models and rounder shape for oil tank and toolbox except for CSR, 18 in. wheels except for CSR, D section mudguards for standard model only.

1964   Norton front forks and front and rear full-width light-alloy hubs, 12-volt electrics, CSR with rounder shape for oil tank and toolbox plus 18 in. wheels as standard one.

1965   646 cc models no change. 745 cc models with Norton Atlas engine, standard as 646 cc, CSR with low bars, rearsets, folding footrests, swept-back exhaust, forks with gaiters, no rear unit lower covers.

1967   CSR model with 19 in. wheels, CS with small tank, trail tyres, capacitor ignition.

1968   G15 Mk 2 and CSR with capacitor ignition.

1969   No changes.

Light singles

1958   Engine with gearbox strapped to back of crankcase, pivoted-fork frame, light telescopic forks, headlamp hung from top fork crown, 17 in. wheels, full-width hubs, dualseat, side covers, rear chaincase option.

1959   No changes to standard model; CS introduced with tuned engine, energy transfer ignition, stronger frame, AMC telescopic forks, 19 in. wheels, offset hubs, dualseat, no lights, light-alloy mudguards.

1960   Standard 248 cc model with headlamp supported from fork shroud lugs, roll-on centre stand; 348 cc model introduced with taller engine, AMC telescopic front forks, 18 in. wheels but otherwise as 248 cc machine; CS model with no changes.

1961   248 and 348 cc models with rear chaincase as standard, S model introduced with dropped bars, CS model with coil ignition and Varley battery.

1962   Longer kickstart lever for all models, narrower handlebars for S model, no other changes for 248 cc, 348 cc or CS models.

During year CSR model introduced with sports engine, polished engine cases, AMC front forks, 17 in. wheels, full-width hubs, air scoop in front-brake backplate, low handlebars.

1963–4   No changes.

1965   Coil-valve springs, silencer with no tail pipe.

1966   Light-alloy mudguards, semi-swept-back exhaust pipe.

4 Colours

Singles

1945   Black frame, forks, hubs, oil tank, toolbox, mudguards, chaincase, chainguard, wheel rims, headlamp shell, handlebars and all painted details. Chrome-plated exhaust system, pushrod tubes, fork cappings, headlamp rim and controls. Petrol tanks in black with lining in gold for AJS and silver with black pinstriping for Matchless, marque name in gold for AJS and in silver with letter M transfer for Matchless.

1946   As 1945.

1947   As 1945 except chrome-plated handlebars and chrome-plated letter M badge for Matchless petrol tank.
Wheel rims chrome-plated with black centres, lined gold for AJS and silver for Matchless.

1948   As 1947 except chrome-plated front-brake backplate and battery strap.
Export singles had wheel rims chrome-plated and for AJS with black centres lined either in gold or silver, and for Matchless with red centres lined in silver. Also they had the AJS petrol tank chrome-plated with panels formed with wide, black lines edged in gold and marque name as gold transfer. Matchless tank chrome-plated with crimson top and side panels lined in silver, fitted with chrome-plated letter M badge on each side.

1949   As 1948 except chrome-plated rear light body.

1950   As 1949 except chrome-plated fork oil seal holders.

1951   As 1950 except oval tank badge for AJS.

1952   Black frame, forks, hubs, oil tank, toolbox, mudguards, chaincase, chainguard, headlamp shell and all painted details. Chrome-plated exhaust system, pushrod tubes, fork cappings, fork oil seal holders, headlamp rim, handlebars and controls. Polished front-brake backplate and lower fork legs. Wheel rims Argenized to give matt aluminium effect and this finish also used for fork cappings, fork oil seal holders and jampot lower spring covers in some cases. Petrol tanks in black with lining and light-alloy, die-cast badges. AJS lining in gold and badge formed as marque name. Matchless lining in silver with red pinstripe and thinner inner silver line and alloy badge round with letter M on red background and flying wings to each side.

1953   As 1952. Export models with chrome-plated wheel rims and tanks as for 1948, other than badges with AJS fitted with 1951 oval badge and Matchless with 1952 round badge.

1954   As 1952 except natural front-hub finish, wheel rims as 1947 and plastic tank badges. AJS badge round with gilt letters and held by bronze finished screws and Matchless in form of 1952 alloy badge. Export models as 1953 with 1954 badges of which the AJS one was in silver with chrome-plated fixing screws.

1955   As 1954 except natural rear hub finish.

1956   As 1955 except AJS badge $\frac{1}{4}$ in. larger in diameter but still used in two forms in gilt or silver.

1957   As 1956. Option for tank with this in black with separate chrome-plated side panels. AJS with light blue panel beading and silver badge and Matchless with red beading. No chrome-plated tanks as before and wheel rims with red centres listed for export Matchless only.

1958   Black frame, forks, mudguards, oil tank, toolbox, chainguard, headlamp shell and all painted details. Chrome-plated exhaust system, pushrod tubes, fork cappings, fork oil seal holders, headlamp rim, handlebars and controls. Natural finish to hubs, polished lower fork legs and chaincase. Chrome-plated wheel rims. Tank black with lining gold for AJS and silver with red pinstripe for Matchless. AJS tank badge round and in gilt with bronze fixing screws. Matchless badge round with letter M and flying wings to each side.
Option of chrome tank panels and beading as 1957. Further option with panel for AJS in gold with blue bead or for Matchless in off-white with red bead.

1959   As 1958 including chrome tank panel option. Colour option with petrol tank, oil tank, mudguards and toolbox in blue for AJS or arctic white (listed as off-white) for Matchless and with chrome-plated panels fitted to the petrol tank with blue bead for AJS and black for Matchless. Further option of coloured parts as listed, plus petrol tank in two-tone with chrome-plated embellishing strip between the colours. For AJS the tank top was blue with the lower in light grey (listed as birch grey) and for Matchless the top was arctic white and the lower in red. Tank badges were as 1956 with gilt for the standard AJS and silver for the options with chrome panels.

| 1960 | As 1959 with two-tone finish for tank also used without other coloured parts which were mudguards, oil tank and toolbox, which thus remained in black. |

1961   As 1959 and 1960 except that larger badges were fitted and the option colours were reversed. Thus single colour for petrol tank, oil tank, mudguards and toolbox was birch grey for AJS and red for Matchless. Two-tone tanks were birch grey upper and blue lower for AJS and red upper and off-white lower for Matchless.

1962   Much larger tank badges die-cast in zinc alloy for both marques. Black frame, fork top covers, mudguards, oil tank, toolbox, chainguard, headlamp shell and all painted details. Chrome-plated wheel rims, exhaust system, headlamp rim, fork cappings, fork oil seal holders, handlebars and controls. Polished lower fork legs and chaincase. Natural hubs.

Option of all painted parts in blue for AJS and tartan red for Matchless except mudguards which were in white for both marques. With the option went a grey seat. 348 cc Sports model with chrome-plated mudguards and chainguard.

1963   As 1962 but double zigzag lines on tank shoulders with thick lower and thin upper in gold for AJS and silver for Matchless. Option colours apply to petrol tank, oil tank and toolbox only.

1964   As 1963 with AJS option in polychromatic blue.

1965   As 1963 with diamond badge for AJS and small M badge for Matchless. No colour options for singles.

1966   As 1965.

Competition singles

1946   Black frame, forks, hubs, oil tank, toolbox, alloy mudguards, chaincase, chainguard, wheel rims, headlamp shell, handlebars and all painted details. Chrome-plated exhaust system, pushrod tubes, fork cappings, headlamp rim and controls. Petrol tanks in black with lining in gold for AJS and silver with black pinstriping for Matchless, marque name in gold for AJS and in silver with letter M transfer for Matchless.

1947   As 1946 except chrome-plated handlebars and chrome-plated letter M badge for Matchless petrol tank.

Wheel rims chrome-plated with black centres, lined gold for AJS and silver for Matchless.

1948   As 1947 except chrome-plated front-brake backplate and battery strap plus polished alloy mudguards.

Export competition singles with wheel rims chrome-plated and for AJS with black centres lined either in gold or silver and for Matchless with red centres lined in silver. Also AJS petrol tank chrome-plated with panels formed with wide, black line edged in gold and marque name as gold transfer. Matchless tank chrome-plated with crimson top and side panels lined in silver, fitted with chrome-plated letter M badge on each side.

1949   As 1948 except chrome-plated rear light body.

1950   As 1949 except chrome-plated fork oil seal holders and M transfer on petrol tank for Matchless.

1951   As 1950 except oval tank badge for AJS and metal M badge for Matchless.

1952   Black frame, forks, hubs, oil tank, toolbox, chaincase, chainguard, headlamp shell and all painted details. Chrome-plated exhaust system, pushrod tubes, fork cappings, fork oil seal holders, headlamp rim, handlebars and controls. Polished front brake backplate, lower fork legs and alloy mudguards. Wheel rims Argenized to give matt aluminium effect and this finish also used for fork cappings, fork oil seal holders and jampot lower spring covers in some cases. Petrol tanks in black with lining and light-alloy, die-cast badges. AJS lining in gold and badge formed as marque name. Matchless lining in silver with red pinstripe and thinner inner silver line and alloy badge round with letter M on red background and flying wings to each side.

1953   As 1952. Export models with chrome-plated wheel rims and tanks as for 1948, other than badges with AJS fitted with 1951 oval badge and Matchless with 1952 round badge.

1954   As home for 1952 except chrome-plated wheel rims, natural front hub finish and petrol tank transfers in gold for AJS and silver for Matchless.

1955   As 1954 except natural rear hub finish.

1956   As 1955 except AJS badge $\frac{1}{4}$ in. larger in diameter.

1957   As 1956.

1958   As 1956. Option for petrol tank for AJS in blue and for Matchless in red with road model badges. This colour option extended to include the oil tank and toolbox in blue or red for the CS models.

1959   Black frame, forks, hubs, oil tank, toolbox, chaincase, chainguard, headlamp shell and all painted details. Chrome-plated wheel rims, exhaust system, pushrod tubes, fork cappings, fork oil seal holders, headlamp rim, handlebars and controls. Polished lower fork legs and alloy mudguards. Petrol tanks in black with lining and transfers in gold for AJS and silver with red pinstripe for Matchless.

Option of petrol tank, oil tank and toolbox in blue for AJS models. Option of petrol tank in red and oil tank in off-white for Matchless with toolbox in off-white for CS singles only.

1960   As 1959.

1961   As 1959.

1962   As 1959 with options only for petrol tank in blue for AJS and red for Matchless plus grey seat for CS models.

1963   As 1959 but no options.

1964   As 1963.

1965   As 1963.

1966–9 G85CS with red tank, silver frame and polished alloy mudguards.

Bernal Osborne with a 1960 G12 fitted out for the Canadian police and with the brake and gear pedals reversed

Twins

1949   Black frame, forks, mudguards, oil tank, toolboxes, hubs, chaincase, chainguard and all
painted details. Chrome-plated exhaust systems,
fork cappings, fork oil seal holders, battery strap,
headlamp rim, handlebars and controls.

Wheel rims chrome-plated with black centres
lined gold for AJS and red centres lined silver for
Matchless.

AJS petrol tank chrome-plated with black top
panel and side panels formed with wide black line
plus outer silver line with blue pinstripe. AJS
transfer on tank sides.

Matchless tank chrome-plated with red top and
side panels lined in silver. Letter M badge on tank
sides.

1950   As 1949.

1951   As 1949 except oval tank badge for AJS.

1952   Black frame, forks, hubs, oil tank, toolbox,
mudguards, chaincase, chainguard, headlamp
shell and all painted details. Chrome-plated
exhaust system, pushrod tubes, fork cappings,
fork oil seal holders, headlamp rim, handlebars
and controls. Polished front brake backplate and
lower fork legs. Wheel rims Argenized to give
matt aluminium effect and this finish also used for
fork cappings, fork oil seal holders and jampot
lower spring covers in some cases. Petrol tanks in
black with lining and light-alloy, die-cast badges.
AJS lining in gold and badge formed as marque
name. Matchless lining in silver with red pinstripe
and thinner inner silver line and round alloy
badge with letter M on red background and flying
wings to each side.

1953   As 1952. Export models with chrome-plated
wheel rims and tanks as for 1949, other than
badges with AJS fitted with 1951 oval badge and
Matchless with 1952 round badge.

1954   As 1952 except natural front-hub finish, petrol
tanks, wheel rims as 1949 and plastic tank badges.
AJS badge round with silver letters and held by

1955	As 1954 except natural rear hub finish.
1956	498 cc models as 1955 except AJS badge $\frac{1}{4}$ in. larger in diameter. 593 cc models as 498 cc except with chrome-plated tank sides with painted tank top in black for AJS and red for Matchless.
1957	As 1956 except petrol tanks which were painted with separate chrome-plated side panels edged with beading. The 498 cc tanks were black with a light blue bead for AJS and a red bead for Matchless. The 593 cc AJS tank was royal blue with a light blue bead and the Matchless tank was red with a black bead. The AJS tank had the silver badge.

chrome-plated screws and Matchless in form of 1952 alloy badge.

1955   As 1954 except natural rear hub finish.

1956   498 cc models as 1955 except AJS badge $\frac{1}{4}$ in. larger in diameter. 593 cc models as 498 cc except with chrome-plated tank sides with painted tank top in black for AJS and red for Matchless.

1957   As 1956 except petrol tanks which were painted with separate chrome-plated side panels edged with beading. The 498 cc tanks were black with a light blue bead for AJS and a red bead for Matchless. The 593 cc AJS tank was royal blue with a light blue bead and the Matchless tank was red with a black bead. The AJS tank had the silver badge.

1958   Black frame, forks, mudguards, oil tank, toolbox, chainguard, headlamp shell and all painted details. Chrome-plated exhaust systems, fork cappings, fork oil seal holders, headlamp rim, handlebars and controls. Natural finish to hubs, polished lower fork legs and chaincase. Chrome-plated wheel rims except 593 cc AJS which had blue centres on chrome-plated rims. Tanks as 1957. Export twins with blue for AJS or red for Matchless oil tank cover and toolbox.

1959   As 1958 without export listing but including chrome tank panel option. All wheel rims chrome-plated. Colour option with petrol tank, oil tank, mudguards and toolbox in blue for AJS or arctic white (listed as off-white) for Matchless and with chrome-plated panels fitted to the petrol tank with blue bead for AJS and black for Matchless. Further option of coloured parts as listed plus petrol tank in two-tone with chrome-plated embellishing strip between the colours. For AJS the tank top was blue with the lower in light grey (listed as birch grey), and for Matchless the top was arctic white and the lower in red. Tank badges were as 1956 with gilt for the standard AJS and silver for the options with chrome panels.

Standard twins in basic finish with all three options available and de luxe fitted with chrome tank panels as standard with other two options available.

1960   As 1959 with two-tone finish for tank, also used without other coloured parts which were mudguards, oil tank and toolbox, which thus remained in black.

1961   As 1959 and 1960 except that larger badges were fitted and the option colours were reversed. Thus single colour for petrol tank, oil tank, mudguards and toolbox was birch grey for AJS and red for Matchless. Two-tone tanks were birch grey upper and blue lower for AJS and red upper and off-white lower for Matchless.

1962   Much larger tank badges die-cast in zinc alloy for both marques. Black frame, fork top covers, mudguards, oil tank, toolbox, chainguard, head-lamp shell and all painted details. Chrome-plated wheel rims, exhaust systems, headlamp rim, fork cappings, fork oil seal holders, handlebars and controls. Polished lower fork legs and chaincase. Natural hubs.

Option of all painted parts in blue for AJS and tartan red for Matchless except mudguards which were in white for both marques. With the option went a grey seat.

1963   As 1962 but double zigzag lines on tank shoulders with thick lower and thin upper in gold for AJS and silver for Matchless. Option colours apply to petrol tank, oil tank and toolbox only.

1964   As 1963 with AJS option in polychromatic blue.

1965   As 1963 with diamond badge for AJS and small M badge for Matchless. No colour options for standard twins.

1966   As 1965.

CS twins

1958   Black frame, forks, oil tank, toolbox, chainguard, headlamp shell and all painted details. Chrome-plated exhaust systems, fork cappings, fork oil seal holders, headlamp rim, handlebars and controls. Natural finish to hubs, polished lower fork legs, chaincase and light-alloy mudguards. Chrome-plated wheel rims. Tanks black with lining in gold for AJS or silver for Matchless with marque transfer in same colour. Option of road type tank in blue for AJS or red for Matchless with chrome-plated side panels with light blue or black beads. Export models with blue or red oil tank cover and toolbox.

1959   No export listing but same options for oil tank, tank cover and toolbox in blue for AJS and off-white or red for Matchless.

1960   As 1959.

CSR twins

1958   Black frame, fork crowns, chainguard, headlamp shell and all painted details. Chrome-plated wheel rims, exhaust systems, front fork shrouds, front fork top covers, front fork cappings, front fork oil seal holders, rear-unit covers, handlebars and controls. Natural hubs, polished fork legs and chaincase. Polished light-alloy mudguards. Petrol tank, oil tank cover and toolbox in Mediterranean blue for AJS and red for Matchless with chrome-plated tank panels with blue or black bead.

1959   As 1958 except black upper forks and rear-unit top covers plus oil tank in colour as well as its cover.

Options of petrol tank in two-tone with chrome-plated embellishing strip between the colours. For AJS the tank top was blue with the lower in light grey (listed as birch grey) and for Matchless the top was arctic white and the lower in red. Also, option of finish as de luxe twins other than alloy mudguards and for Matchless with oil tank, tank cover and toolbox in off-white. Tank badges were as 1956 with gilt for the standard AJS and silver for the options with chrome panels.

1960   As 1959.

A 1951 Matchless single far from home in sunny California with a double complement of riders

1961　As 1959 except that larger badges were fitted and the option colours were reversed. Thus single colour for petrol tank, oil tank and toolbox was birch grey for AJS and red for Matchless. Two-tone tanks were birch grey upper and blue lower for AJS and red upper and off-white lower for Matchless.

1962　Much larger tank badges die-cast in zinc alloy for both marques. Black frame, fork top covers, chainguard, headlamp shell and all painted details. Chrome-plated wheel rims, exhaust systems, headlamp rim, fork cappings, fork oil seal holders, handlebars and controls. Polished light-alloy mudguards, lower fork legs and chaincase. Natural hubs. Petrol tank, oil tank and toolbox in blue for AJS and red for Matchless. Option of all painted parts in blue for AJS and tartan red for Matchless, except mudguards which remained in light alloy. With the option went a grey seat.

1963　As 1962 but double zigzag lines on tank shoulders with thick lower and thin upper in gold for AJS and silver for Matchless. No options as 1962 but tank sides below zigzag could be chrome-plated.

1964　As 1963 with AJS option in polychromatic blue, tank sides chrome-plated as standard, tank top and oil tank plus toolbox remained in colour and mudguards chrome-plated.

221

1965   As 1963 with diamond badge for AJS and small M badge for Matchless. No chrome-plated tank sides.

1966   As 1965.

745 cc twin

1965   Standard model as 1964 646 cc CSR twin but with 1965 badges. CSR model with black frame and forks, polished light-alloy mudguards, chrome-plated tank sides below smooth tank lining, chrome-plated headlamp shell, chainguard, instrument panel and wheel rims. Petrol tank top, oil tank and toolbox in blue for AJS and red for Matchless.

1966   As 1965.

1967   Standard model with black frame and fork uppers, chrome-plated mudguards and petrol tank in blue for AJS and either black or red recorded for Matchless. Parts list gives red and chrome for Matchless which indicates the use of the tank with plated sides.

CSR model as for 1965.

CS model in black with candy apple red tank and chrome-plated mudguards.

1968–9   All as 1967.

Light singles

1958   Black frame, forks, mudguards, rear chaincase and side covers. Chrome-plated wheel rims, headlamp rim, exhaust system, handlebars and controls. Petrol tank and engine side flashes in blue for AJS and red for Matchless with tank lining in gold and silver. Round plastic tank badges.

1959   As 1958.

CS as standard model except for polished light-alloy mudguards.

1960   Standard model as 1958 with option of tank in black or the colour with integral chrome-plated side panels. CS as 1959 and 348 cc model as standard one with its options.

1961   All models with larger tank badges and otherwise as 1960.

S model as standard except chrome-plated mudguards and chainguard plus petrol tank in colour with plated sides fitted as standard.

1962   All road models with tanks with white band on each side. Otherwise as 1961, plus option of all painted parts in blue for AJS or red for Matchless. S as 1961 plus 1962 changes and also with polished engine sides without side flashes. CS as 1961.

CSR with black frame and forks, chrome-plated parts as standard plus mudguards and chainguard, polished engine sides without flashes, silver-painted cylinder barrel and petrol tank in blue or red with integral chrome-plated side panels. All colour option as for standard models.

1963   Standard and CSR model as 1962, no options listed.

1964   CSR model as 1963.

1965   CSR model with black side covers but otherwise as 1963.

1966   CSR model as 1965 except polished light-alloy mudguards.

5 Pistons

Note that compression ratio was affected by the plates fitted under the barrel and there were two thicknesses available. A chrome-plated top ring was fitted to the 497 cc engine for 1951 and the 348 cc single and 498 cc twin for 1952.

Capacity	Bore	Part no.	Ratio	Years	Capacity	Bore	Part no.	Ratio	Years
Singles							011930	9.0	1948–52
348 cc	69 mm	D3-E312	6.35	1945–6			018172	8.30	1953
		011848	6.35	1947			013505	6.3	1954–5
		013504	6.35	1948–54			013505	7.3	1954–5
		011880	9.0	1948–53			018926	8.3	1954–9
		013504	6.5	1954–61			018172	8.3	1954–5
		018924	7.5	1954–63			018172	9.8	1954–5
		011880	9.4	1954–5			026769	7.3	1960–3
	72 mm	022349	9.9	1956–9		86 mm	022350	8.7	1956
		030148	9.0	1964–6			023119	8.7	1957–9
	74 mm	028107	8.5	1962–3			026328	8.7	1958–69
497 cc	82.5 mm	38-G9-E12	6.0	1945–6			026811	12.0	1960–2
		011849	6.0	1947					
		013505	6.0	1948–53					

Capacity	Bore	Part no.	Ratio	Years
Light singles				
248 cc	69.85 mm	043201	7.8	1958–9
		043320	7.8	1960–1
		043748	7.8	1962
		043747	8.0	1962–6
		043203	10.0	1960
		043040	10.0	1961
348 cc	72 mm	044054	7.5	1960–1
		043749	7.5	1962
Twins				
498 cc	66 mm	015518	7.0	1949–55
		018109	8.0	1954–5
		022598	8.0	1956–9
		026323	8.0	1960–1
593 cc	72 mm	022226	7.5	1956–8
		023503	8.5	1958
646 cc	72 mm	026848	6.75	1960–2
		026324	7.5	1960–4
		025042	7.5	1959
		025045	8.5	1959
		026325	8.5	1960–6

Capacity	Bore	Left	Right	Ratio	Years
745 cc	73 mm	24246	23186	7.6	1965
		25389	25390	7.5	1966–9

The 745 cc pistons were all handed with valve-head cutaways machined into the crown.

6 Camshafts

Model	Years	Inlet	Exhaust	Timing data
16M, 18, G3L, G80	1945–53	010837	010836	32, 63, 65, 30
16MS, 18S, G3LS, G80S	1949–53	010837	010836	32, 63, 65, 30
16M, 16MS, G3L, G3LS	1954–5	012695	012694	36, 51, 50, 30
18, 18S, G80, G80S	1954–5	012695	012694	18, 69, 50, 30
16MS, G3LS	1956–7	012695	022565	36, 51, 50, 30
18S, G80S	1956–7	012695	022565	18, 69, 50, 30
16MS, G3LS	1958–63	024147	012695	36, 51, 50, 30
18S, G80S	1958–63	024147	012695	18, 69, 50, 30
16, G3	1964–6	030200	030204	
18, G80	1964–6	030201	030204	
16MC, 18C, G3LC, G80C	1946–53	010837	010836	32, 63, 65, 30
16MC, G3LC	1954	012695	012694	36, 51, 50, 30
18C, G80C	1954	012695	012694	18, 69, 50, 30
16MC, 18C, G3LC, G80C	1955	010836	010837	32, 63, 65, 30
16MCT, G3LCT	1956–63	010836	022566	26, 53, 64, 25
16C, G3C	1964	030203	030206	
16MCS, 18CS, G3LCS, G80CS	1951–3	010837	010836	32, 63, 65, 30
16MCS, 18CS, G3LCS, G80CS option	1951–3	012695	012694	
16MCS, 18CS, G3LCS, G80CS racing	1953	018833	018834	
16MCS, 18CS, G3LCS, G80CS	1954–5	018833	018834	
16MCS, 18CS, G3LCS, G80CS	1956–9	018833	022567	59, 69, 69, 48
18CS, G80CS	1960–1	024534	022567	67, 81, 69, 48
18CS, G80CS	1962–3	028191	028193	67, 81, 69, 48
18CS, G80CS, G85CS	1964–9	030202	030205	60, 69, 74, 46
G80R		024534	024535	67, 81, 83, 60
20, G9	1949–54	011784	011785	35, 65, 65, 35
20, 30, G9, G11	1955–8	018961	018962	24, 65, 63, 25
20, 31, G9, G12	1959–66	025084	025085	37, 77, 73, 43
20, G9 race kit				64, 68, 72, 44
G45				57, 70, 60, 50
Light singles	1958–62	42090		40, 75, 70, 40

7 Sparking plugs

Model	Year	KLG	Listed recommendation Lodge	Champion
Singles				
350 road	1945–6			L10
500 road	1945–6		H14	L7
All	1947–9		H14	L7
Road models	1950	F80		L7
Comp models	1950	FE80		N5
All	1951–9	FE80		N5
Road	1960–2	FE80		N5
Road	1963	FE220		N5
350 road	1964–6	FE220		N3
500 road	1964–6	FE220		N4
Trials	1960–3	FE80		N5
Trials	1964	FE80		N4
Scrambles	1960–2	FE220		N5
Scrambles	1963	FE80		N5
Scrambles	1964–5	FE220		N57R
Scrambles	1966–9			N57R
MX racing	1950–64			N57R
G50 racing				N54R
Twins				
498 cc	1949	FE80	HL14S	
498 cc fast use	1949	FE220		
498 cc	1950–61	FE80		
498 cc G45		FE290		NA12 or NA14
593 cc	1956–8	FE80		
646 cc standard	1959–66	FE80		N4
646 cc CS	1959–60	FE220		
646 cc CSR	1959–65	FE220		N3
646 cc CSR	1966			N3
745 cc standard	1965–9	FE75		N4 or N6Y
745 cc CSR	1965–9			N4 or N6Y
745 cc CS	1967–9			N6Y
Light singles				
standard	1958–63	FE80		
CS	1959–62	FE220		
350	1960–2	FE80		
CSR	1962–4	FE80		
CSR	1965–6	FE220		

Plug equivalents

Original Make	Type	Modern NGK	Champion
KLG	FE75	B6ES	N4
	F80	B7HS	L82
	FE80	B7ES	N3
	FE220	B9ES	N2
	FE290	B10EN	N57R
Lodge	H14	B7HS	L85
	HL14S	B7ES	N3
Champion	L10	B6HS	L10
	L7	B7HS	L85
	N3	B8ES	N3
	N4	B7ES	N4
	N5	B6ES	N5
	N6Y	BP8ES	N6Y
	N57R	B10EN	N57R
	N54R	B11EN	N54R

Three 1948 competition models setting out for a road test from the works

8 Carburettor settings and spacers

AJS	Matchless	Year	Type	Size	Main	Pilot	Slide	pos.	Needle jet
14 14S	G2 G2S	1958–63	376/99	$1\frac{1}{16}$	180	25	$3\frac{1}{2}$	3	.106
14CS	G2CS	1959–62	376/250	$1\frac{1}{16}$	180	25	3	4	.106
14CSR	G2CSR	1962–6	389/82	$1\frac{1}{8}$	200	20	3	3	.106
8	G5	1960–1	389/42	$1\frac{1}{8}$	220	25	$3\frac{1}{2}$	3	.106
		1962	389/68	$1\frac{1}{8}$	230	25	$3\frac{1}{2}$	3	.106
	G3 (ex-WD)	1940	276B	1	150		6/4	3	std
	G3L (ex-WD)	1941–5	275F	$\frac{7}{8}$	160		5/5	4	std
16M 16MS 16MC	G3L G3LS G3LC	1945–9	76D	1	150		6/4	3	std
		1950	76AL	1	150		6/4	3	std
		1951–3	76AE	1	150		6/4	3	std
		1954	76AV	$1\frac{1}{16}$	150		6/4	3	std
		1955	376/1	$1\frac{1}{16}$	210	30	$3\frac{1}{2}$	3	.106
16MS	G3LS	1956–8	376/5	$1\frac{1}{16}$	210	30	$3\frac{1}{2}$	3	.106
16	G3	1959–61	376/5	$1\frac{1}{16}$	210	30	$3\frac{1}{2}$	3	.106
		1962–3	389/68	$1\frac{1}{8}$	230	25	$3\frac{1}{2}$	3	.106
		1964–6	389/208	$1\frac{1}{8}$	260	25	3	3	.106
16S	G3S	1962	389/68	$1\frac{1}{8}$	230	25	$3\frac{1}{2}$	3	.106
16MCT	G3LCT	1956	376/5	$1\frac{1}{16}$	210	30	$3\frac{1}{2}$	3	.106
		1957–8	376/59	$1\frac{1}{16}$	210	30	3	3	.107
16C	G3C	1959–64	376/59	$1\frac{1}{16}$	210	30	3	3	.107
16MCS	G3LCS	1951–3	76AE	1	150		6/4	3	std
		1954	76AV	$1\frac{1}{16}$	150		6/4	3	std
	G3LCS	1954–5	TT	$1\frac{1}{16}$	300		5	4	.109
16MCS	G3LCS	1956	376/55	$1\frac{1}{16}$	200	30	$3\frac{1}{2}$	3	.106
		1957–8	389/18	$1\frac{1}{8}$	280	30	3	3	.106
16CS	G3CS	1959	389/18	$1\frac{1}{8}$	280	30	3	3	.106
18 18S 18C	G80 G80S G80C	1945–9	89B	$1\frac{3}{32}$	180		29/4	3	std
		1950	89M	$1\frac{3}{32}$	180		29/4	3	std
		1951–3	89B	$1\frac{3}{32}$	180		29/4	3	std
		1954	89N	$1\frac{5}{32}$	180		29/4	2	std
		1955–8	389/1	$1\frac{5}{32}$	260	30	$3\frac{1}{2}$	3	.106
18	G80	1959	389/1	$1\frac{5}{32}$	260	30	$3\frac{1}{2}$	3	.106
		1960–3	389/52	$1\frac{5}{32}$	300	25	$3\frac{1}{2}$	3	.106
		1964–6	389/209	$1\frac{1}{8}$	290	25	$3\frac{1}{2}$	3	.106
18CS	G80CS	1951–3	89B	$1\frac{3}{32}$	180		29/4	3	std
		1954	89N	$1\frac{5}{32}$	180		29/4	2	std
18CS	G80CS	1955	TT	$1\frac{3}{16}$	340		7	4	.109
		1956–9	389/12	$1\frac{3}{16}$	440	30	3	3	.106
		1960–5	GP	$1\frac{1}{8}$	290	25	6	5	.109
		1965	389/12	$1\frac{3}{16}$	440	30	3	3	.106
	G80R	1957–61	GP	$1\frac{3}{8}$	320		7	3	.109
		1959	GP	$1\frac{1}{2}$	450		4	3	.109
	G85CS	1966–8	GP	$1\frac{3}{8}$	310	25	6	5	.109
		1967–9	R932/7	32 mm	270	30	3	2	.107

Model AJS	Matchless	Year	Type	Size	Main	Pilot	Slide	Needle pos.	jet
20	G9	1949–53	76AG	1	180		6/4	3	std
20	G9 2 carb	1953	76AP 76AQ	1	180		6/4	3	std
		1954	76AT	1	180		6/4	3	std
		1955–8	376/6	1	220	30	4	3	.106
20 20CS 20CSR	G9 G9CS G9CSR	1959–61	376/209	1	220	30	4	3	.106
30	G11	1956	376/6	1	220	30	4	3	.106
		1957–8	376/78	$1\frac{1}{16}$	280	30	$3\frac{1}{2}$	3	.106
30CS	G11CS	1958	376/78	$1\frac{1}{16}$	280	30	$3\frac{1}{2}$	3	.106
30	G11 2 carb	1957–9	376/95 376/96	$1\frac{1}{16}$	220	25	$3\frac{1}{2}$	3	.106
31	G12	1959	389/29	$1\frac{1}{8}$	400	30	3	3	.106
		1960–1	389/50	$1\frac{1}{8}$	390	20	4	4	.106
		1962–6	389/91	$1\frac{1}{8}$	390	20	4	4	.106
31CS	G12CS	1959	389/29	$1\frac{1}{8}$	400	30	3	3	.106
		1960	389/49	$1\frac{1}{8}$	450	20	4	4	.106
31CSR	G12CSR	1959	389/29	$1\frac{1}{8}$	400	30	3	3	.106
		1960–1	389/49	$1\frac{1}{8}$	450	20	4	4	.106
		1962–6	389/92	$1\frac{1}{8}$	450	20	4	4	.106
646 cc 2 carbs		1962–5	389/73 389/74	$1\frac{1}{8}$	280	25	3	4	.106
	G15/45	1962	389/77	$1\frac{1}{8}$	410	20	4	4	.106
		1963	389/93	$1\frac{1}{8}$	410	20	4	4	.106
33	G15	1965	389/87 389/88	$1\frac{1}{8}$	420	20	3	3	.106
	G15CS	1964–5	389/210 389/211	$1\frac{1}{8}$	380	20	3	3	.106
33CS	G15CS	1966	389/237 689/237	$1\frac{1}{8}$	380	20	3	3	.106
33CSR	G15CSR	1965	389/222 389/223	$1\frac{1}{8}$	360	20	3	3	.106
		1966	389/242 689/242	$1\frac{1}{8}$	360	20	3	3	.106
33P	G15P	1965	389/87 389/88	$1\frac{1}{8}$	420	20	3	3	.106
	G15P	1966	389/241 689/241	$1\frac{1}{8}$	420	20	3	3	.106
33 33CSR		1967–8	R930/7 L930/8	30 mm	220	25	2	2	.106
	G15 G15CSR	1967–9	R930/5 L930/6	30 mm	230	25	2	2	.106

Carburettor spacers

Part number	Thickness (in.)	Bore (in.)	Engine size	Road	Used Comp	CS
41-G3L-E167	$\frac{3}{4}$	1	350	1945–9	1946–50	
36-G8C-E167	$\frac{7}{8}$		500	1945–7	1946–7	
001217	$\frac{7}{8}$		500	1948–9	1948–9	
010676	$\frac{3}{4}$	1	350	1951–3	1951–3	1951–3
015875	$\frac{3}{4}$	$1\frac{1}{8}$	500	1951–3	1950–3	1951–3
021346	$\frac{3}{4}$	$1\frac{1}{16}$	350	1954–61	1954–61	1954, 56, 59
021252	$\frac{3}{4}$	$1\frac{5}{32}$	500	1954–62	1954	1954
021002	$\frac{3}{4}$	$1\frac{3}{16}$	500		1955	1955–6, 59–60
022103	$\frac{3}{4}$	$1\frac{1}{16}$	350			1955
023427	$\frac{1}{4}$	$1\frac{3}{16}$	350			1957–8
023428	$\frac{1}{4}$	$1\frac{3}{16}$	500			1957–8
024533			500			1960–2
015875	$\frac{3}{4}$	$1\frac{1}{8}$	350	1962–6	1962–4	
015875	$\frac{3}{4}$	$1\frac{1}{8}$	500	1963–6		
023496	$\frac{1}{8}$	1	500 twin	1957–61		1959
024308	$\frac{1}{8}$	$1\frac{1}{8}$	650 twin	1959–66		1959–60

9 Capacities

Petrol tank (UK gallons)

Model	Type	Year	Size
Singles	Road	1945–53	3
	350 road	1954	3
	500 road	1954	3.75
	Road	1955–9	3.75
	Road	1960–2	4.25
	Road	1963–6	4
	Comp	1946–9	3
	Comp	1950–5	2.25
	Comp	1956–69	2
	Comp option	1958–62	3
Light	250	1958–9	2.75
	250, 350	1960–1	3.5
	250, 350	1962–6	3.25
	CS	1959–62	2.75
Twins	AJS	1949–53	4
	Matchless	1949–53	3
	500, 600	1954–8	3.75
	600CS	1958	2 or 3
	500, 650CS	1959–60	2 or 3
	500, 650	1959–62	4.25
	650	1963–6	4
	750	1965–6	4
	750	1967–9	4.25
	750CS	1967–9	2.25

Oil tank (UK pints)

Model	Year	Size
Road singles	1945–55	4
	1956–63	5
	1964–6	4
Comp singles	1946–58	4
Trials	1959–64	2.75
CS	1959–65	4
CS	1966–9	5
Twins	1949–55	4
	1956–69	5
Light singles	1958–66	2.5

Gearbox (UK pints)

Model	Year	Amount
Singles	1945–7	1.75
Singles and twins	1948–69	1
Light singles	1958–66	3

Front forks (cc)

Model	Year	Amount
Singles	1945–7	184
Singles and twins	1948–50	284
	1951–63	184
	1964–9	142
250 light single	1958–63	70

10 Transmission

Sprockets, boxes and overall gear ratio

Model AJS	Matchless	Year	Sprockets E	C	G	R	Overall ratio	Box type
16M	G3L	1945–51	18	40	16	42	5.833	1
		1952–5	18	40	16	42	5.833	4
16MS	G3LS	1949–51	18	40	16	42	5.833	1
		1952–6	18	40	16	42	5.833	4
		1957–8	19	42	16	42	5.803	8
16	G3	1959	19	42	16	42	5.803	8
		1960–3	19	42	16	42	5.803	10
		1963–6	20	42	16	42	5.512	10
16S	G3S	1962	19	42	16	42	5.803	10
16MS s/c	G3LS s/c	1958	17	42	16	42	6.485	8
16 s/c	G3 s/c	1959–61	17	42	16	42	6.485	8
		1963–6	18	42	16	42	6.125	10
16MC	G3LC	1946–7	17	40	16	42	6.176	2
		1948–51	16	40	16	42	6.562	2
16MC	G3LC	1952–3	16	40	16	42	6.562	5
		1954–5	16	40	16	42	6.562	6
16MCT	G3LCT	1956	16	40	16	42	6.562	6
		1957–8	17	42	16	42	6.485	9
16C	G3C	1959	17	42	16	42	6.485	9
16C	G3C	1960–4	17	42	16	42	6.485	11
16MCS	G3LCS	1951	16	40	16	42	6.562	3
		1952–3	16	40	16	42	6.562	4
		1954	16	40	16	42	6.562	7
		1955–6	16	40	16	42	6.562	4
		1957–8	17	42	16	42	6.485	8
16CS	G3CS	1959	17	42	16	42	6.485	8
16C s/c	G3C s/c	1959	15	42	16	42	7.350	9
16CS s/c	G3CS s/c	1959	15	42	16	42	7.350	8
18	G80	1945–51	21	40	16	42	5.000	1
		1952–5	21	40	16	42	5.000	4
18S	G80S	1949–51	21	40	16	42	5.000	1
		1952–6	21	40	16	42	5.000	4
		1957–8	22	42	16	42	5.011	8
18	G80	1959	22	42	16	42	5.011	8
		1960–2	22	42	16	42	5.011	10
		1963–6	23	42	16	42	4.793	10
18 s/c	G80 s/c	1945–51	18	40	16	42	5.833	1
		1952–5	18	40	16	42	5.833	4
18S s/c	G80S s/c	1949–51	18	40	16	42	5.833	1
		1952–6	18	40	16	42	5.833	4
		1957–8	20	42	16	42	5.512	8
18 s/c	G80 s/c	1959	20	42	16	42	5.512	8
		1960–2	20	42	16	42	5.512	10
		1963–6	21	42	16	42	5.250	10

18C	G80C	1946–7	19	40	16	42	5.526	2
		1948–51	18	40	16	42	5.833	2
		1952–3	18	40	16	42	5.833	5
		1954–5	18	40	16	42	5.833	6
18CS	G80CS	1951	18	40	16	42	5.833	3
		1952–3	18	40	16	42	5.833	4
		1954	18	40	16	42	5.833	7
		1955–6	18	40	16	42	5.833	4
		1957–8	18	42	16	42	6.125	8
		1959	19	42	16	42	5.803	8
		1960–5	19	42	16	42	5.803	10
	G85CS	1966–9	19	42	16	54	7.460	10
18CS s/c	G80CS s/c	1959	17	42	16	42	6.485	8
		1963–4	17	42	16	42	6.485	10
20	G9	1949–51	20	40	16	42	5.250	1
		1952–6	20	40	16	42	5.250	4
		1957–9	21	42	16	42	5.250	8
		1960–1	21	42	16	42	5.250	10
20CS	G9CS	1959	19	42	16	42	5.803	8
20CSR	G9CSR	1959	21	42	16	42	5.250	8
20 s/c	G9 s/c	1953–6	18	40	16	42	5.833	4
		1958–9	19	42	16	42	5.803	8
		1960–1	19	42	16	42	5.803	10
20CSR s/c	G9CSR s/c	1959	19	42	16	42	5.803	8
30	G11	1956	20	40	16	42	5.250	4
		1957–8	22	42	16	42	5.011	8
30CS	G11CS	1958	22	42	16	42	5.011	8
30CSR	G11CSR	1958	22	42	16	42	5.011	8
30 s/c	G11 s/c	1956	19	40	16	42	5.526	4
31	G12	1959	23	42	16	42	4.793	8
		1960–2	23	42	16	42	4.793	10
		1963–6	24	42	16	42	4.594	10
31CS	G12CS	1959	21	42	16	42	5.250	8
		1960	21	42	16	42	5.250	10
31CSR	G12CSR	1959	23	42	16	42	4.793	8
		1960–5	23	42	17	42	4.511	10
		1966	24	42	17	42	4.323	10
31 s/c	G12 s/c	1959	21	42	16	42	5.250	8
		1960–2	21	42	16	42	5.250	10
		1963–6	22	42	16	42	5.011	10
31CSR s/c	G12CSR s/c	1959	21	42	16	42	5.250	8
		1960–5	21	42	17	42	4.941	10
		1966	22	42	16	42	5.011	10
33	G15	1965–7	23	42	17	42	4.511	10
	G15 Mk II	1968–9	22	42	17	42	4.717	10
	G15 Mk II s/c	1967–8	20	42	17	42	5.188	10
	G15CS	1967–9	21	42	17	42	4.941	10
33CSR	G15CSR	1965	23	42	17	42	4.511	10
		1966–9	22	42	19	42	4.220	10
14	G2	1958–62	21	50	19	55	6.892	12
		late 1962–3	22	46	17	55	6.765	12
14CS	G2CS	1959	17	37	19	70	8.019	12
		1960–2	17	37	17	70	8.962	13
		late 1962	22	46	17	73	8.979	13
CS road use		1961–2	17	37	17	62	7.938	13
14S	G2S	1961–2	21	50	19	55	6.892	12
		late 1962	22	46	17	55	6.765	12
14CSR	G2CSR	1962–4	22	46	18	55	6.389	12
		1965–6	22	46	18	56	6.505	14
8	G5	1960–2	22	46	18	55	6.389	12

Chains

Singles and twins: primary 0.50 × 0.335 × 0.305 in.
final drive 0.625 × 0.400 × 0.380 in.

For these models the parts lists state that the number of links includes the connecting spring link. The numbers given are as in the parts lists.

Gearbox internal ratios

Gearbox	Used	Mainshaft				Layshaft				Gear ratios		
		4	3	2	1	4	3	2	1	3rd	2nd	1st
1 CP road	1945–51	30	27	23	18	20	23	27	32	1.278	1.761	2.667
2 CP trials	1946–51	32	29	23	18	18	21	27	32	1.287	2.087	3.160
3 BA	1951	33	30	26	20	21	24	28	34	1.257	1.692	2.671
4 B52	1952–6	28	25	22	17	18	21	24	29	1.307	1.697	2.654
5 B52 trials	1952–3	30	25	21	17	17	21	24	30	1.482	2.017	3.114
6 Trials	1954–6	30	25	20	17	16	21	26	29	1.575	2.437	3.199
7 Scrambles	1954	28	25	20	17	18	21	26	29	1.307	2.022	2.654
8 AMC	1957–9	24	21	18	14	18	21	24	28	1.333	1.778	2.667
9 AMC trials	1957–9	25	21	16	13	17	21	26	29	1.471	2.390	3.281
10 AMC (1960)	1960–9	23	21	18	14	18	20	24	28	1.217	1.704	2.556
11 Tri (1960)	1960–4	25	21	16	14	16	21	25	29	1.562	2.441	3.237
12 Lwt A	1958–64	28	25	21	16	18	21	25	30	1.307	1.852	2.917
13 Lwt B	1960–2	28	25	21	18	18	21	25	28	1.307	1.852	2.420
14 Lwt C	1965–6									1.23	1.79	2.76

Model AJS	Matchless	Year	Primary	Final drive
16M	G3L	1945–8	66	91
		1949–55	66	94
16MS	G3LS	1949–56	66	98
		1957–8	67	98
16	G3	1959–62	67	98
		1963–6	68	98
16S	G3S	1962	67	98
16MC	G3LC	1948–9	65	91
		1950–5	65	90
16MCT	G3LCT	1956	65	96
		1957–8	66	97
16C	G3C	1959–64	66	94
16MCS	G3LCS	1951–5	65	98
		1956	65	96
		1957–8	66	97
16CS	G3CS	1959	66	97
18	G80	1945–8	67	91
		1949–55	67	94
18S	G80S	1949–56	67	98
		1957–8	68	98
18	G80	1959–62	69	98
		1963–6	69	99
18C	G80C	1948–9	66	91
		1950–5	66	90
18CS	G80CS	1951–5	66	98
		1956	66	96
		1957–8	67	97
		1958	67	98
		1959	67	97
		1960–5	67	98
	G85CS	1966–9	67	104
20	G9	1949–51	67	96
		1952–6	66	96
		1957–61	67	97
20CS	G9CS	1959	66	97
20CSR	G9CSR	1959	67	97
30	G11	1956	66	96
		1957–8	68	97
31	G12	1959–62	68	97
		1963–6	69	96
31CS	G12CS	1959–60	67	97

Model AJS	Matchless	Year	Primary	Final drive
31CSR	G12CSR	1959	67	97
		1960	68	98
		1961–3	68	97
		1964–6	69	97
33	G15	1965–9	68	97
33CSR	G15CSR	1965–9	68	98
	G15CS	1967–9	68	97
	G15 s/c	1966–8	67	97

Lightweight singles: primary 0.375 × 0.250 × 0.225 in. single or duplex or 0.500 × 0.335 × 0.205 in. single strand; final drive 0.500 × 0.335 × 0.305 in.

A 1956 AJS model 16MC fitted out with skis for the Swedish army

Model AJS	Matchless	Year	Primary	Final drive
14	G2	1958–62	73 of $\frac{3}{8}$ in. single	123
		late 1962–3	72 of $\frac{3}{8}$ in. duplex	123
14S	G2S	1961–2	73 of $\frac{3}{8}$ in. single	123
		late 1962	72 of $\frac{3}{8}$ in. duplex	123
14CS	G2CS	1959–62	55 of $\frac{1}{2}$ in. single	131
		late 1962	72 of $\frac{3}{8}$ in. duplex	133
14CSR	G2CSR	1962–6	72 of $\frac{3}{8}$ in. duplex	124
8	G5	1960–2	72 of $\frac{3}{8}$ in. duplex	123

The change to $\frac{3}{8}$ in. duplex primary chain took place at engine 12128 built late in 1962.

Singles: magneto and dynamo 0.375 × 0.250 × 0.225 in.

Magneto AJS	1945–64	46 links
Matchless	1945–51	58 links
	1952–69	46 links
Dynamo	1945–8	47 links 17-tooth dynamo drive
	1949–56	49 links 21-tooth dynamo drive
	1957–63	50 links 21-tooth dynamo drive

Norton twin: Camshaft 0.375 × 0.250 × 0.225 in. with 38 links

Ignition 0.375 × 0.250 × 0.155 in. with 42 links.

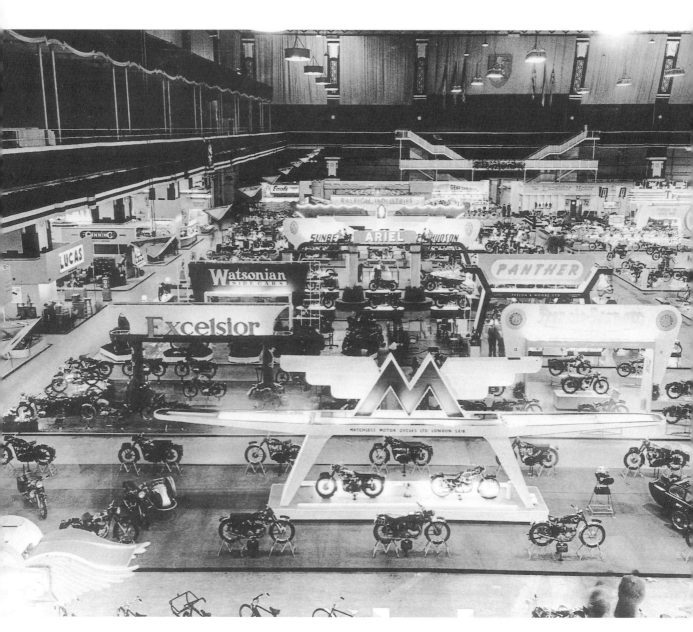

Earls Court in November 1954 with the models awaiting the public

11 Wheels, brakes and tyres

Brake diameters

Model	Year	Front	Rear
Singles	1945–7	$6\frac{1}{2} \times \frac{7}{8}$	$6\frac{1}{2} \times \frac{7}{8}$
	1948–62	$7 \times \frac{7}{8}$	$7 \times \frac{7}{8}$
	1963	$7 \times 1\frac{1}{8}$	$7 \times \frac{7}{8}$
	1964–6	$8 \times 1\frac{1}{4}$	$7 \times 1\frac{1}{4}$
Comp	1946–7	$6\frac{1}{2} \times \frac{7}{8}$	$6\frac{1}{2} \times \frac{7}{8}$
	1948–58	$7 \times \frac{7}{8}$	$7 \times \frac{7}{8}$
Trials	1959–64	$5\frac{1}{2} \times \frac{3}{4}$	$5\frac{1}{2} \times \frac{3}{4}$
CS	1959–62	$7 \times \frac{7}{8}$	$7 \times \frac{7}{8}$
	1963–5	$7 \times 1\frac{1}{8}$	$7 \times \frac{7}{8}$
	1966–9	$7 \times 1\frac{1}{8}$	$8\frac{1}{4} \times 1\frac{1}{4}$
Twins	1949–62	$7 \times \frac{7}{8}$	$7 \times \frac{7}{8}$
std 1963		$7 \times 1\frac{1}{8}$	$7 \times \frac{7}{8}$
CSR 1963		$7 \times \frac{7}{8}$	$7 \times \frac{7}{8}$
	1964–9	$8 \times 1\frac{1}{4}$	$7 \times 1\frac{1}{4}$
Light singles			
Standard	1958–63	6×1	6×1
CS	1959–62	$7 \times \frac{7}{8}$	$5\frac{1}{2} \times \frac{3}{4}$
350	1960–2	6×1	6×1
CSR	1962–6	$6 \times 1\frac{1}{8}$	6×1

Size	Year	Front	Rear
650	1959–62	3.25 × 19	3.50 × 19
650	1963–6	3.25 × 18	3.50 × 18
650CS	1959–60	3.00 × 21	4.00 × 19
650CSR	1959–63	3.25 × 19	3.50 × 19
650CSR	1964–6	3.25 × 18	3.50 × 18
750	1965–6	3.50 × 18	4.00 × 18
750	1967–9	3.25 × 18	4.00 × 18
750CS	1967–9	3.50 × 18	4.00 × 18
750CSR	1965–6	3.25 × 18	3.50 × 18
750CSR	1967–9	3.25 × 19	3.50 × 19

Tyre equivalents

Section

Original	Low profile	Metric
2.75	3.10	80/90
3.00	3.60	90/90
3.25	3.60	90/90
3.50	4.10	100/90
4.00	4.25/85	110/90

Revolutions per mile

3.25 × 17	865
3.25 × 18	831
3.50 × 18	812
4.00 × 18	787
3.25 × 19	794
3.50 × 19	777
4.00 × 19	758
3.50 × 19 s/c	790

Date from Avon Tyres Ltd
Sidecar tyre included for reference.

Tyre sizes

Model	Size	Year	Front	Rear
Single	350	1945–62	3.25 × 19	3.25 × 19
		1963–6	3.25 × 18	3.25 × 18
	500	1945–62	3.25 × 19	3.50 × 19
		1963–6	3.25 × 18	3.50 × 18
Comp	350,500	1946–7	2.75 × 21	4.00 × 19
	350,500	1948–53	3.00 × 21	4.00 × 19
Trials	350	1954–64	2.75 × 21	4.00 × 19
	500	1954–5	2.75 × 21	4.00 × 19
Scrambles	500CS	1954–65	3.00 × 21	4.00 × 19
	500CS	1966–9	3.00 × 21	4.00 × 18
Light singles	std	1958–63	3.25 × 17	3.25 × 17
	CS	1959–62	3.00 × 19	3.50 × 19
	350	1960–2	3.25 × 18	3.25 × 18
	CSR	1962–6	3.25 × 17	3.25 × 17
Twin	500	1949–61	3.25 × 19	3.50 × 19
	500CS	1959	3.00 × 21	4.00 × 19
	500CSR	1959	3.25 × 19	3.50 × 19
	600	1956–8	3.25 × 19	3.50 × 19
	600CS	1958	3.50 × 19	4.00 × 19
	600CSR	1958	3.25 × 19	3.50 × 19

12 Headlamp, ammeter and switches

These varied over the years and while the data given below is also to be found in the main text, a summary may help. Competition models had a quickly detachable headlamp. These were normally supplied with the trials machines but not the scrambles ones after 1955, although they were listed as an option for the CS singles and twins for 1959–62.

Road singles

1945–51   Small panel in headlamp shell carrying ammeter and light switch with speedometer on fork top.
1952–3   As 1945 except for underslung pilot lamp.
1954   Twin pilot lights added with one each side of the headlamp.
1955–7   Deeper headlamp shell made in three parts with pilot lights and speedometer mounted to rear with light switch ahead to the left and ammeter to the right.
1958–9   As before but without pilot lights and with ignition switch in centre of lights one.
1960–1   More compact one-piece headlamp shell with speedometer to rear with ammeter ahead of it flanked by light switch to left and ignition switch to right.
1962–6   Separate ignition key added to switch.

Competition singles

1946–63   Small panel in headlamp shell carrying ammeter and light switch with speedometer on fork top. Often headlamp not fitted but remained available as an option.

Standard twins

1949–51   Small panel in headlamp shell carrying ammeter and light switch with speedometer on fork top.
1952–3   As 1949 except for underslung pilot lamp.
1954   Twin pilot lights added with one each side of the headlamp.
1955–7   Deeper headlamp shell made in three parts with pilot lights and speedometer mounted to rear with light switch ahead to the left and ammeter to the right.
1958   As before but without pilot lights.

1959   As 1958 plus ignition switch in centre of lights one.
1960–1   More compact one-piece headlamp shell with speedometer to rear with ammeter ahead of it flanked by light switch to left and ignition switch to right.
1962–6   Separate ignition key added to switch.

De luxe twins

1959–61   As 1958 standard twins.

CS twins

1958–60   Small panel in headlamp shell carrying ammeter and light switch with speedometer on fork top.

CSR twins

1958   Small panel in headlamp shell carrying ammeter and light switch with speedometer on fork top.
1959   Headlamp shell with speedometer mounted to rear with light switch ahead to the left and ammeter to the right.
1960–6   More compact headlamp shell but otherwise as 1959.
1962   Cowl listed as option with ammeter in centre, light switch behind it and rev-counter to left and speedometer to right.

750 twins

1965–9   Headlamp shell with ammeter only as light switch mounted between rev-counter and speedometer on fork top bracket. CSR with same layout but different parts.

Light singles

1958–66   Headlamp shell with speedometer to rear and ammeter ahead of it flanked by light switch to left and ignition switch to right.

Picture indexes

These are compiled in date order, by machine and by item to give the maximum benefit. Because of space restrictions it is not possible to have a picture of each side of every model for every year, but by using these indexes it is often possible to find a picture that helps. This is because the cycle parts were often common for several models in any one year, so any picture from that year will help. Thus one of a 1955 Matchless will help with an AJS of the same year while a single can help with the cycle side of a twin.

So look for your model and year but also check other models of the same year. It can also be worth looking at the same model in the years before and after as the feature you are checking may not have changed. Some of the references are for detail parts only so check the index, list the relevant pages and have a look at each to see if it helps.

Picture index by year

Picture index by model

Matchless

Component picture index

Index